MW01254055

TREATY IMPLEMENTATION: FULFILLING THE COVENANT

Office of the Treaty Commissioner
Saskatoon, Saskatchewan

© Office of the Treaty Commissioner 2007. No part of this publication may be reproduced, stored in a retrieval system, or transmitted in any form or by any means, electronic, mechanical, photocopying, recording, or otherwise without the prior written permission of the Office of the Treaty Commissioner.

ISBN 978 – 0 – 9782685 – 0 – 3

Printed in Canada

Published by the Office of the Treaty Commissioner
Saskatoon, Saskatchewan, Canada

Publication of this book has been made possible with the cooperation
of the Saskatchewan Institute of Public Policy

SASKATCHEWAN INSTITUT DE POLITIQUES
INSTITUTE OF D'INTÉRÊT PUBLIC
PUBLIC POLICY DE LA SASKATCHEWAN

TABLE OF CONTENTS

LETTER OF TRANSMITTAL

February 15, 2007

Chief Lawrence Joseph
Federation of Saskatchewan Indian Nations
Executive Office
Suite 200 – 103A Packham Avenue
Saskatoon, Saskatchewan
S7N 4K4

The Honourable Jim Prentice
Minister of Indian Affairs and
Northern Development
10 Wellington Street, Room 2100
Gatineau, Quebec
K1A 0H4

Dear Minister and Chief:

Re: *Treaty Implementation: Fulfilling the Covenant*

I am pleased to provide you with the following report, *Treaty Implementation: Fulfilling the Covenant.* The objective of this report is to assist the Parties in setting the foundation for a revitalized treaty relationship, which will lead to treaty implementation in a modern context, thereby, honouring the solemnity and sacred underpinnings of the treaties.

In Saskatchewan, the Federation of Saskatchewan Indian Nations and the Government of Canada are leading the country in creating a new path toward treaty implementation. Revitalizing the treaty relationship has much promise and hope, not only for the First Nations but for all Canadians. The Parties are to be commended for their progress to date and encouraged to continue their journey toward fulfilling the covenant.

The treaties are an integral part of the fabric of our Constitution. They form the bedrock foundation of the relationship between the Treaty First Nations and the Government of Canada. It is from the treaties that all things must flow in the treaty relationship. They represent the common intersection both historically and politically between nations. They created a relationship which is perpetual and unalterable in its foundation principles. The treaties are the basis for a continuous intergovernmental relationship.

The First Nations and Canada had their own goals and objectives when they came together to make treaties. Their collective common goals were to determine how they were going to live in harmony, with mutual benefit based on mutual respect, and to determine how First Nations were going to be part of the new economy that the newcomers were bringing. Unfortunately, these common goals have not been defined or achieved within a comprehensive treaty-based framework. The objective of the Crown, to settle and prosper on this new land without conflict from First Nations, has been achieved. Those of the First Nations, to share economic prosperity with the new society, secure a brother-to-brother relationship with the Crown, continue to nurture their communities and protect their right to govern themselves, have not. In order to implement the treaty relationship and fulfill the promise of the treaties, there needs to be revitalization based upon four pillars of reconciliation: political, legal, socio-economic, and spiritual. Each of these is equally important and should be given equal weight by the Parties.

This report suggests that the Parties build on the good work they have created in past discussions at the Exploratory Treaty Table. At that table, the Parties built common understandings on fourteen principles underlying the treaty relationship, as reported in the *Statement of Treaty Issues*. The Parties recognized that all of the principles might not have been identified and agreed that further discussion might have to occur in order to fully address the nature of the existing, agreed-upon principles. They also agreed that further principles might be identified and, in turn, be the subject of further discussions.

Treaty Implementation: Fulfilling the Covenant presents a comprehensive treaty-based approach that will enable the Parties to fulfill their obligations to each other. It includes four salient features. First, it articulates the treaty obligation, on both Parties, to act to implement the treaties and fulfill the promise of the treaty relationship. Second, it sets out a vision, a mission and a set of goals for treaty implementation and the fulfillment of the treaty relationship. Third, it sets out a plan of action for accomplishing the vision. Fourth, it presents an implementation agenda for the future. Through this approach, I believe the Parties will be able to fulfill the covenant.

Based on this broad framework, this report sets out a number of recommendations for the implementation of the treaties and the treaty relationship. I encourage the Parties to take careful, confident, incremental steps to ensure that the understandings created in the treaty relationship are properly implemented for the benefit of future generations. As Treaty Commissioner, I am optimistic that the goodwill of the Parties will guide a new process that allows the treaties to be accorded their rightful place in the Canadian state, thereby allowing Treaty First Nations people to take their rightful place in Canadian society.

Yours respectfully,

The Honourable Judge David M. Arnot
Treaty Commissioner for Saskatchewan

ACKNOWLEDGMENTS

For over a year, the Office of the Treaty Commissioner's primary mission has been to prepare this report on *Treaty Implementation: Fulfilling the Covenant* and provide advice on ways to further the treaty implementation process. This would not have been possible without the dedicated, professional and personal support of many individuals. Those involved in the preparation of this report have made their contribution because they believe in Canada, they believe in the treaties, they believe treaty implementation must be based on the original spirit and intent of treaties, and they believe that First Nations people must take their rightful place in Canada.

It is with honour and gratitude that the Office of the Treaty Commissioner acknowledges those who contributed to the preparation of this report. The staff of the Office of the Treaty Commissioner contributed by arranging meetings, collecting material, reviewing documents, distributing numerous materials, and drafting portions of the report. Policy advisors assisted in drafting and redrafting the content and the Interim Report released on March 31, 2006. Elders, representatives from the Federation of Saskatchewan Indian Nations and the Government of Canada, and observers from the Government of Saskatchewan at the Exploratory Treaty Table provided advice on, and exhibited much patience in, the development of this report.

In addition to these individuals, the Office of the Treaty Commissioner would like to thank all those who contributed by coming to meetings with First Nations youth and First Nations communities, meetings with Federation of Saskatchewan Indian Nations officials, meetings with federal officials both in Ottawa and Regina, and meetings with provincial officials. Although there are too many to name, they need to know that their contribution made this report possible. Not only did they provide valuable insight into the issues, their participation added strength to the report. Readers and participants should be aware that in addition to all the research and study, what was heard at the various meetings with front-line and community people fundamentally influenced our thinking.

More specifically, from the Office of the Treaty Commissioner, thank you to Ken Horsman, Darrell Seib, Colleen Cameron, Krysta Japp, Wendy Hoknes, and Sharon Ahenakew.

Policy and spiritual advisors included: Elder Alma Kytwayhat, Elder Jacob Bill, Elder Amelia Potts, Elder Simon Kytwayhat, Kay Lerat, Alan Pratt, Eleanore Sunchild, David Hawkes, Paul Favel, Ian Peach, Merrilee Rasmussen, James Scharfstein, Loraine Thompson, John Borrows, Ernie Lawton, Jim Miller, and Dan Bellegarde.

From the Exploratory Treaty Table, our thanks to: Elders Alma Kytwayhat (Makwa Sahgaiehcan First Nation), William Dreaver (Big River First Nation), Danny Musqua (Keeseekoose First Nation), Jimmy Myo (Moosomin First Nation), Richard Poorman (Kawacatoose First Nation), Lawrence Tobacco (Kawacatoose First Nation), Jean Oakes (Nekaneet First Nation), Dolly Neapetung (Yellow Quill First Nation), Fred Wahpoosywan and Florence Wahpoosywan (Sakimay First Nation), and Jonas Bird (Lac La Ronge Indian Band). Federation of Saskatchewan Indian Nations representatives: Chief Lawrence Joseph, Chief Denton George, Chief Irvin Starblanket, Chief Henry Daniels, Chief Henry Lewis, Chief Ben Weenie, Jake Tootoosis, Paul Favel, Dorothy Myo, Jacob Sanderson, Murray Long, Darrell Buffalo, Lorna Arcand, Doris Greyeyes, Tamara Starblanket, Leona Tootoosis, Sylvia McAdam, Carla Nokusis, Chris Morin, Roxanne Baldwin, Treena Knight, Lloyd Martell, Lindsay Cyr, Allery Carrier, Tom McKenzie, and Alex Ahenakew. Representatives from the Government of Canada: David Hawkes, Victoria De La Ronde, Keith Sero, Peggy Martin McGuire, Murray Wagner, John Barg, Sandra Wabagijig, Jason Haviland, and Angela Bishop. Observers from the Government of Saskatchewan: John Reid, Jan Joel, Mark LaRocque, David Gullickson, Mitch McAdam, Curtis Talbot, Jack Kinnear, and Glenn McKenzie.

We are especially grateful to the Elders who helped us in the past by providing guidance and advice, and who have since left us to join the spirit world. In 2004, the Office of the Treaty Commissioner made a commitment to honour the following Elders in four annual Treaty Elders Memorial Round Dances: the late Elders Gordon Oakes, Hilliard Ermine, Norman Sunchild, Alpha Lafond, Fred Martell, Kaye Thompson, Henry Whitstone, Joe Stick, Marie Kay, and Douglas Rabbitskin. They all deserve our sincere and heartfelt thanks.

Our deepest gratitude must go to Elder Alma Kytwayhat, the spiritual and inspirational resident Elder at the Office of the Treaty Commissioner; and to the Creator who guided the original treaty making process and whose guidance was sought in preparing this report.

We also wish to thank former Chief Alphonse Bird and former Minister Andy Scott for giving the Office of the Treaty Commissioner this opportunity to provide them with advice on treaty implementation.

Finally, we thank current Chief Lawrence Joseph and Minister Jim Prentice for considering this report. We pray the Creator will provide them with the wisdom and courage to act on the recommendations it contains so that the original spirit and intent of the treaties is brought to fulfillment for First Nations people and all people in Saskatchewan.

EXECUTIVE SUMMARY

On July 18, 2005, Chief Alphonse Bird of the Federation of Saskatchewan Indian Nations and the Honourable Andy Scott, Minister of Indian Affairs and Northern Development, asked the Office of the Treaty Commissioner to produce a report on treaty implementation. *Treaty Implementation: Fulfilling the Covenant* is the Office of the Treaty Commissioner's response.

In fulfilling its obligations, the Office of the Treaty Commissioner undertook three primary activities: workshops, research, and policy analysis. Information gathering workshops were conducted with federal officials, First Nations youth, communities and political and administrative officials. A number of research and policy studies were commissioned to explore the various contextual, historical, statistical, socio-economic, policy and legal aspects of treaty implementation. On March 31, 2006, the Office of the Treaty Commissioner released an interim report and sought reaction from the Parties, the Exploratory Treaty Table and others on the ideas and challenges identified. During this deliberation and fact-finding process, the Office of the Treaty Commissioner constantly relied on Elders and the previous ten years of Treaty Commission work to provide inspiration and direction.

Fundamentally, the workshops, research and policy analysis provided a much better understanding of treaty implementation. Through the research, the original intentions of the treaty Parties were examined and found to be honourable. By accommodating and reconciling two very different cultures, they contained the key to success in the future. That key is the covenantal nature of the treaties. The covenant formed a brother-to-brother relationship and committed the treaty Parties to reconciling differences through a continuing treaty relationship.

A review of the historical experience of the treaty relationship demonstrates the failure of past efforts at treaty implementation. The summary of the socio-economic circumstance in which First Nations people find themselves documents what is well known – First Nations people do not have socio-economic parity with non-First Nations people and one of the keys to overcoming this situation is education. Through discussions with First Nations communities and federal and provincial officials, the Office of the Treaty Commissioner arrived at the essence of the recommendations. It was clear that participants in the discussions were concerned about the socio-economic conditions of First Nations people; they recognized the need for a common understanding of treaties and called for greater accountability by the Parties on several levels, including the need for a plan of action that produced results.

The other major influence on the recommendations was the analysis of a wide ranging set of treaty implementation issues. These include the legal perspectives of First Nations and Canada, the Constitution, the evolution and pattern of Supreme Court decisions of the last 30 years and the divergent and common views of the Parties. This analysis led to the conclusion that there is a need for reconciliation – for the Parties to sit together again to overcome their differences. Further, there are four pillars to this reconciliation: political reconciliation, legal reconciliation, socio-economic reconciliation and spiritual reconciliation.

Through this work, the Office of the Treaty Commissioner holds great hope for the future, but this hope emerges from over 130 years of little hope, little action and great disappointment with respect to treaties and treaty implementation.

The Office of the Treaty Commissioner found that since the making of the treaties the following conditions have prevailed:

• Treaties have been ignored, marginalized and subverted.

• For the most part, treaty implementation has not occurred either in practice or in spirit.

- Efforts to implement treaties have been fragmented, unfocused and characterized by a lack of urgency.

- First Nations people and all Canadians have paid dearly for this lack of treaty implementation in political, legal, socio-economic and spiritual ways.

The Office of the Treaty Commissioner found reason for great hope because:

- The treaties represent remarkable agreements between nations. They are based on mutual respect, mutual benefit, good relations and honour. Treaties represent the Parties' vision that First Nations people would participate in the new economy emerging at the time of treaty making. Fundamentally, the treaties affirm a commitment between the Parties that they would work together in a continuing relationship to reconcile differences between them. They are based on peace, harmony and good relations.

- The political commitment by both Parties has steadily increased, particularly since the adoption of section 35 of the Constitution which states: "The existing Aboriginal and treaty rights of the Aboriginal peoples of Canada are hereby recognized and affirmed."

- The legal decisions of the Supreme Court of Canada over the past 30 years have consistently found treaties to be building blocks of the Canadian state. These decisions demonstrate a clear direction – that the treaties are more than their written word, that the spirit and intent of both Parties must be considered when developing policy, designing implementation strategies or resolving differences in interpretation, and that Canada has a duty to address and bring meaning to section 35 of the Constitution.

- The socio-economic circumstance of First Nations people, although dire, provides reason for optimism. These circumstances along with the demographics of Saskatchewan put treaties and treaty implementation at the top of the priority list.

- The treaties are a covenant: a commitment by both Parties made in the presence of the Creator and with the honour of the Crown and the honour of the First Nations. Indeed, the spirit of the treaties remains alive with First Nations Elders. The ultimate goal was to sit together to develop a common understanding of the spirit and intent of the treaties.

For this hope to become a reality, the Parties need a plan for moving forward. This document, *Treaty Implementation: Fulfilling the Covenant*, sets out such a plan in its 26 recommendations. The recommendations follow the outline of a strategic plan. The intention is to be clear about what the Office of the Treaty Commissioner believes needs to be done in order for treaty implementation to occur.

The recommendations identify a vision, mission, principles and set of goals for treaty implementation.

Vision:
> The treaties find their rightful place in the Canadian state and Treaty First Nations find their rightful place in Canadian society.

Mission:
> To implement the treaties and the treaty relationship in a way that respects their spirit and intent, and brings certainty and clarity in a modern context.

Principles:
> Principles draw and expand upon the principles already agreed to in the *Statement of Treaty Issues* published in 1998.

This report also reframes the four pillars of reconciliation as the goals of treaty implementation. Those goals are:

Goal 1: Political
That the Parties renew the treaty relationship.

Goal 2: Legal

That Canada and First Nations give meaning and content in a Saskatchewan context to section 35 of the *Constitution Act, 1982* with a view to bringing certainty and clarity to the promises of the past.

Goal 3: Socio-economic

That First Nations people achieve socio-economic parity with other Canadians.

Goal 4: Spiritual

That the Parties fulfill their covenant by coming to agreement on a common understanding of the spirit and intent of the treaties in a modern context.

The Office of the Treaty Commissioner believes these are reasonable and achievable goals that will bring focus to the treaty implementation process and provide an opportunity for the Parties to feel a sense of accomplishment in the process. To translate these goals into measurable outcomes, the recommendations go on to identify a more detailed plan of action. This plan includes a set of objectives for treaty implementation, a set of operational guidelines and perspectives, and the following five strategic initiatives.

Strategic Initiative 1: Acknowledgment of the Importance of Treaties, Treaty Implementation and First Nations Culture

> The recommendations under this initiative call for the Parties to sign a joint declaration acknowledging their obligation to maintain the treaty relationship and to share responsibility. The recommendations call for a statement and actions which affirm First Nations culture.

Strategic Initiative 2: Structures and Mechanisms

This initiative is designed to establish the structures and mechanisms needed for the ongoing efforts intended to achieve treaty implementation. These structures and mechanisms are summarized as follows:

- Establishing a forum for discussion – the Table for Treaty Implementation.

- Defining a role for Saskatchewan.

- Identifying a senior representative for all Parties.

- Establishing powerful internal decision making and capacity building processes within each of the Parties.

- Re-mandating an Office of the Treaty Commissioner whose role, among other things, is to advocate for treaties, facilitate discussions, monitor progress and hold the Parties accountable.

Strategic Initiative 3: Opportunities for Early Progress

Under this initiative, three high priority areas are identified as targets for early agreement: education, child and family services and the Dakota/Lakota adhesion.

Strategic Initiative 4: Treaty Implementation Framework Agreement

This initiative outlines five components for an overall Treaty Implementation Framework Agreement, which would set out the general areas for long-term action by the Parties. The five components are: adopting a strategic plan, bringing meaning to section 35 of the Constitution, working toward socio-economic parity, addressing self-government and sharing responsibility.

Strategic Initiative 5: Accountability

> This initiative addresses the need for accountability of the treaty implementation process to First Nations people and all Canadian citizens. It is recommended that the Parties establish an evaluation and accountability plan which focuses on outcomes, requires reporting to the Parties and their legislative assemblies, and mandates the Office of the Treaty Commissioner to publicly report on progress.

The recommendations conclude with timelines for implementation.

The time has come for a comprehensive treaty-based approach that will enable the Parties to fulfill their obligations to each other. The Office of the Treaty Commissioner believes:

> That treaties must find their rightful place in the Canadian state and Treaty First Nations must find their rightful place in Canadian society.

This can be achieved if:

> The Parties fulfill their covenant by coming to agreement on a common understanding of the spirit and intent of treaties in a modern context.

If this occurs, the Parties will have achieved treaty implementation and will have fulfilled the covenant entered into with the Creator and our forefathers.

SUMMARY OF RECOMMENDATIONS

It is recommended that:

Recommendation 1 – Vision

The vision for treaty implementation is that the treaties find their rightful place in the Canadian state and Treaty First Nations find their rightful place in Canadian society.

Recommendation 2 – Mission

The mission for treaty implementation is to implement the treaties and the treaty relationship in a way that respects their spirit and intent, and brings certainty and clarity in a modern context.

Recommendation 3 – Principles

Treaty implementation is to be based upon the following foundational principles, which direct and govern the interaction between the Parties:

a) Treaty making incorporated the customs of the respective Parties and created a fundamental political relationship between Treaty First Nations and the Crown. Treaties gave shape to this relationship, creating obligations and expectations on both sides.

b) The treaty relationship is perpetual and unalterable.

c) The treaties are political agreements that are properly dealt with in a political forum.

d) The treaty relationship is one in which the Parties expect to resolve differences through mutual discussion and decision.

e) The treaty making process between the Parties involved the exchange of solemn promises, based on respect for the spiritual and traditional values of the other. The Crown and Treaty First Nations entered into the agreements freely and of their own accord as the best possible means of advancing their respective interests.

f) The treaty relationship acknowledges the solemnity of the treaties.

g) The treaty relationship embodies mutual benefit, mutual respect, reciprocity and mutual responsibility.

h) Treaty implementation is a shared responsibility.

i) The act of treaty making was indicative of mutual recognition of the authority vested in the Treaty Commissioners on behalf of the Crown and in the Chiefs and Headmen on behalf of their First Nations to enter into treaties.

j) In entering into these agreements, both the representatives of the Crown and the Treaty First Nations recognized each other's authority and capacity to enter into treaties on behalf of their respective people.

k) The treaty making process contains within it the treaty principle of maintaining the honour of the Crown and the honour of Treaty First Nations in maintaining the treaty relationship. Equally important was the conduct and behaviour of the Parties to honour and respect the commitments made in treaties.

l) The treaty relationship embodies the honour of the Crown and the honour of the Treaty First Nations and supports the trust-like, non-adversarial, brother-to-brother relationship.

m) The treaty making process was a means of building lasting and meaningful alliances between the Parties that would foster the future well-being of the people they represented.

n) The treaties were foundational agreements entered into to provide the Parties with the means of achieving survival and stability, anchored on the principle of mutual benefit.

o) The treaties were designed to provide equal opportunity between First Nations and newcomers.

p) The treaties were designed to provide the First Nations with the education required to integrate them into the economy of the newcomers; they were not designed to assimilate them culturally, linguistically or spiritually.

q) The treaties were to provide for peace and good order between the Parties and among the First Nations.

r) The relationship between the Treaty First Nations and the Crown is one in which the Parties have both benefits and responsibilities with respect to one another. The treaties created mutual obligations that were to be respected by the Parties.

s) The Parties share a common commitment to reinvigorate the treaty relationship and to build on their partnership to address the well-being of both Parties in a respectful and supportive way.

t) Canada and Treaty First Nations can enter into arrangements whereby Treaty First Nations exercise jurisdiction and governance over their lands and people, building upon the foundation of their treaty relationship with Canada. These agreements should not alter the treaties; rather they should implement the treaty partnership in a contemporary way while respecting the principles of treaty making.

u) The Parties recognize that the participation of the Government of Saskatchewan is required for there to be significant progress on the implementation of Treaty First Nations' jurisdiction and governance within Saskatchewan, and they believe that the principles of the treaty relationship are beneficial for all people in Saskatchewan.

Recommendation 4 – Goals

The Parties adopt the following four goals for treaty implementation in Saskatchewan:

Goal 1 – Political
That the Parties renew the treaty relationship.

Goal 2 – Legal
That Canada and First Nations give meaning and content in a Saskatchewan context to section 35 of the *Constitution Act, 1982* with a view to bringing certainty and clarity to the promises of the past.

Goal 3 – Socio-economic
That First Nations people achieve socio-economic parity with other Canadians.

Goal 4 – Spiritual
That the Parties fulfill their covenant by coming to agreement on a common understanding of the spirit and intent of the treaties in a modern context.

Recommendation 5 – Objectives

The Parties adopt the following objectives for treaty implementation in Saskatchewan.

● To implement the Treaty First Nations right to livelihood.

● To fundamentally restructure the relationship between the Parties.

● To reconcile the Parties from political, legal, socio-economic and spiritual perspectives.

- To revitalize the treaty relationship.

- To recognize that the treaty relationship is perpetual and unalterable in its principles.

- To reverse the damage done by the non-implementation of the spirit and intent of the treaties.

- To reverse the damage done by the assimilation policy inherent in the *Indian Act*.

- To provide the Treaty First Nations with equality of opportunity.

- To recognize that equality of benefit may require differential treatment.

- To ensure that the Treaty First Nations have healthy families and communities.

- To ensure that the Treaty First Nations create economic development and diversification opportunities.

- To clarify the respective jurisdictions of the Parties.

- To establish certainty in the treaty relationship.

- To implement the Treaty First Nations right of governance.

- To ensure there is accountability by both Parties in a brother-to-brother relationship.

Recommendation 6 – Operational Guidelines and Perspectives

The Parties adopt the following operational guidelines and perspectives for treaty implementation in Saskatchewan.

- That the brother-to-brother treaty relationship implies a fundamentally political relationship that can only be revitalized at the political level, through a political commitment to fulfill the Parties' obligations to the treaties in a modern context.

- That the spirit and intent of treaty implementation has not been achieved.

- That the implementation strategies of the past have provided many important lessons, and have provided a greater common understanding upon which the Parties can build.

- That the modern context is vastly different from the time when the treaties were made.

- That the modern context, in part, means bringing certainty and clarity to the rights and obligations of each party in the treaty relationship.

- That the largely unproductive, frustrating and stalled treaty implementation strategies of the past are damaging to First Nations people and indeed to all Canadians.

- That the principles that underlie the *Indian Act* are the antithesis of the principles that underlie treaty implementation.

- That the past has been a problem, but it is time to turn the page on the past and move on to revitalize the treaty relationship.

- That we now have a greater legal understanding of the treaty relationship upon which the Parties can build.

- That the treaty relationship is a trust relationship based on a non-adversarial brother-to-brother relationship that must proceed on an interest-based approach.

- That accountability by both Parties is one of the salient features of the brother-to-brother relationship in a modern context.

- That treaty implementation is a developmental and incremental process that must proceed with urgency while remaining realistic and conscious of the largely sequential and iterative nature of such a process.

- That it is time for the exploratory process to end and discussions to begin to explicitly address the need to implement the treaties and fulfill the treaty relationship; while at the same time new avenues must be identified for reaching a shared understanding of the principles that will take the discussions forward.

Recommendation 7 – Obligation to Treaties and the Treaty Relationship

The Parties sign a Joint Declaration on the treaty relationship, which would acknowledge that the treaties created an obligation on both Parties to maintain a treaty relationship between the Crown and First Nations people, and that the treaty relationship requires a continuing dialogue between the First Nations and Canada in order to address differences in treaty interpretation and implementation. The signatories to this Joint Declaration should be the Crown as represented by the Governor General of Canada and the First Nations as represented by the Chief of the Federation of Saskatchewan Indian Nations.

Recommendation 8 – Shared Responsibility

The Parties make a joint declaration on their shared responsibility for treaty implementation, either as part of the Joint Declaration on the treaty relationship or separately signed as a supplement to it.

Recommendation 9 – Affirmation of First Nations People

The Parties and Saskatchewan prepare a formal joint statement describing, affirming and acknowledging the place of the cultural, linguistic and spiritual traditions of the First Nations in Saskatchewan, and prepare an action plan to secure their rightful place in modern Canadian society. Elders must have a prominent role in the development of this statement.

Recommendation 10 – Table for Treaty Implementation

The Parties establish a Table for Treaty Implementation that oversees treaty discussions in Saskatchewan.

Recommendation 11 – Role for Saskatchewan

The Parties come to agreement between themselves and with the Government of Saskatchewan on the role of the provincial government in treaty implementation discussions.

Recommendation 12 – Senior Representatives

The Parties and Saskatchewan each appoint a senior representative to lead the treaty implementation process.

Recommendation 13 – Canada – Policy Processes

The Government of Canada create a Cabinet Committee on Treaty Implementation and a committee of senior officials, including central agency officials, to develop a "treaty implementation policy" and mandate that will guide their representatives during treaty implementation discussions and monitor progress.

Recommendation 14 – Canada – Treaty Education

The Government of Canada engage in a process of education for government officials to improve their understanding of their role in facilitating treaty implementation.

Recommendation 15 – Saskatchewan – Policy Processes

The Government of Saskatchewan create a Cabinet Committee on Treaty Implementation and a committee of senior officials, including central agency officials, to develop a "treaty implementation policy" and mandate that will guide their representatives during treaty implementation discussions and monitor progress.

Recommendation 16 – Saskatchewan – Treaty Education

The Government of Saskatchewan engage in a process of education for government officials to improve their understanding of their role in facilitating treaty implementation.

Recommendation 17 – Federation of Saskatchewan Indian Nations – Policy Processes

The Federation of Saskatchewan Indian Nations create a Treaty Implementation Commission to develop a "treaty implementation policy" and mandate that will guide their representatives during treaty implementation discussions and monitor progress.

Recommendation 18 – Federation of Saskatchewan Indian Nations – Treaty Education

The Federation of Saskatchewan Indian Nations engage in a process of education for their officials to improve their understanding of their role in facilitating treaty implementation.

Recommendation 19 – Office of the Treaty Commissioner

The Parties re-mandate the Office of the Treaty Commissioner as part of a new "made-in-Saskatchewan" treaty implementation process. This Office should be empowered to:

a) Be a neutral and independent office.

b) Advocate for the treaties, the treaty relationship and treaty implementation.

c) Facilitate discussions at the Table for Treaty Implementation.

d) Establish, foster and participate in treaty celebrations, commemorations and other acts of renewal.

e) Enhance public education and understanding of treaties, the treaty relationship and treaty implementation.

f) Foster treaty implementation by engaging the Parties in discussions aimed at resolving different views on the following matters as well as others the Parties may identify: education; child welfare; shelter; health; justice; treaty annuities; hunting, fishing, trapping and gathering; and lands and resources.

g) Conduct research and prepare reports, which will contribute to the resolution of treaty implementation and other matters within its mandate.

h) Establish and implement dispute resolution mechanisms.

i) Monitor and audit agreements and the independent actions of the Parties with respect to the treaties, the treaty relationship and treaty implementation.

j) Make recommendations to the Parties.

Recommendation 20 – Education Action Plan

The Parties and Saskatchewan develop an action plan for:

a) Strengthening First Nations control of First Nations education.

b) Enhancing the quality of First Nations education by:

- The establishment of shared standards for the education of First Nations children in both First Nations and provincial education systems.

- The expansion of support systems at primary, secondary and tertiary levels.

- The support of innovative development in mathematics and science education, distance learning, special education, gifted education, alternative education and accountability.

Recommendation 21 – Child and Family Services System

The Parties and Saskatchewan establish a province-wide First Nations child and family services system that would operate both on and off reserves and address the need for mutual recognition of standards and interjurisdictional protocols.

Recommendation 22 – Dakota/Lakota Adhesion Claim

The Parties focus their attention on resolving the matter of the Dakota/Lakota adhesion to treaty.

Recommendation 23 – Treaty Implementation Framework Agreement

The Parties work toward a Treaty Implementation Framework Agreement, which would be an over-arching, comprehensive umbrella agreement with the following components:

a) As a starting point for discussion, the Parties agree upon a vision, a mission, principles, goals for treaty implementation and operational guidelines and perspectives (such as those set out in recommendations 1 through 6).

b) That section 35 of the *Constitution Act, 1982* be given content and meaning in a Saskatchewan context through a negotiated effort to define and implement the inherent and treaty rights of First Nations people in Saskatchewan.

- That the Parties to the treaties have an agreed-upon working definition of the content of treaty rights in a modern, Saskatchewan-specific context that allows for effective implementation of the treaties.

- That outstanding land claims issues are resolved through negotiation.

- That agreements are reached to allow for the orderly exercise of First Nations' rights to hunt, fish, trap and gather renewable resources.

- That First Nations' access to non-renewable resources and revenues from resource exploitation are settled through negotiation.

- That First Nations' right to govern themselves is recognized as an inherent right contained within section 35 of the Constitution.

- That the Parties create improved processes to address past injustices.

- That public education programs be established to increase awareness of the treaties. These programs should strive to emphasize the treaty relationship in all its complexity, but with a strong emphasis on the positive contribution of the treaties to a harmonious Canadian society.

c) That First Nations people achieve socio-economic parity with other Canadians.

- That First Nations people have access to primary, secondary and post-secondary education that is both culturally relevant and adequate to ensure their full participation in modern Canadian society.

- That First Nations people are provided with the support needed to build self-sustaining economies on First Nations lands and to participate in the provincial economy as employers, partners and employees.

- That the over-representation of the First Nations people in the justice system and their reliance on social assistance are addressed by equal access to education, health and employment.

d) That the right of First Nations to be self-governing is realized within the Canadian federation.

- That First Nations have the jurisdiction and authority to govern their members on matters internal to those Nations, integral to their cultures, and essential to their operation as a government.

- That First Nations have institutions of governance and administration that are recognized by their members/citizens as culturally appropriate, legitimate and effective.

- That First Nations governments have the capacity to effectively operate their institutions and exercise their jurisdictions.

- That First Nations governments are accountable to their members/citizens for their decisions.

e) That responsibility for ensuring a mutually respectful, brother-to-brother relationship be shared by the treaty Parties.

- That the *Indian Act* relationship of legislated dependency is replaced by an intergovernmental relationship of equals.

- That the Parties and Saskatchewan involved in the brother-to-brother relationship are accountable to one another and their electorates for the effective implementation and ongoing management of the relationship.

- That the Parties and Saskatchewan work to include First Nations in their intergovernmental relations, so that federal-provincial-First Nations relations become normalized and institutionalized, while at the same time remaining effective and efficient.

- That intergovernmental mechanisms for policy coordination, mutual recognition of laws and standards, and dispute avoidance and resolution are established.

- That all governments involved in the brother-to-brother relationship are committed to providing one another with advance notice of a policy or program change that will likely have a significant impact on the policies and programs of other governments, and consult with potentially affected governments on the implementation of these changes.

- That the Crown's fiduciary obligation to First Nations peoples is reduced and modified incrementally, as is appropriate in response to First Nations' exercise of self-government.

- That certainty and clarity on the meaning of treaties and the treaty relationship in a modern context are achieved.

Recommendation 24 – Accountability Characteristics

The Parties and Saskatchewan design an evaluation and accountability plan for treaty implementation. The characteristics of the accountability plan include:

- A focus on the outcomes of the treaty implementation process.

- Reporting of outcomes by the Parties to the other Parties, to the Office of the Treaty Commissioner and to the public through the Parliament of Canada, the Federation of Saskatchewan Indian Nations legislative assembly and the Saskatchewan legislature.

- A public report of outcomes on progress of treaty implementation by the Office of the Treaty Commissioner to the Parties and Saskatchewan.

Recommendation 25 – Funding Agreement

That the Government of Canada and the Federation of Saskatchewan Indian Nations work in cooperation to establish a joint five year work plan and the required funding arrangements to allow the Parties to fully engage in the recommended comprehensive treaty implementation process.

Recommendation 26 – Implementation

The Parties and Saskatchewan implement the recommendations in this document between now and March 2012, according to the following timeline:

April 2007 – the Parties agree to re-establish a mandate for the Office of the Treaty Commissioner (recommendation 19).

June 2007 – the Parties and Saskatchewan begin creating internal processes to develop "treaty implementation policies" and mandates for treaty implementation discussions, and establish capacity building processes to prepare for treaty implementation (recommendations 10 to 18).

January 2008 – the Governor General of Canada and the Chief of the Federation of Saskatchewan Indian Nations sign a Joint Declaration affirming their mutual commitment to the treaty relationship, to sharing responsibility and to revitalizing First Nations communities and cultures (recommendations 7-9).

- *The Parties and Saskatchewan come to an agreement clarifying the role of the Government of Saskatchewan in treaty implementation discussions (recommendation 11).*

- *The Parties each appoint a senior representative to lead treaty implementation discussions on their behalf (recommendation 12).*

September 2008 – the Parties and Saskatchewan begin the establishment of an education action plan (recommendation 20).

January 2009 – the Parties resolve the Dakota/Lakota adhesion to treaty (recommendation 22).

September 2009 – the Parties and the Government of Saskatchewan begin the establishment of the province-wide First Nations child and family services system (recommendation 21).

March 2010 – the Parties sign a Treaty Implementation Framework Agreement (recommendation 23).

- *The Parties and the Government of Saskatchewan sign an evaluation and accountability plan for treaty implementation.*

March 2012 – the first phase of the treaty implementation is completed.

My father used to tell me, we need to make a thanksgiving...[he said,] you know my son, we are alone and you may think we are the first persons in this area, but our great-grandfathers were here before us...I am going to sing to bring a thanksgiving to the Creator and to Mother Earth who has supplied us. Now, you sing with me if you can. So he starts singing and I start repeating his song with him and he would tell me to stop. So we would stop, now listen to our grandfathers and great-grandfathers. You can hear them singing with us. In every hill around us you could hear the echo, even further, now you hear that? We are not the first persons in this country. They were our forefathers, our great-grandfathers that were here. I could hear all the echo around us and that the spirit of our great grandfathers and also that is the Mother Earth supporting us. [1]

Senator Frank McIntyre, August 7, 1997.

It was the will of the Creator that the White Man would come here to live with us, among us, to share our lives together with him, and also both of us collectively to benefit from the bounty of Mother Earth for all time to come.[2]

Elder Jacob Bill, November 12, 1997.

---

[1] Cardinal, Harold and Walter Hildebrandt, *Treaty Elders of Saskatchewan* (Calgary: University of Calgary Press, 2000), p. 12.

[2] Ibid., p. 7.

The whole world has lived through sweeping changes since the days, almost 100 years ago, when your predecessors signed the treaties with the representatives of the government of my great-grandmother, Queen Victoria.

Here in the West of Canada, the changes have been particularly marked. Thousands of newcomers came to this land in search of a new life, yet in spite of the disruption this brought to their ways, the Indian people gave them much needed help.

How the land is transformed and life has completely changed. Large cities, intensive cultivation and all the products of this technological age have appeared as part of the new civilization which has been developed here.

It is unfortunately true that during this rapid transformation and in spite of the wealth that has been created, many Indian people have been left to live in poverty and distress. This and many other problems arising from these changes still need to be addressed.

You may be confident of the continued cooperation of my government which represents your people as it represents all of the people of Canada. You may be assured that my government recognizes the importance of full compliance with the spirit and terms of your treaties.

Let us look to the future. The Indian people of Canada are entering into a new phase in their relationship with other Canadians. It is my hope that in the coming years you will together find a means to combine a way of life, which suits your culture, and social aspirations, with full participation in the creation and enjoyment of the growing material wealth of Canada today.[3]

Her Majesty Queen Elizabeth II, July 5, 1973.

There is nothing, so far as I can see, to warrant any distrust by the Indians of the Government of Canada. But, in case there should be, the discussion in this case will strengthen their hand so as to enable them to withstand any onslaught. They will be able to say that their rights and freedoms have been guaranteed to them by the Crown – originally by the Crown in respect of the United Kingdom – now by the Crown in respect of Canada – but, in any case, by the Crown. No Parliament should do anything to lessen the worth of these guarantees. They should be honoured by the Crown in respect of Canada "so long as the sun rises and the river flows." That promise must never be broken.[4]

Lord Denning of the English Court of Appeal, 1981.

[3] Her Majesty Queen Elizabeth II, reply to an address by Harold Cardinal, President of the Indian Association of Alberta, as quoted in Price, Richard, *Legacy: Indian Treaty Relationships* (Edmonton:1991), p. 85.
[4] *R v. Secretary of State for Foreign and Commonwealth Affairs, Ex p. Indian Association of Alberta,* [1982] 1 Q.B. 892.

1. INTRODUCTION

Canadians pride themselves on being a country uniquely favoured among all the nation-states of the world. As a nation, we are blessed with abundant land, renewable and non-renewable natural resources, fresh water and clean air. The majority of citizens are healthy, well-educated and economically productive. Canada is a democracy governed by a legal system that guarantees equality and the rights of minorities. It is a nation that has embraced the diversity of all peoples of the world and welcomed people from all nations, all races and all religions to share this land. Canadians are a peaceable, law abiding and tolerant people, an honourable people.

Canadians share this country with the peoples who are indigenous to the land. From 1874 to 1906, in areas of the Northwest Territories that would become the Province of Saskatchewan, the Crown entered into Treaty Nos. 4, 5, 6, 8 and 10 with the Chiefs and Headmen of the Cree, Saulteaux, Nakota and Dene — nations indigenous to the territory. Not until 1905, the year before the last of these treaties was made, was the Province created. By 1906, the entire territory of the province had become "treaty territory." Every square metre of the Province of Saskatchewan is covered by the "sacred blanket" of the treaties and the treaty relationship.[5] The Crown agreed, through these treaties, that if its citizens came into the territories of the First Nations, all people would benefit, the indigenous and the newcomer peoples alike. The Crown and the First Nations agreed, in treaty making, that their citizens would not only survive but prosper, that the unique benefits of the coming together of two ways of life would be shared, that they would both benefit from the land and resources.

Today in Saskatchewan, First Nations comprise an important and growing segment of society. According to the 2001 census, 102,290 of Saskatchewan's 963,150 people identified themselves as "North American Indian."[6] This means that 10.6 percent of Saskatchewan's

---

[5] Elder Alma Kytwayhat of Makwa Sahgaiehcan, Office of the Treaty Commissioner resident Elder.

[6] Statistics Canada, Profile of Citizenship, Immigration, Birthplace, Generation Status, Ethnic Origin, Visible Minorities and Aboriginal Peoples, for Canada, Provinces, Territories, Census Divisions and Census Subdivisions, *2001 Census of Population* (Ottawa: Statistics Canada, 2003). Statistics Canada notes, however, that Aboriginal population figures may be somewhat under-reported due to the difficulty in enumerating some reserves in the province.

people were First Nations, the highest percentage of any of the provinces. In a recent publication, Dr. Eric Howe, a professor of economics at the University of Saskatchewan, predicted that 50 percent of Saskatchewan's population would be Aboriginal by 2050.[7] This makes achieving the Parties' intentions during the original treaty negotiations an imperative for the entire province, namely, anchored on the principle of mutual benefit that First Nations people share in economic prosperity with Canadian society and foster the future well-being of First Nations families and communities.

Many First Nations people have prospered and enjoy the quality of life that was envisaged in the treaties. For example, four of Saskatchewan's top 100 companies, the Saskatchewan Indian Gaming Authority, NorSask Forest Products, Kitsaki Management Ltd. Partnership and Northern Resource Trucking Limited Partnership, are First Nations-owned.[8] These four companies alone employ over 2,000 people.[9] Yet many First Nations people are struggling to overcome generations of poor economic opportunity, of social, linguistic and cultural damage, of poverty and of ill-health. The First Nations in Saskatchewan have a young and expanding population. They are struggling to retain their languages, cultures and important teachings of their elders, to achieve practical forms of governance, to achieve economic self-reliance, and to live as healthy individuals within healthy families and communities. These are not the conditions that the treaties promised.

In 2006, as the Province of Saskatchewan entered into its second century with prosperity and confidence, many First Nations communities still endured third-world living conditions. They also endured many of the consequences of a colonial political system. These facts are sources of concern that demand immediate, practical public policy reform in a nation-state as well-favoured and profoundly compassionate as Canada.

This report has been commissioned by the Parties to these treaties to advise them on what it means to embark upon a process of treaty implementation. The document seeks to identify

---

[7] Howe, Eric, "Saskatchewan with an Aboriginal Majority; Education and Entrepreneurship" *SIPP Public Policy Paper 44* (Regina: Saskatchewan Institute of Public Policy, 2006), p. 4.
[8] "Top 100: Saskatchewan's Top 100 Companies of 2006," *Saskatchewan Business Magazine*, Vol. 27, issue 4 (Aug. 2006), pp. 18-23.
[9] Ibid·

the numerous reasons why, as a Canadian society, we must act to implement the treaties; to define what "treaty implementation" would be; to set out an agenda and a plan for treaty implementation; to propose processes to achieve that plan; and to identify short-term achievable results that will generate momentum for the full implementation of the treaties. The first step, though, is to state, and to have Canadian society accept, that the treaties have not been implemented in the more than 130 years since the first treaty was made.

For the purposes of this report, the term "Parties" refers to the Treaty First Nations, who are represented by the Federation of Saskatchewan Indian Nations, and the Crown in right of Canada. Recognizing the primary role of the federal Crown in the treaty relationship, the Government of Saskatchewan has been and continues to be a willing and interested observer at the Exploratory Treaty Table, but is not included in the term "the Parties" as it is used in this report.

The treaty Parties have found substantial common ground in their examination of treaty issues, but a considerable gap still exists in their understanding of the relevance of the treaties to many important matters. The existing rights that are conferred by the treaties have been given recognition and affirmation by the Constitution of Canada, the supreme law of the land, and that constitutional recognition and affirmation has been given an interpretation by the courts that must be taken into account.

The Exploratory Treaty Table

Since January 1, 1997, the Office of the Treaty Commissioner has coordinated and facilitated discussions with representatives of the Crown and the Federation of Saskatchewan Indian Nations about the relationships created by the treaties, and about the relevance of treaties and the treaty relationship to the future of Saskatchewan.

The Exploratory Treaty Table was established in 1997. From the outset, it has been guided by these principles:

- The treaties are a fundamental part of the relationship between Treaty First Nations in Saskatchewan and the Crown.

- It is desirable to arrive at a common understanding of Treaties 4, 5, 6, 8 and 10 as they apply in Saskatchewan.

- There are differences of views over the content and meaning of the treaties, which the Parties are committed to exploring. The Treaty First Nations believe the treaties have not been implemented according to their spirit and intent, including oral promises, while the Government of Canada relies primarily on the written text of the treaties as the embodiment of the Crown's obligations.

- Respect for First Nations and treaty rights is an important part of maintaining the honour of the Crown in its relations with Treaty First Nations.

- The Office of the Treaty Commissioner is an effective intergovernmental mechanism to assist both Parties in the bilateral process, and in the identification and discussion of treaty and jurisdictional issues.

By October 1998, after intensive consultation with the Parties and the commissioning of independent research, the Office of the Treaty Commissioner released its report entitled *Statement of Treaty Issues: Treaties as a Bridge to the Future.* The present report builds upon the Parties' work, which was facilitated by the Office of the Treaty Commissioner, and endeavours to lay the groundwork for a process of treaty implementation.

Two Perspectives on the Treaties

Discussions at the Exploratory Treaty Table have made it clear that Treaty First Nations in Saskatchewan have always maintained that the treaties are covenantal in nature. The treaties with the Crown are sacred covenants, made among three parties – the First Nations and an undivided Crown, as sovereign nations, and the Creator. In their view, a permanent relationship of mutual respect and sharing was thus established. The unwavering conviction of the Treaty First Nations is that the treaties include not only the written texts recorded by the Crown and the oral agreements made at the time of each treaty, but also their very spirit and intent, and that the treaties govern every aspect of their relationship with the Crown and, through the Crown, with all non-First Nations peoples. In this view, the treaties are holistic in their relevance to all dealings between the Parties and have political, legal and sacred status. It is through these agreements with the Crown that the First Nations gave their consent to sharing their territories with newcomers from overseas and their descendants, and that a unique and eternal relationship between the First Nations and the Crown was forged.

For its part, the Crown entered into the treaties for a complex set of reasons, including establishing peaceful relations with Treaty First Nations, obtaining First Nations' consent to the settling of their territories by European populations, and ensuring the First Nations would make a transition into the new economy.[10] There is a fundamental Crown policy of consensual dealings and respect for First Nations and treaty rights, much of which is embodied in the common law. But to this day, the Government of Canada has developed no general policy guidelines for use in its treaty relations with First Nations.

The Statement of Treaty Issues

The *Statement of Treaty Issues* described treaties as a "bridge to the future." This perspective was and is an explicit rejection of any notion that the treaties are artifacts frozen in the past. Instead, it sees in the treaties the basis of a healthy future relationship in which Treaty First Nations coexist with non-Aboriginal people in harmony and in a way that economic and other opportunities are equitably shared. This future relationship, though, is rooted in the shared principles and mutual promises that underlay the making of the treaties.

---

[10] Ray, Arthur J, Jim Miller and Frank Tough, *Bounty and Benevolence*, (Montreal & Kingston: McGill-Queen's University Press, 2000).

The *Statement of Treaty Issues* was accepted by the Parties and thus provides an important foundation for the current report. In particular, the *Statement of Treaty Issues* formulated the following treaty principles, which have been accepted by both the Federation of Saskatchewan Indian Nations and the Government of Canada:

i.   Treaty making incorporated the customs of the respective parties and created a fundamental political relationship between Treaty First Nations and the Crown. Treaties gave shape to this relationship, creating obligations and expectations on both sides.

ii. The treaty making process between the Parties involved the exchange of solemn promises, based on respect for the spiritual and traditional values of the other. The Crown and Treaty First Nations entered into the agreements freely and of their own accord as the best possible means of advancing their respective interests.

iii. The act of treaty making was also indicative of mutual recognition of the authority vested in the Treaty Commissioners on behalf of the Crown and in the Chiefs and Headmen on behalf of their First Nations to enter into treaties.

iv. In entering into these agreements, both the representatives of the Crown and those of Treaty First Nations recognized each others' authority and capacity to enter into treaties on behalf of their respective people.

v.   One of the fundamental treaty principles is the acknowledgment by the treaty Parties of the solemnity of the treaties.

vi. The treaty making process contains within it the treaty principle of maintaining the honour of the Crown and the honour of Treaty First Nations in maintaining the treaty relationship. Equally important was the conduct and behaviour of the Parties to honour and respect the commitments made in treaties.

vii. The treaties were to provide for peace and good order between the Parties and among the First Nations.

viii. The treaty making process was a means to build lasting and meaningful alliances between the Parties that would foster the future well-being of the people they represented.

ix. The treaties were foundational agreements that were entered into for the purpose of providing the Parties with the means of achieving survival and stability, anchored on the principle of mutual benefit.

x. The relationship between the Treaty First Nations and the Crown is one in which the Parties have both benefits and responsibilities with respect to one another. The treaties created mutual obligations that were to be respected by the Parties.

xi. The treaty relationship is one in which the Parties expect to resolve differences through mutual discussion and decision.

xii. The Parties share a common commitment to reinvigorate the treaty relationship, and to build on a partnership that can address the well-being of both Parties in a respectful and supportive way.

xiii. Canada and Treaty First Nations can enter into arrangements whereby Treaty First Nations exercise jurisdiction and governance over their lands and people, building upon the foundation of their treaty relationship with Canada. These agreements should not alter the treaties; rather they should implement the treaty partnership in a contemporary way while respecting the principles of treaty making.

xiv. The Parties recognize that the participation of the Government of Saskatchewan is required for significant progress on implementation of Treaty First Nations' jurisdiction and governance within Saskatchewan. They also believe that the principles of the treaty relationship are beneficial for all people in Saskatchewan.

The "Made in Saskatchewan" Process

The principles underlying the treaty relationship have guided the Parties' discussions at the Exploratory Treaty Table and served them well. Since the *Statement of Treaty Issues* was released, several other reports have been finalized. Referred to as "treaty context" reports, they outline the Parties' views, goals and objectives on specific treaty issues – education, child welfare, annuities, health and shelter. Discussions are under way on justice, lands and resources, and hunting, fishing, trapping and gathering. The treaty context reports were intended to feed into a broader "made in Saskatchewan process" in which discussions on First Nations governance and jurisdiction were occurring.

The treaty Parties, along with the Government of Saskatchewan, also developed a comprehensive process to address First Nations governance and jurisdiction in Saskatchewan. Their challenge was finding a way to move forward within each of their positions and mandates. The representatives of Canada were constrained by Canada's inherent right to self-government policy and its long-standing position that treaty rights must be defined by the courts. The representatives of the

Federation of Saskatchewan Indian Nations had to uphold their mandate of treaty promotion, protection and implementation. And the representatives of Saskatchewan had to approach the negotiations within their policy positions recognizing the right to self-government as an existing inherent right but maintaining that the treaty relationship and treaty implementation were matters to be dealt with between First Nations and the Government of Canada.

In an attempt to come to meaningful and pragmatic outcomes within these legal and policy constraints, the Federation of Saskatchewan Indian Nations, Canada and Saskatchewan concluded a complex web of agreements: a bilateral (Federation of Saskatchewan Indian Nations-Canada) Exploratory Treaty Table joint work plan; a bilateral Memorandum of Agreement reconstituting the Office of the Treaty Commissioner and authorizing exploratory treaty discussions; and a tripartite (Federation of Saskatchewan Indian Nations-Canada-Saskatchewan) Protocol Agreement to Establish a Common Table to facilitate negotiations on self-government and fiscal arrangements. Flowing from the Protocol Agreement, a tripartite Governance Table, where negotiations on governance and jurisdiction would take place, and a tripartite Fiscal Relations Table were established.

Between 1997 and 2003, the Parties expended substantial resources through these processes. The Exploratory Treaty Table undertook exploratory treaty discussions and completed its treaty context reports, while the Parties at the Governance and Fiscal Relations Tables engaged in negotiations to move toward draft governance agreements in principle.

The Governance Agreements in Principle

On May 27, 2000, the Federation of Saskatchewan Indian Nations, the Government of Canada and the Government of Saskatchewan entered into a Framework for Governance of Treaty First Nations. The Office of the Treaty Commissioner was not involved in the negotiation of that Framework nor in subsequent negotiations that eventually led to the July 2003 initialling of a bilateral (i.e. Federation of Saskatchewan Indian Nations-Canada) Agreement-in-Principle and a Tripartite-Agreement-in-Principle that included Saskatchewan as a party. Initialling was a preliminary step to signing the Agreement-in-Principle and the Tripartite-Agreement-in-Principle, which in turn would authorize formal negotiations toward bilateral and tripartite governance agreements.

In late 2003 and early 2004, the Federation of Saskatchewan Indian Nations and Canada consulted with the member First Nations communities and leadership of the Federation of Saskatchewan Indian Nations on the recently initialled Agreement-in-Principle and Tripartite-Agreement-in-Principle. The Federation of Saskatchewan Indian Nations reported significant concern on the part of First Nation communities that the Agreement-in-Principle and Tripartite-Agreement-in-Principle did not sufficiently reflect the principles of the treaties or the goal of honouring, fulfilling or implementing the spirit and intent of the treaties, and that linkages to the treaties in the agreements were inadequate. As a result of these concerns, no progress has been made toward approval of the Agreement-in-Principle and the Tripartite-Agreement-in-Principle by First Nations, which is required before they can be signed. Without a signed Agreement-in-Principle and Tripartite-Agreement-in-Principle, the work of developing the formal governance agreements could not begin.

The emerging impasse between the Federation of Saskatchewan Indian Nations and Canada over the relationship between the treaties and negotiations on Treaty First Nations governance led the Parties to commission the Office of the Treaty Commissioner to prepare a report specifically on treaty implementation with respect to treaties within Saskatchewan.

About This Report

This report builds upon the hard work of the Parties at the Exploratory Treaty Table and on the dedicated and honest participation of many government officials who have had to grapple with issues that often appear elusive. It also builds upon the heartfelt and sincere participation of many Treaty First Nations Elders, youth, political leaders and policy-makers to whom these issues are a birthright and who have brought deep reservoirs of optimism and patience. The Exploratory Treaty Table evolved into a place where important issues are discussed respectfully and that, in itself, is evidence of what the spirit and intent of the treaties really means.

The report also builds upon important developments in policy and law since the *Statement of Treaty Issues* was published and the treaty principles were adopted by the Parties, developments that have made the issue of treaty implementation of even greater contemporary relevance. There is no longer a real debate as to whether the treaties in Saskatchewan *should* be implemented, nor should there be any debate over the statement that they *have not* been implemented. But there is great uncertainty about how the process of implementing them can be mandated and achieved and, of course, what the end result of such a process should mean for the Parties and for Canadian society.

The progress made by officials at the Exploratory Treaty Table and elsewhere is not necessarily reflected in equal progress in public understanding, despite a concerted effort by the Parties and the Office of the Treaty Commissioner to raise public awareness of treaty issues. For some members of the public, the treaties remain curiosities of the historical past, to be remembered and perhaps re-enacted on anniversaries as pieces of the distant past; for others, the treaties embody the very founding and living principles of the nation. The successful realization of treaty implementation will require broad public support both for the conceptual basis of treaty implementation and for the actions required to make it a reality. The Government of Saskatchewan, too, will have an important role to play in this endeavour.

Some can only conceive of treaties as artifacts of the particular historical moments they were made. This limited view blinds those who need to understand the treaties' nature as constitutional documents that embody principles of a relationship promised to last "as long as the sun shines, the grass grows and the rivers flow." The Parties, through their representatives at the Exploratory Treaty Table, have also agreed with this perspective. By the same token, those who read such words only as the quaint expression of sentiments of a distant, simpler time cannot feel their power to bind and link the peoples of our country, and all the generations of those peoples, or their power not only to explain our past but also to guide our future.

Unlike most other jurisdictions, treaties continue to be made in Canada. The rights of Aboriginal peoples under modern comprehensive land claims agreements are deemed to be included with the term "existing Aboriginal and treaty rights" by virtue of subsection 35 (3) of the *Constitution Act, 1982*. Unlike Treaties 4, 5, 6, 8 and 10, though, modern comprehensive claims agreements contain extensive implementation agreements and dispute resolution mechanisms.

Even in the case of modern-day treaty-like agreements, however, serious implementation difficulties can and do arise. In November 2003, the Office of the Auditor General of Canada observed:

> • Signing a land claim agreement is a major accomplishment. Managing it afterward is an ongoing challenge that requires collaboration by all parties. That collaboration must begin with Indian and Northern Affairs Canada (INAC) taking a leadership role in making the claims work. It must also manage federal responsibilities set out under the agreements in a way that achieves results. We found that with respect to the two claims we looked at, the Gwich'in people of the Northwest Territories (NWT) and the Inuit of Nunavut, Indian and Northern Affairs Canada's performance on both counts has left considerable room for improvement.
>
> • For example, Indian and Northern Affairs Canada seems focused on fulfilling the letter of the land claims' implementation plans but not the spirit. Officials may believe they have met their obligations, but in fact they have not worked to support the full intent of the land claims agreements.
>
> • Also, the various mechanisms for managing the claims are not effective in resolving all disputes. Land claims arbitration panels have not dealt with any of the long-standing disagreements since the claims were settled over 10 years ago.[11]

---

[11] Auditor General of Canada, *2003 Report of the Auditor General of Canada to the House of Commons*, chapter 8 "Indian and Northern Affairs Canada – Transferring Federal Responsibilities to the North," p. 1.

The detailed analysis of the Office of the Auditor General reveals that even in cases where the parties to what are often called "modern treaties" have negotiated implementation agreements, an inappropriate focus upon fulfilling "the letter" of those implementation agreements can frustrate fulfilling their "full intent." Inconsistent implementation can damage the relationships that comprehensive claims agreements seek to build:

> • All Parties generally agree that many of the obligations on the land claim agreements have been met and have led to positive outcomes. However, when there are disagreements that the oversight framework and the dispute resolution process do not resolve, unhealthy relationships can develop.[12]

It is hardly surprising, then, that an examination of the implementation of treaties made more than a century ago reveals similar difficulties and gives rise to similar strains upon the relationship of the treaty Parties. In treaty implementation, we are proposing that the Parties now negotiate implementation agreements more than a century after the fact. In approaching that task, we can certainly learn from the challenges of implementing contemporary land claims agreements and from the incisive advice of the Office of the Auditor General. Having an implementation plan is necessary, but it is not enough. The Parties will need to make sure that the plan itself is implemented and that progress toward the performance goals in a treaty implementation agreement can be measured, reviewed and verified.

This report explores what the treaty relationship was intended to be from the perspective of both Parties, and also why the intentions of the treaty Parties for mutual benefit and prosperity failed to come to pass and why many of the challenges facing Treaty First Nations may be ascribed to that failure. The purpose is, above all, to encourage the Parties to accept responsibility for implementing the treaties and fulfilling the treaty relationship rather than to impose blame. The report also offers answers to the questions: What does treaty implementation mean? Why is treaty implementation necessary? What are the impediments to treaty implementation? What would a plan for treaty implementation look like? What mechanisms are necessary to make treaty implementation a reality?

---

[12] Ibid., p.9.

Our peaceable and prosperous Canadian society is a product of the treaties. We must all remember that the making of the treaties were acts of hope and declarations of optimism. By making the treaties, the Parties undertook to work together in the shared enterprise of building a Canadian society in which First Nations and newcomers could live with mutual respect, dignity and opportunity. All citizens of Canada have a collective responsibility to ensure that their governments act with honour, on their behalf, to implement the treaties, and that a harmonious treaty relationship is continuously maintained. This responsibility is a duty of citizenship.

The process will take time, building on consensus as it is achieved issue by issue. The public needs to understand why this process is so important. It is an issue of justice and basic human rights. Our very honour as a Canadian society demands that it be done, and done well.

2. THE INTENTIONS OF THE TREATY PARTIES

The treaties need to be honoured in accordance with their original spirit and intent. The courts have said that rights under the treaties are not limited to words in treaty documents. The term "spirit and intent" is used in this report to include both the meaning of the written text and aspects of the treaties and treaty relationship that the written word alone cannot always capture. The term "spirit and intent" captures the essence of the treaty relationship, including the mutual promises made by the Parties and the spiritual foundation. But if it is to serve as more than a poetic motto, it needs to be given specific meaning that can be adopted by both Parties.

Spirit and Intent of Treaties: The Elders' Understanding

Through a series of five Elders' forums coordinated and facilitated by the Office of the Treaty Commissioner in 1997 in each of the province's treaty regions, the Office of the Treaty Commissioner has gained a comprehensive view of Elders' perspectives on the meaning of the treaties. The information gathered at the Elders' forums provided the First Nations' view on what the treaties mean. That perspective was documented by the late Harold Cardinal and Walter Hildebrandt in *Treaty Elders of Saskatchewan*. The authors state:

> The result, we believe, is a text that contains a traditional First Nations
> theoretical framework to be used as a guide for approaching the question
> of treaty implementation in Saskatchewan.[13]

For the first time, the First Nations perspective on the meaning of the treaties from all five treaty regions within Saskatchewan had been documented. As a result, there now exists in Saskatchewan a written record of a perspective that has been transmitted orally through the generations.

To understand the Elders' perspective on the treaties, one must be prepared to acknowledge the world views of the First Nations:

---

[13] Cardinal and Hildebrandt, *Treaty Elders of Saskatchewan*, page ix.

> The Elders made it clear that, in their view, those who seek to understand Indian Treaties must become aware of the significance of First Nations spiritual traditions, beliefs, and ceremonies underlying the treaty making process. [14]

Critical to that understanding is the relationship between First Nations people and the Creator. Their belief that they were placed on the North American continent by the Creator, where they developed their political, social, educational, economic and spiritual structures and institutions, is fundamental to that understanding. It is within this context that the First Nations' view of the treaties must be considered.

The Elders presented similar descriptions of their belief systems. A theme common to the Dene, Cree, Assiniboine and Saulteaux peoples was the focus on their relationship with the Creator. The late Elder Norman Sunchild of the Thunderchild First Nation provided the following insight:

> ... Our Old Ones spent their lifetime studying, meditating, and living the way of life required to understand those traditions, teachings and laws in which the treaties are rooted. In their study, they rooted their physical and spiritual beings directly on Mother Earth as the way of establishing a "connectedness" to the Creator and his creation. Through that "connectedness", they received the conceptual knowledge they required, and the capacity to verbalize and describe the many blessings bestowed on them by the Creator. They were meticulous in following the disciplines, process and procedures required for such an endeavour.[15]

Thus, one of the primary objectives of the treaty making process was to have the First Nations' relationship with the Creator recognized and affirmed:

> In the view of the Elders, the treaty nations – First Nations and the Crown – solemnly promised the Creator that they would conduct their relationships with each other in accordance with the laws, values and principles given to each of them by the Creator.[16]

This basic principle underlying the treaties, that they were formulated with the guidance of the Creator and are protected by the Creator, is critical to the First Nations' understanding of the Treaties. It leads to the belief that this sacred underpinning of the treaties cannot be altered or

---

[14] Ibid., p. 1.

[15] Office of the Treaty Commissioner, *Statement of Treaty Issues: Treaties as a Bridge to the Future* (Saskatoon, Office of the Treaty Commissioner, 1998), p. 12.

[16] Cardinal and Hildebrandt, *Treaty Elders of Saskatchewan*, p. 1.

changed. They are to continue as long as the sun shines, the rivers flow and the grass grows. Elder Peter Waskahat of the Frog Lake First Nation expressed it this way, "The [treaties] can only be broken through the will of the Creator."[17] This principle was expressed in a similar manner by the late Elder George Ryder of Carry the Kettle First Nation: "The pipe is holy and it is a way of life for Indian people. The treaty was made with a pipe and that is sacred, that is never to be broken...never to be put away."[18] This connection to the Creator and the spiritual basis for the treaties translates into a strong conviction that the treaty relationship cannot be altered or changed.

(a) Elders' Understanding of Treaty Principles

The Elders unequivocally stated their belief that the treaties were a recognition by the Crown of the First Nations' relationship with the Creator. The treaties, according to the Elders, were based on several principles. First and foremost was the joint acknowledgment by the treaty-makers of the supremacy of the Creator. The second principle related to the maintenance of peace between the Parties; the third to the Parties entering into a familial relationship based on *wâhkôhtowin* (good relations). The fourth undertaking was the guarantee of each other's survival and stability based on mutual sharing. The fifth principle identified mutual sharing as including the First Nations' continuing right to livelihood.

These five principles guided the First Nation treaty-makers as they negotiated the treaties, and thus, "They provide the contextual framework for the Indian understanding of the collective and individual relationships created by treaty."[19]

Elders throughout five treaty areas expressed these principles in remarkably similar language. They are summarized in the following statement provided by Elder Peter Waskahat of the Frog Lake First Nation:

> Elders from many different tribes say they knew about the coming of the White man long before he arrived. They say that Elders and holy men among them prophesied that men would come with different ways, that

---

[17] Ibid., p. 25.
[18] Ibid., p. 28.
[19] Ibid., p. 38.

these men would want to live among them. Long before the arrival of the White man, the First Nations discussed how they would live with the White man. There were extensive discussions to determine how the First Nations could peacefully co-exist with the newcomers. The Elders say they knew the White man was coming across the sea from places where there was much bloodshed. On the island of the new world created by *Wisahkêcâhk*, that way of life could not prevail. The island of North America was created so that peace could prevail. When the newcomers arrived, peace treaties would need to be negotiated.

It was decided long before the White man arrived that the First Nations would treat the newcomers as relatives, as brothers and sisters. The First Nations had decided that they would live in peace and that they would share the land with these newcomers. The sacred earth could never be sold or given away, according to the principles of the First Nations, but it could be shared. The First Nations decided that the earth could be shared with the newcomers and that it could be shared to the depth of a plough blade. The earth could be shared so everyone could peacefully co-exist.[20]

(b) Witaskêwin – Living Together on the Land

In order to allow for the peaceful settlement of the fertile prairie lands by newcomers, the Canadian government soon after Confederation embarked upon a vigorous campaign to negotiate treaties with the original inhabitants of North America:

> In devising a format for new treaties in Rupert's Land, Canada was informed by two streams of diplomatic precedent. One was the practice established between the First Nations and the HBC [Hudson's Bay Company]. Many of these diplomatic protocols were carried over into the negotiation of Canada's post-Confederation treaties, such as the use of the sacred pipe, formal exchange of gifts and distribution of uniforms, medals and flags. Canada was also mindful of another stream of precedent: Crown treaties concluded with First Nations east and north of the Great Lakes prior to Confederation...[21]

That land was the central impetus for these negotiations is undisputed, but the resulting agreement on how land was to be dealt with remains one of the major differences in interpretation between the Parties. Elders firmly believe that the land was to be shared with the newcomers but that did not mean a loss of ownership. Historically, First Nations had

---

[20] Ibid., p. 31.
[21] Office of the Treaty Commissioner, *Statement of Treaty Issues*, p. 19.

entered into agreements with other First Nations to share lands for trapping or hunting or gathering purposes. They were prepared to enter into a similar agreement with the Crown that would allow for *Witaskêwin*, living together on the land.

The result has been vastly different interpretations on land ownership as a result of Treaties 4, 5, 6, 8 and 10. Elders expressed their views on this matter in a variety of ways, but the underlying theme was that First Nations never consented to the blanket extinguishment of First Nations title. The Royal Commission on Aboriginal Peoples stated the Elders' perspective in the following manner:

- treaty nations did not intend to consent to the blanket extinguishment of their Aboriginal rights and title by entering into the treaty relationship;

- treaty nations intended to share the territory and jurisdiction and management over it, as opposed to ceding the territory, even where the text of an historical treaty makes reference to a blanket extinguishment of land rights.[22]

Elders enunciated their belief that the treaties were nation-to-nation agreements. First Nations welcomed the newcomers to their land and agreed through the treaties to accommodate them by sharing the land with them. The treaties, from the Elders' perspective, were negotiated within the conceptual framework and understanding of the relationship between the Creator, his children and all elements of his creation: "Hence, in this context, the Elders utilize the knowledge, teachings, laws, doctrines and values symbolically represented in part by the following: sun, grass, river, rock, sweetgrass and pipe stem."[23]

In their view, the circle has been widened to accept the Crown. The treaties acknowledge this acceptance and the willingness of the First Nations to share the land with the newcomers – to live together on the land.

---

[22] Cardinal and Hildebrandt, *Treaty Elders of Saskatchewan*, p. 58.
[23] Ibid., p. 54.

(c) Elements of Treaty that Require Flexibility and Adaptability

According to the Elders, the treaties were designed to guarantee to the First Nations their liberty, freedom, independence and economic self-sufficiency. In order to accomplish this in a modern context, some elements of the treaties require flexibility and adaptability. All of the treaties guaranteed that the First Nations' way of life would continue. Elders suggest that *Pimâcihowin*, making a living or the duty to provide for one's needs,[24] and *Pimâcihisowin*, making one's own living, are treaty guarantees.[25] The Elders believe that the livelihood arrangements were made to enable them to continue their relationship to the land. When necessary, it would result in adapting to, and becoming part of, new livelihoods. That adaptation was made necessary by the influx of thousands of settlers who made it impossible for First Nations people to pursue their traditional ways. The Elders indicated their clear understanding that the treaties promised that First Nations would receive the required assistance to enable them to participate in economic environments as they changed in the future. This would enable First Nations people to make their own living, thereby maintaining their self-reliance, or *Pimâcihisowin*.

Another element of the treaties that requires flexibility and adaptability is the education clause. Education was included in the treaties to enable First Nations to obtain the skills needed to participate in the new economic system that newcomers were implementing in Canada. It would be the basis of self-sufficiency for First Nations people. As Canadian society evolved, so must the treaty education system. First Nations need to direct the evolution of that system, so they can ensure that it results in an education system that is effective and appropriate for their people.

Equally important is the need to view governance as an area that requires adaptability and flexibility. Elders firmly conveyed the message that the treaties were concluded between sovereign nations. Based on that premise, the Elders believe it is time to renew the government-to-government relationship that existed at the time treaties were negotiated. Inherent in this is the need for First Nations to have the opportunity to rebuild governance

[24] Ibid., p. 44.
[25] Ibid., p. 45.

structures that are legitimate in the eyes of their citizens; accountable, transparent and responsible to those citizens; culturally appropriate; and flexible enough to evolve over time. As well, since Elders are the keepers of so much sacred knowledge, a renewed government-to-government relationship must also include an ongoing role for Elders in interpreting the spirit and intent of the treaties and resolving the disputes that arise in any ongoing relationship. This will ensure that the spirit and intent of the treaties continues to be understood and respected well into the future.

Achieving this renewed relationship will only be possible if the full "spirit and intent" of the treaties is implemented, as "the Elders cannot see how self-governance is going to be viable unless it is implemented on the land-sharing principles contemplated by First Nations at the time treaty was signed."[26] According to the Elders, it is on this basis that governance discussions must proceed.

The Numbered Treaties: Canada's Understandings

If the spirit and intent of the treaties from the First Nations' perspective involves an understanding of the languages, laws and traditions that informed an oral agreement, the Crown's understanding is largely derived from the written texts understood within the broader context of Crown policy as it related to indigenous peoples.

The current understanding of the federal government about treaties, treaty rights and treaty relationships is by no means straightforward. While the history of the Crown's relationship with First Nations will be explored in more detail in a later section, for the purpose of understanding the Government of Canada's views on the intent of the treaties, three main eras in the policy approach of the Government of Canada are identified:

• First, the policies of the *Royal Proclamation of 1763*, which established certain legal and political principles upon which the treaty making process was founded.

---

[26] Ibid., p. 67.

- Second, the overt and covert policies fostering assimilation that have been given effect through the *Indian Act* and other means.

- Third, recognition within the past generation that past policies based on a goal of assimilation caused harm and need to be replaced with more respectful approaches, as evidenced by the inclusion of First Nations and treaty rights in section 35 of the *Constitution Act, 1982,* the conclusion of Treaty Land Entitlement agreements in the 1990s and the establishment of the Office of the Treaty Commissioner itself in 1989 and its renewed mandate in 1997.

The conduct of Crown officials demonstrates the same pattern of assuming certain fundamental truths that may not have been shared by First Nations during the treaty councils:

- It was widely assumed by Crown officials, that, prior to the treaties, the Crown was already sovereign over First Nations' traditional territories through unilateral assertion or through treaties with European powers.

- It was assumed, therefore, that the Crown had the power to extend its laws to First Nations.

- It was widely assumed that the benefits of "civilization" and Christianity to First Nations were self-evident.

These assumptions informed the conduct of the Crown's treaty commissioners and form part of the context of the making of the treaties.

(a) The Policy of the Royal Proclamation of 1763

The *Royal Proclamation of 1763* was a landmark in establishing the Crown's policy that:

> ... the several Nations or Tribes of Indians with whom We are connected, and who live under our Protection should not be molested or disturbed in the Possession of such Parts of Our Dominions and Territories as, not having been ceded to nor purchased by Us, are reserved to them, or any of them, as their Hunting Grounds.

The Proclamation established a treaty making process that focused upon, but was not limited to, the acquisition of First Nations lands through consensual purchase. The Treaty of Niagara in 1764 cemented the central policies of the Proclamation as the key to the Crown's approach to relations with First Nations, as described by the Ontario Court of Appeal in *Chippewas of Sarnia v. Canada*.

> The Royal Proclamation was an important, albeit not the first, manifestation of Crown imperial policy as it applied to Indian lands. The Royal Proclamation:
>
> - recognized that First Nations had rights in their lands;
> - established imperial control over settlement on Indian lands whether those lands were within or beyond the boundaries of the established British colonies in North America;
> - prohibited private purchase of Indian lands and required that alienation of Indian rights in their lands be by way of surrender to the Crown; and
> - established a process by which surrenders of Indian land would be made to the Crown. The surrender process accepted that Indian rights in their lands were collective and not individual.
>
> After setting out its policy in the Royal Proclamation, the Crown took extraordinary steps to make the First Nations aware of that policy and to gain their support on the basis that the policy as set down in the Royal Proclamation would govern Crown-First Nations relations. In the summer of 1764, at the request of the Crown, more than 2,000 First Nations chiefs representing some twenty-two First Nations, including chiefs from the Chippewa Nation, attended a Grand Council at Niagara. Sir William Johnson, the Crown representative, who was well known to many of the chiefs present, read the provisions of the Royal Proclamation respecting Indian lands and committed the Crown to the enforcement of those provisions. The chiefs, in turn, promised to keep the peace and deliver up prisoners taken in recent hostilities. The singular significance of the Royal Proclamation to the First Nations can be traced to this extraordinary assembly and the treaty it produced. [27]

Thus, the policy of the *Royal Proclamation* not only became part of the common law, but informed Imperial diplomacy and established high ideals for honourable dealings between the Crown and First Nations people. The policies of the *Royal Proclamation* were also pragmatic and served the interests of the Imperial authorities as they consolidated British

---

[27] Chippewas of Sarnia Band v. Canada (2000), 51 O.R. (3d) 641 paras. 53-6.

jurisdiction and influence in British North America. An orderly land acquisition process would overcome earlier frauds and abuses and minimize friction between First Nations and settlers and traders.

(b) Legislative Policies and the Indian Act

The treaties that apply in Saskatchewan were made at a time when the policy objectives of assimilation and containment on reserves were already well established. Thus, even as treaties continued to be made under the principles established by the *Royal Proclamation*, colonial governments and after 1867 the federal government enacted legislation that intruded greatly upon the internal affairs of Indian bands. By the time the treaties were made in the area that is now Saskatchewan, federal government policy had begun to deviate, at least in part, from the spirit of the *Royal Proclamation* enacted more than a century earlier.

Nonetheless, the first Prime Minister recognized the need to deal with the First Nations pursuant to the policies established by, or at least reaffirmed by, the *Royal Proclamation*. The Rupert's Land and North-Western Territory Order that transferred the land to the Dominion of Canada relieved the Hudson's Bay Company of any responsibilities for First Nations stating, "Any claims of the Indians to compensation for lands required for purposes of settlement shall be disposed of by the Canadian Government in communication with the Imperial Government..." In their address to the Queen, the Senate and House of Commons stated, "...upon the transference of the territories in question to the Canadian Government, the claims of the Indian tribes to compensation for lands required for purposes of settlement will be considered and settled in conformity with the equitable principles which have uniformly governed the British Crown in its dealings with the aborigines." Prime Minister John A. Macdonald wanted to ensure the successful implementation of his "National Policy." Important aspects of the policy included populating the western territories with thousands of European settlers and connecting British Columbia with the eastern provinces by a transcontinental railway. In order to accomplish these goals, peace and harmony with the First Nations had to be established. Macdonald did not want a repeat of the American experience, in which settlement was only possible after years of bloody warfare between the United States and First Nations. The peaceful settlement of the western territories was to be carried out based on political diplomacy, compromise and accommodation inherent in the negotiated treaties between Canada and First Nations.

To implement the treaty making process, Macdonald looked to treaty commissioners such as Adams Archibald and Wemyss Simpson. By the time the treaties that apply in Saskatchewan were made, the chief treaty commissioner was Alexander Morris, the Lieutenant Governor of Manitoba, the North-West Territories and Kee-wa-tin. Morris shared the Prime Minister's desire to have a stable political foundation on which to settle the western territories with newcomers. "One of the gravest of the questions presented for solution by the Dominion of Canada...was securing the alliance of the Indian tribes, and maintaining friendly relations with them."[28]

Morris also looked to the model established between the Hudson's Bay Company and the First Nations as best suited for future treaties. Canada's intent in negotiating the numbered treaties can be summarized as follows:

> Each of the western or numbered treaties began by stressing "The desire of Her Majesty, to open up to settlement" a particular tract of country by obtaining the consent of "her Indian subjects inhabiting the said tract" through a treaty resulting in "peace and goodwill" between the Indians and Her Majesty, since they could be assured of "Her Majesty's bounty and benevolence." In effect, this language indicates the objectives of the treaty making process: opening areas for settlement in exchange for the Crown's bounty and benevolence thereby ensuring peace and goodwill.[29]

A primary objective for Canada was to clear First Nations title to the land:

> The Dominion's main interest in formally treating with Indians – to clear what it understood to be 'Indian title' to facilitate an agricultural and commercial frontier is well known.[30]

---

[28] Morris, Alexander. *The Treaties of Canada with Indians of Manitoba and the North-West Territories*. (Toronto: Belfords, Clark and Co., 1880), p. 9.

[29] Ray et al., *Bounty and Benevolence*, p. 59.

[30] Ibid., p. 64.

In exchange for the clearing of the "Indian title" that stood in the way of settlement, Canada intended to reciprocate in a generous and benevolent manner. Reserves would be set aside for the exclusive use of First Nations. First Nations people would continue to pursue their traditional lifestyles; hunting, fishing and trapping would not be jeopardized. If First Nations people decided to take up agricultural activities, assistance would be provided. From the Crown's perspective, each First Nation person would be entitled to an annual annuity as well as education and health care. The intent of all these commitments was to gain title to the land in a peaceful manner, thereby facilitating the influx of settlers and, in turn, ensuring the First Nations would gain the skills necessary to participate in and benefit from the new economy.

(c) Treaties in the Modern Era

Three events highlight the Crown's current renewed, if yet incomplete, acceptance that the treaties have not yet been fully implemented and that it needs to begin implementing its treaty commitments. The first event is the inclusion of an explicit constitutional recognition of existing Aboriginal and treaty rights in section 35 of the *Constitution Act, 1982*. While it was not clear in 1982 what rights section 35 contained, subsequent experience has demonstrated that it is important in making treaty implementation an imperative for governments.

The second event in Saskatchewan was the negotiation of a Treaty Land Entitlement Framework Agreement with the Federation of Saskatchewan Indian Nations and Treaty Land Entitlement agreements with First Nations in the 1990s. These constituted an acceptance by the federal and provincial governments that treaty promises to land had not been fully implemented and this failure had to be rectified. While progress in completing the Treaty Land Entitlement process has been slow, negotiation of the agreements and efforts made to implement them demonstrate a renewed recognition by governments of the importance of abiding by the terms of the treaties.

The third event was the creation of the Office of the Treaty Commissioner and the beginning of the Exploratory Treaty Table process in 1997. The discussions represented the first time in 123 years that the Government of Canada agreed to explore, in a meaningful way, the treaties and the treaty relationship with First Nations in Saskatchewan. These three events have created the momentum on which future processes to negotiate treaty implementation and fulfillment of the treaty relationship can and must build.

Conclusion: Identifying Common Intentions as a Guide to the Future

A full understanding of the spirit and intent of the treaties from both Parties' perspectives includes:

- The principles identified by Elders, such as matters that were implicitly fundamental to each of the Parties and thus to remain unaffected by the treaties, matters that were to change as time and circumstances evolved, and the promise that treaty promises would be eternal.
- The assurances made at the time of the treaty negotiations about the creation of a relationship based on mutual respect.
- The sharing of economic opportunity and the preservation of traditional livelihood.
- The principle of the honour of the Crown, which requires the treaties to be fulfilled with a view to their underlying beneficial purposes.

The analysis of the treaty Parties' perspectives indicates two types of agreements were reached:

- An agreement that First Nations would share the benefits of the land with newcomers and, in exchange, the Crown would provide the necessities of life and opportunity to share in the prosperity that the newcomers would bring to the land, such as through education, health care and continued access to the resources of the land.
- An agreement to act together in the future in a brother-to-brother relationship wherein conflicts would be resolved cooperatively, on the basis of mutual respect for the autonomy and interdependence of the Parties.

These understandings of the intentions of the treaty Parties come directly from the Parties and their contributions to the Exploratory Treaty Table over more than ten years. This will be discussed in the next section. The Parties need to continue discussing the spirit and intent of treaties in order to agree on a common "spirit and intent" which will govern their relationship, and to agree on the principles and practical implications of that relationship in the modern context. Only when the Parties share a common intention and act upon it to ensure that the treaties find their rightful place in the state and that Treaty First Nations people find their rightful place in Canadian society will we have achieved treaty implementation.

3. APPROACHES AT THE EXPLORATORY TREATY TABLE

If the spirit and intent of the treaties is to be implemented in a meaningful, respectful way and the promise of the treaty relationship fulfilled, the treaty Parties need a neutral space in which to discuss their understandings of the treaties and how they might be implemented in a modern context. It is also essential for them to have a neutral source of research and analysis to support their discussions. It was not until the 1990s that the federal government agreed to enter into a dialogue around the treaties in a "made in Saskatchewan" process, and even then, as we have already seen, that agreement was only to *explore*:

> Between May of 1997 and March of 1998, Canada and the Federation of Saskatchewan Indian Nations engaged in discussions, through the auspices of the Office of the Treaty Commissioner, to explore each other's understanding of the nature of the treaty relationship and to examine the policy implications of building on the treaty relationship.[31]

Despite limitations on the federal government, this was an historic development. For the first time in over a century, Canada had agreed formally to engage in an exploration of the meaning of treaties and the treaty relationship with First Nations in Saskatchewan.

Exploratory discussions have achieved as much as they can, especially as the impasse in discussions at the Governance and Fiscal Relations Table means there is no process for the results of these discussions to contribute to. It is time for the Parties to move from exploratory to results-orientated discussion, the result being implementation of the treaties and fulfillment of the promise of the treaty relationship. The neutral space and support that the Office of the Treaty Commissioner provides to the Parties will be more important than ever as the Parties begin to engage seriously in what will sometimes be difficult discussions on treaty implementation – discussions that will require them to make accommodations and reconcile competing interests and points of view. The relationships the Parties have established at the Exploratory Treaty Table and the lessons they and the Office of the Treaty Commissioner have learned over the last ten years, however, provide a solid foundation for progress.

---

[31] Office of the Treaty Commissioner, *Statement of Treaty Issues*, p. 36.

Federation of Saskatchewan Indian Nations Approach

The Federation of Saskatchewan Indian Nations approached the Exploratory Treaty Table in a way that placed the treaties within a broader context:

> The Federation of Saskatchewan Indian Nations emphasized that it was important to contextualize the discussion in terms of how they conceived the treaty relationship, how they understood the history of the treaties, how they view the purposes of treaty making and how they interpret the objectives of the parties. [32]

In other words, the Federation of Saskatchewan Indian Nations would not be entering discussions confined to the written text of the treaties. Neither would they accept the courts' interpretation as the sole basis for discussions. First Nations views, particularly those of the Elders, would have to be recognized and accepted as legitimate perspectives. The broader dimensions of the treaties and treaty relationships, including economic, political and spiritual aspects, guided the Federation of Saskatchewan Indian Nations at the Exploratory Treaty Table just as they had guided the making of treaties themselves.

The Federation of Saskatchewan Indian Nations stated that First Nations believe the treaty making process guaranteed three key elements:

• governance

• livelihood

• brother-to-brother relations.

In the case of governance, the Federation of Saskatchewan Indian Nations adopted the principle that First Nations would govern themselves according to the comprehensive body of laws given to them by the Creator. They asserted that traditional authority over areas such as responsibility for children, family well-being, education and spiritual beliefs were retained by First Nations at the time of treaty making. This authority was to be exercised through the retention of their social, political and cultural organizations as self-governing First Nations.

---

[32] Ibid., p. 38.

The Federation of Saskatchewan Indian Nations also linked governance to the second guarantee of the treaty making process, livelihood. They indicated that, through their own laws and their own system of justice, First Nations would govern their own people as they pursued the traditional activities of trapping, hunting and fishing and the new livelihood activities introduced to their lands.

Finally, the Federation of Saskatchewan Indian Nations stated that First Nations would approach the relationship with the Crown in the spirit of the brother-to-brother relationship, which was an integral part of the spirit and intent of the treaties:

> In their description of the relationship forged by the treaties, First Nations emphasized that they expected the treaty partners to come together regularly to discuss matters of mutual concern.[33]

These matters of mutual concern include such issues as child and family well-being, education, justice and livelihood issues of access to lands and resources, both for traditional purposes of hunting, fishing, trapping and gathering and for an opportunity to participate in new livelihood activities introduced by the Europeans. The Exploratory Treaty Table finally, if belatedly, provided that opportunity.

Canada's Approach

By agreeing to participate in the Exploratory Treaty Table discussions, Canada made a commitment to come to Saskatchewan to listen to First Nations' Elders and leaders in order to better understand the implications of the treaty relationship. Federal representatives stated at the outset that Canada's relationship with First Nations is most often based on social policy:

> ... the Government of Canada, as a matter of public policy, seeks to provide a basic level of health care, access to education, economic opportunities, and the like to all citizens, regardless of treaty status.[34]

---

[33] Ibid., p. 41.
[34] Ibid., p. 37.

The Exploratory Treaty Table provided an opportunity for Canada to engage in discussions on treaties that would take them beyond social policies on program and service delivery, to try to understand a more relationship-oriented approach to the treaties.

However, Canada also acknowledged that First Nations have constitutionally protected rights such as hunting, fishing and trapping on unoccupied Crown lands and the annual receipt of annuities. The Government of Canada also recognized the special role for the Crown in relation to First Nations, as affirmed in the *Royal Proclamation of 1763* and acknowledged, "... that section 35 of the *Constitution Act, 1982* recognizes and affirms existing Aboriginal and treaty rights of the Aboriginal people of Canada."[35] For an interpretation of Aboriginal and treaty rights, the federal government indicated that it "looks to the courts for guidance regarding the nature of treaties,"[36] particularly the Supreme Court of Canada, and that their decisions guide the government's approach in dealing with treaties and treaty rights. The Canadian government has consistently relied on the written text of the treaties as interpreted by the courts.

Within the context of the various court decisions, the federal government has developed policies and procedures for dealing with issues arising out of treaty interpretations and obligations. For example, the federal government has established specific claims and treaty land entitlement processes. Canada also recognizes the inherent right of self-government as an existing Aboriginal right under section 35 of the 1982 *Constitution Act*. Under the federal inherent right policy, the inherent right to self-government may find expression in treaties, building on the Crown's relationship with Treaty First Nations.[37]

There are other restrictions within which the federal government approached these discussions. Through the terms of the *Natural Resources Transfer Agreement* and the *Constitution Act, 1930*, all federal government interests in Crown lands were transferred to the Province of Saskatchewan. This introduces a third party to the equation that did not exist at the time treaties were made. It also meant that Canada's participation at the Exploratory Treaty Table was to be framed by these other legislative and constitutional obligations.

---

[35] Ibid.
[36] Ibid.
[37] Ibid., p. 37.

Nevertheless, Canada remained committed to the process:

> The federal government wishes to build a stronger and more effective partnership between Canada and the Treaty First Nations of Saskatchewan. By recalling that treaties were made for the mutual benefit of both parties, and by developing common understandings of the treaty relationship, the federal government believes that the treaty relationship may provide a framework for our shared future together.[38]

Common Understandings

There are wide differences of interpretation between the Parties on the intent of various treaty matters. But there is also some common ground that opens the way for further discussion. This common ground is referred to in the preliminary views provided by the partners at the Exploratory Treaty Table.

The Federation of Saskatchewan Indian Nations offered this view:

> Treaties provided us with a shared future, treaties prevented war and guaranteed peace, treaties defined and shaped relations between nations through enduring relations of mutual respect, and treaties guaranteed the shared economic bounty of one of this planet's richest and most productive lands.[39]

Similar views were expressed by Canada:

> The federal government understands that the treaties between Canada and First Nations were intended by the parties to endure into the future. It recognizes that treaties define fundamental aspects of the continuing relationship between Canada and Treaty First Nations and that they are important instruments guiding the way to a shared future for First Nations and other Canadians. The federal government recognizes that, by doing justice to the treaties, it may honour the past and enrich the future.[40]

The fact that both Parties recognize the treaties as a foundation to future relations is an important common understanding that augurs well for ongoing treaty discussions. The treaty Parties in Saskatchewan also arrived at other common understandings, captured in the *Statement of Treaty Issues*, that will assist future relations.

---

[38] Ibid., p. 38.
[39] Ibid., p. 62.
[40] Ibid., p. 63.

The Role of the Office of the Treaty Commissioner

The Office of the Treaty Commissioner has performed a number of roles in support of the discussions at the Exploratory Treaty Table and through this, the discussions between the Federation of Saskatchewan Indian Nations, Canada, and Saskatchewan at the Governance and Fiscal Relations Table. The Office of the Treaty Commissioner's mandate, as an independent and impartial office, has been to facilitate exploratory treaty discussions between the Federation of Saskatchewan Indian Nations and the Government of Canada on treaty issues. The mandate focuses on the nature of the treaty relationship and the requirements and implications of treaty implementation. It also focuses on the specific treaty issues of education, child welfare, health, shelter, justice, treaty annuities, hunting, fishing, trapping and gathering, and lands and resources.

The primary work of the Office of the Treaty Commissioner in support of the Exploratory Treaty Table has been the commissioning of background research on treaty issues and the facilitation of exploratory discussions and other workshops among the Parties. A major contribution of the Office of the Treaty Commissioner has been documenting and publishing research reports, including *Treaty Elders of Saskatchewan* by the late Harold Cardinal and Walter Hildebrandt; *Bounty and Benevolence* by Arthur J. Ray, Jim Miller and Frank Tough; and the *Statement of Treaty Issues*. These works have provided a basic foundation for the analysis in this report.

The Office of the Treaty Commissioner further supports treaty implementation through a program of public education, including a *Teaching Treaties in the Classroom* program, a Speakers Bureau and a Learning Centre. The Speakers Bureau has presented to over 55,000 people; the Learning Centre has had over 1,500 learner visits; and the *Teaching Treaties in the Classroom* program has provided the Treaty Resource Kit to every school in Saskatchewan and trained over one third of the teaching force in Saskatchewan in its use. In March 2005, the Office of the Treaty Commissioner established a Treaty Learning Network comprised of 20 Elders and 50 teachers, who support the *Teaching Treaties in the Classroom* program. These public education programs are designed to improve Canadian society's understanding of the meaning and continuing relevance of treaties, thereby paving the way for all members of society to contribute to implementing the treaties and fulfilling the treaty relationship. The Office of the Treaty Commissioner has evolved into a neutral meeting ground where Elders' views are sought, valued and respected, and where the Parties can openly and freely explore each other's perspectives.

After 10 years of carrying out research, facilitating discussions and conducting broad-based public education programs, there is reason to celebrate successes and draw upon strengths. As the Parties have prepared for expiry of the Office of the Treaty Commissioner mandate and as the Office of the Treaty Commissioner has reviewed this matter with others, a number of common threads have appeared. The first is to build on the public education programs. These programs are regarded as highly successful and should be expanded. The K-12 Teaching Treaties in the Classroom Program is the cornerstone of the public education program, but it needs to be expanded to include greater public education. The population in general needs to have a greater awareness of treaties and their importance to the make-up of Canada.

The Office of the Treaty Commissioner has added greatly to the understanding of treaties through its research programs – these need to be continued. The Exploratory Treaty Table is where the Parties come together to discuss treaty issues. It needs to be refocused, move beyond exploration and become more outcome-oriented. Two actions need to be taken for this to occur. First, the Parties need to re-commit themselves to the treaties, treaty implementation and the treaty relationship. Second, the Office of the Treaty Commissioner needs to be given a stronger mandate and resources to support the Parties in becoming more outcome-focused.

Elements of that stronger mandate are a greater role in advocating for the treaty relationship, more tools for resolving differences of opinion between the Parties and a role in holding the Parties accountable by making recommendations and reporting publicly on outcomes and accomplishments of Treaty Table discussions.

With respect to advocacy, it must be clear that it is advocacy for the treaty relationship, not for either Party's view on issues. Advocacy for particular views can and must occur but it must take place in the appropriate manner and with respect to the stage at which discussions are occurring. Siding with one Party or the other in an untimely way will only destroy the credibility of the Office of the Treaty Commissioner and the entire treaty implementation discussion process.

With this in mind, the Office of the Treaty Commissioner needs other dispute resolution tools which are standard practices in other forums where differences of opinion exist. These tools need to be available to the Office of the Treaty Commissioner and the Exploratory Treaty Table or its replacement. As in other forums, the Parties need to agree upon the kinds of dispute resolution tools most appropriate in this environment.

The Parties need to be held more accountable for the outcomes of the treaty implementation discussions. The Office of the Treaty Commissioner has a part to play in this through reporting to the Parties and the public. Further, as part of the dispute prevention and resolution process, there is value in the Office of the Treaty Commissioner having a role in making recommendations to the Parties, when the Commissioner feels it would be helpful. This is a legitimate role for the facilitator of the treaty implementation discussions.

The role of the Office of the Treaty Commissioner has been important to the approach taken at the Exploratory Treaty Table. This role needs to evolve and grow as the treaty implementation discussions enter a new and more outcome-oriented stage.

Conclusion

While there are certainly different views between the Parties, there are also common understandings developed during almost a decade of Exploratory Treaty Table discussions. These common understandings create a basis for our confidence that the momentum exists to renew the Parties' efforts at achieving treaty implementation.

There will be challenges on the way to treaty implementation. Many of these challenges will be products of the history of First Nations-Crown relations in the period since the treaties were made, a history of broken treaty promises and misguided policies that have caused tremendous harm to First Nations peoples, as well as dependency and distrust. These issues will be explored in the next section. More recent history suggests the Parties are capable of overcoming these challenges and implementing the spirit and intent of the treaties in a modern context.

4. HISTORICAL OVERVIEW OF THE TREATY RELATIONSHIP

This section begins by setting out many of the principal events in the treaty relationship since the making of the treaties. It provides a summary of well-documented facts about the history of relations between the Crown and Treaty First Nations. It is important to understand the unfortunate history and the injustices and grievances created by non-implementation of the treaty relationship. These events and their consequences contribute to present day difficulties in the relationship between Treaty First Nations and others in our Canadian society. Understanding the grievances of the past helps to explain the current reality. This step must occur before we can bridge to the future.

This section also provides an overview of policy changes made within the last 30 years, as well as constitutional changes and attempts to recognize First Nations governance and the significance of treaties. The events of the past 30 years need to be understood, as they demonstrate the importance of properly understanding the treaty relationship and using the values in that relationship to create a harmonious and prosperous future for all people in Saskatchewan.

Post Treaty Era (1870s to 1930s)

(a) Provision of Timely and Full Treaty Land Entitlement

First Nations did not receive, in a timely way, their *full* allotment of reserve lands according to the treaty land entitlement formula. We know that, in many cases, the full provision of land was delayed for many generations. This failure was not addressed until 1990, when the first Office of the Treaty Commissioner wrote a document that led to negotiation of a Framework Agreement in 1992 to complete this crucial treaty promise.[41] The timely provision of treaty land entitlement selected for its economic advantages would have given Treaty First Nations in the province a valuable economic asset as well as a protected homeland for their exclusive use and benefit, on which they might have developed successful communities.

---

[41] Wright, Cliff, *Report and Recommendations on Treaty Land Entitlement* (Saskatoon: Office of the Treaty Commissioner, 1990). An electronic copy of the report can be obtained at http://www.otc.ca/LibraryArchive.htm. See Saskatchewan Treaty Land Entitlement Act, S.C. 1993, c. 11 (in force March 30, 1993); see also R.S.S., c. T-20.1 (in force June 22, 1993) that gave legal effect to the Treaty Land Entitlement Framework Agreement.

Indeed, even with the successful conclusion of the Framework Agreement, First Nations in Saskatchewan are still a considerable distance from enjoying the benefits of this most important treaty right. The Office of the Auditor General of Canada reported in November 2005 that the process of converting lands purchased by First Nations to reserve status was proceeding too slowly, and that only about 58 percent of land selected by Saskatchewan First Nations since 1992 had been converted to reserve status.[42] Despite some shortcomings, though, the outstanding treaty land entitlement issue was addressed by the Parties through a negotiated agreement, which can serve as a guide in addressing the spirit and intent of treaties today.

(b) The Indian Act

In 1876, the federal Parliament enacted the *Indian Act*. It was frequently amended between the year of its enactment and 1951, when a significant revision took place. The *Indian Act* in place today, however, is in most respects the direct descendant of the original 1876 Act. In virtually every instance, both in the original Act and in subsequent revisions, Parliament chose to define, control and regulate the conduct of Treaty First Nations. Governance systems and membership rules were imposed. The traditional roles of the Chiefs and Headmen were circumscribed in the new governance systems to the passage of bylaws on limited subjects. These bylaws are still subject to Ministerial disallowance. The use of reserve land and the sale of crops, timber and minerals were rigidly controlled.[43] From 1895 to 1951, religious ceremonies such as the sundance were outlawed.[44] From 1927 until 1951, in response to certain First Nations claims, the *Indian Act* made it an offence to solicit or give money for the pursuit of Indian claims, a measure intended to make it more difficult for First Nations to have access to legal counsel to press their claims against the federal Crown as their fiduciary. Virtually every aspect of life on Indian reserves was placed under the control of Indian agents who, according to much anecdotal information, could be rigid in their approach to their responsibilities.

---

[42] Auditor General of Canada, *2005 Report of the Auditor General of Canada to the House of Commons,* (Ottawa: Auditor General of Canada, 2005), Chapter 7: "Indian and Northern Affairs Canada – Meeting Treaty Land Entitlement Obligations" p. 11. This Report is available at http://www.oag-bvg.gc.ca/domino/reports.nsf/html/05menu_e.html.

[43] Carter, Sarah, *Lost Harvests: Prairie Indian Reserve Farmers and Government Policy,* (Montreal and Kingston: McGill University Press, 1990), especially chapter four.

[44] Pettipas, Katherine, *Severing the Ties that Bind: Government Repression of Indigenous Religious Ceremonies on the Prairies,* (Winnipeg: University of Manitoba Press, 1994), especially chapters four and six.

The *Indian Act* created economic barriers to Treaty First Nations that prevented them from taking full economic advantage of their reserve lands, barriers which were fundamentally inconsistent with the spirit and intent of the treaties. First Nations people were prohibited from selling their agricultural and other produce from reserves without a permit from their Indian agent. Mining and lumbering were severely impeded by the Act. The Act was also revised to allow for wide discretion to use Indian trust monies for Departmental purposes and for meeting treaty obligations. This practice did not end until after the 1935 court decision in the *Dreaver* case relating to the "medicine chest" referred to in Treaty 6.[45]

Prior to 1985, the *Indian Act* contained provisions to strip First Nations people of their Indian status through the process of "enfranchisement." Indian people were enfranchised or "deemed not to be an Indian within the meaning of the *Indian Act* or any statute of law" if the individual became a doctor, lawyer, clergyman, monk, nun, university graduate or resided in a foreign country without permission. The children and wives of enfranchisement were also deemed to be enfranchised Indians under the provisions of the *Indian Act*.

The *Indian Act* divided families by inducing some members to enfranchise in order to obtain advancement, and it took away a woman's birthright as an Indian with treaty rights if she married a non-Indian. This loss of Indian status was not legislatively addressed until 1985 with the amendments introduced as Bill C-31. Even then, it was concern about gender equality under the *Canadian Charter of Rights and Freedoms*, not honouring treaties, that was the impetus for reform.

That honouring First Nations people's identity as treaty people was not a consideration in Bill C-31 becomes obvious when one considers that the Bill gradually dispossesses First Nations people of their status. By virtue of limitations on status contained in the Bill, the children born of a relationship between a non-status person and a status Indian who was himself or herself the child of a status Indian and a non-status person will lose their status. As Howe has noted, with a lag, the absolute number of children who qualify to be status

---

[45] Dreaver et al. v The King (1935), 5 C.N.L.C. 92 (Exchequer Court of Canada).

Indians will peak and then begin to decrease. In the foreseeable future, the number of children who qualify for status will reach zero and, with mortality, the number of status Indians will, in time, reach zero.[46] This amendment to the *Indian Act* has the effect of continuing the assimilation policy and is of grave concern to First Nations people. This underscores the need for First Nations to determine their own citizenship.

(c) Famine Relief

In the negotiation of the early Saskatchewan treaties, a prominent theme was the need for the Crown to assist in times of famine. The written text of Treaty 6 includes this clause:

> That in the event hereafter of the Indians comprised within this treaty being overtaken by any pestilence, or by a general famine, the Queen, on being satisfied and certified thereof by Her Indian Agent or Agents, will grant to the Indians assistance of such character and to such extent as Her Chief Superintendent of Indian Affairs shall deem necessary and sufficient to relieve the Indians from the calamity that shall have befallen them.[47]

During the 1880s and at other times, severe famine struck Treaty First Nations across southern Saskatchewan. The Crown was obliged to assist them under treaty provisions and Crown promises, yet officials used the rationing of food to weaken the First Nations politically and splinter their ranks. Once settled on reserves, they suffered chronic malnutrition as the result of rationing policies that in some cases led to death from starvation and susceptibility to disease. Their pleas were all too often ignored by Agents and officials in Ottawa, who had the means and the power to provide, or withhold, relief.[48]

Many Treaty First Nations people died unnecessarily. Treaty First Nations communities suffered relocation and fragmentation as they fought to survive. Hardship, poverty and dislocation were the result.

---

[46] Howe, "Saskatchewan with an Aboriginal Majority," pp. 10-11

[47] Canada, *Treaty No. 6* (1876).

[48] St. Germain, Jill, "'Feed or Fight': Rationing the Sioux and the Cree, 1868-1885," *Native Studies Review,* 16, No. 1 (2005): 71-90. St. Germain compares relief in western Canada and the U.S. in this period and concludes that the American policy was more generous.

(d) Lack of Agricultural Assistance

Apart from times of particular hardship, Treaty First Nations were typically not given the equipment, livestock and training necessary to develop an agricultural economy equivalent in productivity to that being developed by settlers. These were promised, in differing terms, by each of the treaties. At treaty talks, the representatives of the Crown promised the means and assistance to make the transition to an agricultural economy, with a livelihood on par with that of their neighbours.[49]

Instead of providing up-to-date farming technology, the Crown tried to train First Nations farmers in the ways of peasant farming. Those First Nations farmers who achieved successes in agriculture were often prevented from selling their goods, lest they compete with other farmers and ranchers. When the Department purchased produce and livestock from First Nations, it paid less than the market price. The inability to market agricultural surpluses at market prices impaired the ability to maintain and replace equipment provided on "once and for all" terms under treaty.[50]

(e) The Saskatchewan Act, 1905

The *Saskatchewan Act* created the Province of Saskatchewan. It was silent with respect to the duty of the new provincial government to honour, fulfill and respect the treaties. It did not subject the province to treaties and treaty rights, and it did not create jurisdictional space for the governance institutions of the Treaty First Nations.

(f) Surrenders of Productive Reserve Land Under Duress

In the early years of the twentieth century, many Treaty First Nations were induced by the adverse circumstances in which they found themselves to surrender the most productive parts of their reserve land allotments.[51] Between 1896 and 1911, more than 30 percent of Indian reserve lands that had been set aside in Saskatchewan under the treaties were surrendered.

---

[49] See Carter, Sarah, *Lost Harvests*, chapter three.
[50] See ibid., chapters four and five.
[51] See generally Martin-McGuire, Peggy, *First Nations Land Surrenders on the Prairies* 1896-1911 (Ottawa: Indian Claims Commission, 1998).

Senior federal Ministers and bureaucrats engaged in behaviour that made it inevitable that prime farmland would be taken from Treaty First Nations and sold to farmers, land speculators, railways, and townsite developers.

In many cases, the surrender of lands was engineered through the use of "special agents" who had the trust of First Nations, by promises of wealth that would flow from the sale of surrendered lands, by withholding agricultural assistance and relief assistance unless surrenders were given, and increasing the initial cash payments offered, often in hard times, to induce a surrender. The opportunity to build sound economies based on agriculture was lost. The reserve lands remaining were often those least suited to any productive agricultural use. Some First Nation communities who had been trying to develop an agricultural economy gave up.

After World War I, unsold, previously surrendered reserve lands were sold to the Soldier Settlement Board for the benefit of returning veterans. A second wave of surrenders then took place between 1918 and 1921 for soldier settlement purposes, although in some cases these lands ended up in the hands of neighbouring farmers who were not veterans.[52]

(g) The Migratory Birds Convention Act

In 1917, Parliament passed the *Migratory Birds Convention Act*. This Act outlawed the hunting of migratory birds such as geese and ducks, an important source of food for Treaty First Nations. The Government of Canada failed to consult Treaty First Nations prior to passing this law and, as a result, failed to respect their hunting rights and the relevance of hunting rights to First Nations both economically and socially.

(h) Residential School Policy

The objective of the residential school policy was to civilize and Christianize First Nations children. Girls were taught home-making skills, boys farming skills. However, there is no longer any debate about whether the residential school policy was wrong. Treaty First

---

[52] See Royal Commission on Aboriginal Peoples, *Gathering Strength: Final Report of the Royal Commission on Aboriginal Peoples* (Ottawa: Queen's Printer, 1996), Volume 1, pp. 553-4.

Nations had their children taken away to residential schools as part of a deliberate policy to destroy First Nations cultures and languages and to assimilate Treaty First Nations people into the mainstream. We now know that the tragic effects of this policy included the irreparable loss of indigenous cultures, languages, spirituality and family structures, as well as widespread abuse of children.

As the Government of Canada stated in a formal announcement of policy in 1997:

> One aspect of our relationship with Aboriginal people over this period that requires particular attention is the Residential School system. This system separated many children from their families and communities and prevented them from speaking their own languages and from learning about their heritage and cultures. In the worst cases, it left legacies of personal pain and distress that continue to reverberate in Aboriginal communities to this day. Tragically, some children were the victims of physical and sexual abuse.
>
> The Government of Canada acknowledges the role it played in the development and administration of these schools. Particularly to those individuals who experienced the tragedy of sexual and physical abuse at residential schools, and who have carried this burden believing that in some way they must be responsible, we wish to emphasize that what you experienced was not your fault and should never have happened. To those of you who suffered this tragedy at residential schools, we are deeply sorry. [53]

Generations of First Nations families suffered the loss of the essential bonds of family due to the residential school policy. The amount of human pain and suffering and the loss of parenting skills that has resulted from the residential school system is incalculable.[54] After many years of litigation and negotiations between First Nations and the Crown, billions of dollars are now being identified to provide after-the-fact compensation to individuals who were affected by this policy.[55] The damage that families suffered in the residential schools period underscores the rationale for having First Nations govern the provision of services and supports to their families and children as part of treaty implementation.

---

[53] Department of Indian and Northern Development, *Gathering Strength: Canada's Aboriginal Action Plan* (Ottawa: Minister of Public Works and Government Services Canada, 1997).

[54] See Royal Commission on Aboriginal Peoples, *Gathering Strength*, Volume 1, chapter 10; Miller, J.R., Shingwauk's Vision, (Toronto: University of Toronto Press, 1996) Milloy, J.S., *A National Crime: The Canadian Government and the Residential School System, 1879 to 1986,* (Winnipeg: University of Manitoba Press, 1999).

[55] See materials on website of Indian Residential Schools Resolution Canada: www.irsr-rqpi.gc.ca.

(i) Education

Education was a vital treaty right and promise, and is mentioned in the text of each numbered treaty. It was a critical tool in the First Nations' treaty tool chest, one that would help them respond to, and to succeed in, the new economic circumstances. Under the spirit and intent of the treaties, education was to help reconcile traditional learning and knowledge with the imported skills and knowledge needed to survive and prosper in a new reality in which indigenous and newcomer cultures would coexist in harmony. Treaty First Nations children would have received the education they needed to deal equally with the descendants of European settlers without being forced to give up their "Indianness." However, the quality of First Nations education lagged far behind the quality of education for the settlers, as unfortunately remains the case, and Treaty First Nations had no input over the curriculum that their children learned. In 1947, Joseph Dreaver of the Union of Saskatchewan Indians told the Special Joint Parliamentary Committee on the *Indian Act*: "Our greatest need today is proper education."[56]

(j) The Natural Resources Transfer Agreement

Until 1930, the public land and natural resources of Saskatchewan (like those of Manitoba and Alberta) were controlled by the federal government. In that year, the *Natural Resources Transfer Agreement* attempted to place the three Prairie provinces on the same footing as the original provinces under section 109 of the *Constitution Act, 1867*. In doing so, the Government of Canada did not fully require the provincial governments to honour and implement the spirit and intent of the treaties. In fact, according to a decision of the Supreme Court of Canada, the *Natural Resources Transfer Agreement* expressly took away the important treaty right of commercial hunting.[57]

Canada did not consult with the Treaty First Nations about the *Natural Resources Transfer Agreement*, which gave the provincial government enormous leverage to delay and frustrate the fulfillment of treaty rights to land as well as game and fish harvesting. It also imposed a

---

[56] Special Joint Parliamentary Committee of the Senate and the House of Commons on the *Indian Act., Minutes of Proceedings and evidence of the Joint Committee of the Senate and the House of Commons on the Indian Act.* (Ottawa: Queen's Printer, 1947).
[57] *R. v. Horseman*, [1990] 1 S.C.R. 901.

number of restrictions on the enjoyment of reserve lands that were imported directly from the 1924 *Indian Lands Agreement* in Ontario, an agreement made after the Government of Canada was compelled to yield to provincial demands upon losing a series of important constitutional cases in the courts.

(k) The Great Depression

The great depression of the 1930s hit Treaty First Nations of the southern Prairies hard, as it did all residents of Saskatchewan. Treaty promises of assistance in times of widespread famine went unfulfilled. Once again, as in the times of earlier famines, the First Nations suffered excessively and unnecessarily. Their meagre trust accounts were depleted to pay for the necessities of life for their members, as well as for education, health care, salaries of Indian Department officials and other treaty expenses, necessities that should have been provided under the promised "bounty and benevolence" of the Crown.

This short, and far from complete, list of major events in the Treaty First Nations-Crown relationship since 1874 is a combination of events that were at the time illegal (breaches of the *Indian Act* for which the Specific Claims Policy or the courts may provide compensation and redress) and events that may have been, strictly speaking, legal at the time in the sense that the courts have upheld the authority of governments to enact legislation in contravention of treaty promises and rights.

Opportunities for Reform (1940s to 1980s)

Proposals to reform the *Indian Act* and other aspects of the Crown-First Nations relationship came to public attention during the twentieth century. In the late 1940s, the House of Commons and the Senate held hearings to consider wholesale amendments to the *Indian Act*. Many Treaty First Nations leaders from Saskatchewan and elsewhere demanded treaty implementation and the settlement of legitimate land claims, for recognition of their right to govern themselves, for economic self-reliance, and for improved education for their children. In short, they asked for the treaties to be fulfilled, not for more rules and more legislation to bind them.[58] When the 1951 *Indian Act* amendments were passed, however, Parliament chose not to make material changes to the legislative template that had prevailed since 1876. [59]

In the early 1960s, Parliamentarians again heard First Nations, provincial government, church and other representatives detail the huge and rapidly growing gap between the distressing social and economic conditions on reserves and the booming economic conditions in post World War II Canada, but made no substantial recommendations to address the situation.[60] In 1969, another great opportunity was missed when a series of consultations with First Nations, including Treaty First Nations, ignored the repeated statements of First Nations leadership that any new policy direction must, first and foremost, fulfill existing treaty obligations.[61] In a major study of the *Indian Act* that was commissioned by the Royal Commission on Aboriginal Peoples, the consultations were described as follows:

> The final consultation meeting with Indians took place in April 1969 in Ottawa. It was a notable gathering, significant because it brought together Indians from all regions of Canada, including a number of those who would figure prominently in later constitutional events. Impatient with what they perceived as the federal government's stalling on claims and a failure to address Indian priorities, they tabled a brief setting out those priorities as follows:
>
>> It has been made abundantly clear, both by the consultations to date and through Indian meetings throughout the land, that the principal concerns of Indian people center around:
>>
>> A) recognition of the treaties and the obligations imposed by same

---

[58] Leslie, John F., "Assimilation, Integration or Termination? *The Development of Canadian Indian Policy*, 1943-1963," (Ph.D. dissertation, Carleton University, 1999), chapter three, "The Special Joint Committee on the *Indian Act*, 1946-1948: The Search for a New Indian Policy," especially pp. 138-53 and 156-65.

[59] Tobias, John L., "Protection, Civilization, Assimilation: An Outline History of Canada's Indian Policy," in Miller, J.R., ed., *Sweet Promises: A Reader on Indian-White Relations in Canada* (Toronto: University of Toronto Press, 1991), pp. 139-40.

[60] Hawthorn, H.B., ed., *A Survey of the Contemporary Indians of Canada: Economic, Political, Educational Needs and Policies,* (Ottawa: Indian Affairs, 1966-7).

[61] Weaver, Sally, *Making Canadian Indian Policy: The Hidden Agenda, 1968-70,* (Toronto: University of Toronto Press, 1981).

B) recognition of Aboriginal rights

C) reconciliation of injustices done by the imposition of restrictions on Indian hunting through the ratification of the Migratory Birds Convention and subsequent federal and provincial legislation

D) Claims Commission

It is our opinion that before meaningful consultation on amendments to the *Indian Act* can take place, these four items must be dealt with and a position of mutual understanding and commitment reached.[62]

Instead, the Government of Canada introduced a policy, widely known as the White Paper, to promote assimilation of First Nations people into the mainstream. A key component of the White Paper's policy was discarding the treaties as irrelevant and anachronistic relics once their promises of "so much twine and so much gunpowder," in the dismissive phrase of Prime Minister Pierre Trudeau, had been discharged. A few years later, due to the overwhelmingly negative reaction from First Nations, the White Paper was formally withdrawn.

In the 1970s, the Crown developed a Specific Claims Policy to negotiate claims in which Canada agreed there had been a "breach of lawful obligation." This policy continues to apply to many treaty breaches, among other matters. In 1991, the Indian Claims Commission was established with the power to make recommendations about claims that had been rejected. Many Saskatchewan and other Prairie surrender claims have been the subject of specific land claims and a number have been settled. However, the specific claims process remains slow, often ineffective and controversial.[63]

In the 1980s, the impetus for reform was renewed. In 1982, when the Constitution of Canada was patriated, the new *Constitution Act, 1982* included a section dealing with the

---

[62] Giokas, John, *The Indian Act: Evolution, Overview And Options For Amendment And Transition*, March 22, 1995, published by Royal Commission on Aboriginal Peoples on CD-ROM For Seven Generations (Ottawa: 1996).

[63] *A Specific Claims Resolution Act, S.C. 2003*, c. 23 has been passed by Parliament but has not come into force.

existing Aboriginal and treaty rights of the Aboriginal peoples of Canada. Section 35 has become the basis of a significant body of Canadian jurisprudence relevant to questions of treaty interpretation and implementation. As well, section 37 of the *Constitution Act, 1982* provided for a First Ministers' Conference on Aboriginal issues. This was an explicit acknowledgment that the bare recognition and affirmation found in section 35 was only a beginning, and that the Aboriginal constitutional agenda contained unfinished business.

First Ministers' Conferences held in 1983, 1984, 1985 and 1987 increasingly focused on the attempt to define a constitutional basis for Aboriginal self-government.[64] The 1987 Conference ended in failure. During these years, the Government of Canada promoted the issue of self-government as a potentially constitutionally protected right, but only after negotiations involving Aboriginal peoples and the federal and provincial or territorial governments.

The issue of First Nations self-government was also given great impetus by the 1983 Report of the Special Committee of the House of Commons, known as the Penner Report.[65] This report was broadly encompassing and touched upon every facet of socio-economic and political life for First Nations people. It was the first Government of Canada publication to advocate the use of the term "First Nation." It recommended the establishment of a new relationship between First Nations and the Crown, premised upon Indian self-government. According to the report's recommendations, First Nations governments were to be established, first pursuant to a federal Indian Nations Recognition Act and then by constitutional amendment. First Nations governments would form one of three orders of government in the Canadian federation.

At the same time as the First Ministers' Conferences, the Treaty 8 Renovation initiative was undertaken. This initiative was explicitly based upon conclusions of the Penner Report and the new constitutional status of existing treaty rights. In its final report, the Royal Commission on Aboriginal Peoples quoted a March 1985 letter from then Minister of

---

[64] Miller, J.R., *Skyscrapers Hide the Heavens: A History of Indian-White Relations in Canada,* (3rd edition). (Toronto: University of Toronto Press, 2000), pp. 240-1.

[65] Special Committee of the House of Commons on Indian Self-Government, *Report of the Special Committee of the House of Commons on Indian Self-Government.* (Ottawa: Queen's Printer, 1983).

Indian Affairs David Crombie to Negotiator Harold Cardinal that succinctly and usefully describes the scope and purpose of a treaty implementation process:

> While I am willing to consider the articles of the treaty, the report of the treaty commissioners and other written contemporary reports, and the Indian understanding of the treaty including written and oral history, I do not believe that we need to be limited in this fashion and that it is much more important that we recognize that the treaty is the expression of a special relationship, which itself needs to be renewed and restored. It is in the spirit and intent of this, rather than a legalistic requirement that you produce evidence, that we should proceed....The exercise, in my view, offers an opportunity to redesign and reconceptualize your relationship with the federal government in a way which reinforces your historical and constitutional rights as Indian First Nations, while at the same time, restoring to you the means to manage your own affairs. [66]

It is not entirely clear why this initiative failed. It did, however, produce an important report authored by then Member of Parliament Frank Oberle on many matters that would have to be addressed in a treaty renovation initiative.[67] Mr. Oberle had been appointed by Minister David Crombie as a "special envoy" to explore the scope of authority that would be needed to address treaty renovation in the Treaty 8 area. The Oberle Report was intended to be the basis of Cabinet authority for treaty renovation within a new policy environment. A promising beginning ended in failure, as the Treaty First Nations and Minister could not agree on how to move the initiative forward.

In the mid 1980s, the Government of Canada concluded its first statutory self-government arrangements with the Cree and Naskapi in Quebec and with the Sechelt First Nation in British Columbia. It also introduced a Community-Based Self-Government Policy designed to enable negotiations on self-government arrangements. These would not acquire the constitutional status of Aboriginal or treaty rights, however. In the late 1980s, the Canadian constitutional agenda was dominated by Quebec issues, with the Meech Lake Accord being signed mere months after the failure of the 1987 First Ministers' Conference on Aboriginal Issues.

---

[66] Royal Commission on Aboriginal Peoples, *Gathering Strength*, Volume 2, p. 55.
[67] Oberle, Frank, *Treaty 8 Renovation Discussion Paper*, January 31, 1986 (unpublished).

The 1990s

The Charlottetown Accord of 1992 would have transformed the relationship between First Nations and other Aboriginal peoples and the Crown. Some of the key features of the Charlottetown Accord are:

- A so-called "Canada clause" would define eight "fundamental characteristics" of Canada including:

> (b) the Aboriginal peoples of Canada, being the first peoples to govern this land, have the right to promote their languages, cultures and traditions and to ensure that the integrity of their societies and their governments constitute one of three orders of Government in Canada ...

- The inherent right of First Nations to self-government within Canada would be recognized, and First Nations governments would be recognized as one of three orders of Government in Canada.

- First Nations laws would displace federal and provincial laws, subject to laws "essential to the preservation of peace, order and good government in Canada."

- The right of self-government would be enforceable and not contingent, but there would be a delay of five years before the specific recognition of the inherent right would be dealt with in any court, although First Nations could, in the meantime, raise issues of self-government in a court, including arguments based on section 35(1) of the *Constitution Act, 1982.*[68]

The Charlottetown Accord also contained a commitment to amend the Constitution with respect to treaties.

> With respect to treaties with Aboriginal peoples, the Constitution should be amended as follows:
>
> - treaty rights should be interpreted in a just, broad and liberal manner taking into account the spirit and intent of the treaties and the context in which specific treaties were negotiated;

---

[68] The complete August 28, 1992, Final Text of the Charlottetown Accord can be found at www.thecanadianencyclopedia.com/index.cfm?PgNm=TCE&Params=A1ARTA0010099.

- the Government of Canada should be committed to establishing and participating in good faith in a joint process to clarify or implement treaty rights, or to rectify terms of treaties when agreed to by the parties. The governments of the provinces should also be committed, to the extent that they have jurisdiction, to participation in the above treaty process when invited by the Government of Canada and the Aboriginal peoples concerned or when specified in a treaty;

- participants in this process should have regard, among other things and where appropriate, to the spirit and intent of the treaties as understood by Aboriginal peoples. It should be confirmed that all Aboriginal peoples that possess treaty rights should have equitable access to this treaty process;

- it should be provided that these treaty amendments shall not extend the authority of any government or legislature, or affect the rights of Aboriginal peoples not party to the treaty concerned.[69]

The Charlottetown Accord was rejected in a national referendum in October 1992. However, in 1995, the Government of Canada introduced a policy to govern negotiations on what it recognized as the "inherent right" of Aboriginal self-government.

The Royal Commission on Aboriginal Peoples Final Report was released in 1996 and contained extensive recommendations on treaty implementation. It addressed both substantive matters and matters of process. There are a number of salient recommendations made by the Royal Commission on Aboriginal Peoples, as set out in Appendix 2 of this report. We would, however, highlight these recommendations:

> With respect to the historical treaties, the Commission recommends that:

>> 2.2.2 The parties implement the historical treaties from the perspective of both justice and reconciliation:

>>> (a) Justice requires the fulfillment of the agreed terms of the treaties, as recorded in the treaty text and supplemented by oral evidence.

>>> (b) Reconciliation requires the establishment of proper principles to govern the continuing treaty relationship and to complete treaties that are incomplete because of the absence of consensus.

---

[69] Ibid. See also Royal Commission on Aboriginal Peoples, *Gathering Strength*, Volume 2, p. 55.

2.2.3   The federal government establish a continuing bilateral process to implement and renew the Crown's relationship with and obligations to the treaty nations under the historical treaties, in accordance with the treaties' spirit and intent.

2.2.4 The spirit and intent of the historical treaties be implemented in accordance with the following fundamental principles:

(a) The specific content of the rights and obligations of the parties to the treaties is determined for all purposes in a just and liberal way, by reference to oral as well as written sources.

(b) The Crown is in a trust-like and non-adversarial fiduciary relationship with the treaty nations.

(c) The Crown's conflicting duties to the treaty nations and to Canadians generally is reconciled in the spirit of the treaty partnership.

(d) There is a presumption in respect of the historical treaties that

- treaty nations did not intend to consent to the blanket extinguishment of their Aboriginal rights and title by entering into the treaty relationship;

- treaty nations intended to share the territory and jurisdiction and management over it, as opposed to ceding the territory, even where the text of an historical treaty makes reference to a blanket extinguishment of land rights; and

- treaty nations did not intend to give up their inherent right of governance by entering into a treaty relationship, and the act of treaty making is regarded as an affirmation rather than a denial of that right. [70]

The New Millennium

In February 2000, the Standing Senate Committee on Aboriginal Peoples issued its report entitled *Forging New Relationships: Aboriginal Governance in Canada*. It, too, recommended significant legislative and structural changes at the federal government level, including the creation of a new Office of Aboriginal Relations that would have a Treaty and

---

[70] Royal Commission on Aboriginal Peoples, *Gathering Strength*, Volume 2, p. 58.

Agreements Negotiations Division and a Treaty and Agreements Implementation Secretariat. It also included the following recommendation, which refers to treaty implementation:

> The Committee recommends that new legislation be introduced by the federal government for the purposes of providing a broad statutory framework to guide the Government of Canada in the negotiation and implementation of relationships by way of treaties and other agreements with Aboriginal peoples. The Minister responsible for the new Office of Aboriginal Relations should have responsibility for administering this legislation.[71]

The common theme in these recent reports is that they have called for a dramatic restructuring of the relationship between First Nations and the Crown. Where treaties are involved, they have called for the implementation of the treaties, often in terms of their spirit and intent. Another common element is that in each case the recommendations were not followed, and a great deal of careful analysis led to little or no concrete change in policy.

In the *First Nations – Federal Crown Political Accord on the Recognition and Implementation of First Nations Governments* signed on May 31, 2005 by the National Chief of the Assembly of First Nations and the Minister of Indian Affairs and Northern Development, in the presence of the entire federal Cabinet, the Government of Canada made a formal commitment to joint policy development with First Nations:

> The intent and purpose of this Accord is to commit the Parties to work jointly to promote meaningful processes for reconciliation and implementation of section 35 rights, with First Nation governments to achieve an improved quality of life, and to support policy transformation in other areas of common interest, affirming and having regard to the following principles.[72]

The Political Accord stated:

> **Whereas** the Prime Minister, at the April 19, 2004 Canada-Aboriginal Peoples Roundtable, stated, "It is now time for us to renew and strengthen the covenant between us", and committed that "No longer will we in Ottawa develop policies first and discuss them with you later. The principle of collaboration will be the cornerstone of our new partnership."[73]

---

[71] Standing Senate Committee on Aboriginal Peoples, *Forging New Relationships: Aboriginal Governance in Canada*, available at: http://www.parl.gc.ca/36/2/parlbus/commbus/senate/Com-e/ABOR-E/REP-E/rep03feb00-e.htm.

[72] First Nations – *Federal Crown Political Accord on the Recognition and Implementation of First Nations Governments* signed on May 31, 2005. The full text is available at http://www.afn.ca/cmslib/general/PolAcc.pdf.

[73] Ibid.

This use of language is revealing. Terms like "covenant" and "partnership" strongly echo Treaty First Nations' expressed views of their existing treaty relationships. Indeed, one of the principles outlined in the Political Accord for future joint policy development is this:

> Implementation of the treaty relationship must be informed by the original understandings of the treaty signatories, including the First Nations' understanding of the spirit and intent.[74]

As its title suggests, the Political Accord addresses the need for the *joint* development of policy to foster First Nations governance. The very reference to the treaty relationship within a governance-oriented Political Accord reveals that the federal government is on the way to recognizing the linkage between treaties and First Nations' self-governance. With the signing of the Political Accord, Canada undertook to develop a policy to enable government officials to engage in the implementation of the treaty relationship, as well as to develop improved policies on First Nations governance. As well, the recent commitment of the Government of Canada to settle outstanding specific land claims quickly and efficiently holds out promise for resolving a long-standing conflict that has interfered with fully implementing the treaties.

Conclusion

Federal policy on First Nations matters has made significant progress in the past 30 years. Although policies remain which could result in assimilation, it is no longer regarded as a legitimate goal. The distinctive Aboriginal and treaty rights of First Nations have achieved constitutional recognition. The inherent right of First Nations to govern themselves has been recognized.

While the intention to reject assimilation seems clear, it is not clear what paradigm of the relationship has replaced assimilation. The ongoing re-evaluation of public policy has, in the last three decades or so, seen the constitutional entrenchment of existing Aboriginal and treaty rights, the rise of self-government as a policy objective through an extended period of constitutional negotiations (including treaty implementation proposals), an expansion of the role of the courts in

---

[74] Ibid.

addressing Aboriginal and treaty rights and the relationships within which they exist, and a heightened but largely uninformed public awareness that too many wrongs litter our past. The Government of Canada has admitted to certain past wrongs, most notably the consequences of its Indian residential school policy, and has undertaken to provide public acknowledgments of the harm that policy has caused, along with significant financial compensation to those harmed by it.

At the same time, while there is an expanding body of self-government legislation, mostly resulting from negotiated self-government agreements and applicable only to specific First Nations, all attempts to replace the *Indian Act* have failed. It is a source of virtually universal consternation that while all observers regard it as inappropriately paternalistic and intrusive on the lives of First Nations, it is still on the statute books. To move forward, we need to understand the complexity of the Crown's intentions in treaty making. In making sense of Canada's interests relating to treaties today, we need to avoid two pitfalls. First, we cannot engage in historical revisionism and pretend that the past did not unfold as it did but as we would have preferred it had. Second, we cannot oversimplify the conduct of the treaty Parties.

The *Royal Proclamation of 1763* constituted a commitment by the Crown to a process of protection of First Nations and consensual dealings with respect to their lands and territories. The fact that some of the high ideals that were official policy were not translated accurately into the actions of all officials does not negate the importance of those ideals, either then or now. Indeed, the honour of the Crown as a legal concept today surely requires us to measure the Crown's conduct in practice against the ideals of enlightened and compassionate Crown policy.

Some policies that we now regard as being misguided and harmful were conducted within the cultural perspective of the time. Crown policies intended to "civilize" First Nations, to protect them by containing them on reserves, to expand the influence of the Christian religion, and to train them in agriculture were promoted out of a genuine desire to improve the condition of First Nations. Although the Crown's policy was assimilation, it was seen as a plausible goal, and seen from the perspective of the day was not overtly duplicitous or contrary to what had been promised in the treaties.

Today, the treaty Party officials charged with the task of re-examining the treaties and treaty implementation have an opportunity to draw upon all we have learned to restore the spirit and intent of the treaties. We must draw upon the inspiration of recent policy development in the direction of self-government and respect for treaties and the distinctive rights of First Nations, and the unique relationship they have with Canada. We must also recognize the importance to Canadian society of having First Nations people enter the modern economy and actively seek to foster their socio-economic inclusion, so that the livelihood promises in the treaties are fully implemented. It is to this issue that we next will turn.

5. ENTERING THE NEW ECONOMY

Intention of the Treaty Parties

During the treaty negotiations, First Nations sought assurances that their way of life and livelihood would continue while they learned the skills required to participate in the new economy being brought to their territories. This concept was described by Elder Danny Musqua of the Keeseekoose First Nation in the following manner:

> We believed that the treaties and the Crown were going to do us good. That they were going to bring the heart [the goodness and wealth] of the Great White Mother, the great Queen Mother, we believed that... In 1905, it hadn't yet materialized. And when treaty implementation materialized, it was very limited. Some of our people became very good at what they had hoped they would acquire through these settlements. They became cattlemen. Animal husbandry was one of the very basic skills that our people had... They knew how to take care of their animals...

> First Nations were clear and told the Crown... We don't want your language. We don't want your [burial] grounds. We don't want your governments...

> The answer from Morris was "What you have shall be. We will maintain what you have and then we will put promises and protection on top of what you have. And what is that on top? All of these things that we said and the protection of the Crown. The Queen's authority shall surround you. She will protect you from all of these people here [newcomers]. She will protect you from encroachment of taxpayers, and land speculators... she will protect you from the certain encroachment on your personal lives and your culture... and from the newcomers that will come... and you will be just as wealthy as they are."[75]

The intent of the Crown during the treaty making process has been captured in the following quotation:

> The Crown agreed to provide a number of social/economic provisions to ensure First Nations well-being. Provision by the Crown of schools and support for agriculture, and the recognition of continuing hunting and fishing rights were designed to compensate for loss of land and to ensure a sustainable livelihood. The Crown justified the provision of small reserves by promising to secure future livelihoods for First Nations.[76]

---

[75] Cardinal and Hildebrandt, *Treaty Elders of Saskatchewan*, p. 47.
[76] Ray, et al., *Bounty and Benevolence*, p. 210.

The livelihood provisions of the treaties were mutually agreed to during treaty negotiations. Not all of the commitments made during these discussions were transferred to the written text of the Numbered Treaties, but ample documentation exists to demonstrate the intent of the treaty Parties. As noted by Ray, et al., "revision to Treaties 1 and 2 demonstrate that the written versions of these treaties were an inadequate summary of the agreement reached at treaty talks."[77] The commitments included in the written text are adequate confirmation of the intent of both Parties to protect the livelihoods of both First Nations people and the newcomers to western Canada.

Unfortunately, this intention has not been implemented equally for both Parties, and treaty objectives have not been met. Soon after the treaties were signed, it became obvious that the traditional way of life of First Nations people would be severely restricted. In the south, the loss of the buffalo proved devastating. The imposition of the *Indian Act* further eroded the traditional economic pursuits in both the southern and northern regions. In the north, the effects of other legislation such as the *Migratory Birds Convention Act* were particularly damaging, as was the impact of provincial laws on trapping, hunting and fishing. These restrictions and other measures imposed on First Nations after the making of treaties, combined with a rapidly changing economy, made the pursuit of traditional occupations economically non-viable. This meant the First Nations people had to look to non-traditional economic activity to gain a livelihood. In the Treaty 4 and 6 areas, this equated to agriculture. Immediately following the making of the treaties, many First Nations people began to adjust to farming and ranching. Initially, many of these operations were successful, but a combination of unreasonable demands from Indian agents and a limited amount of agricultural instruction made sustained progress almost impossible: "Department policy in the south after 1886 bore almost no resemblance to the attitudes that treaty commissioners such as Archibald and Morris had displayed during the 1870s."[78]

In the northern treaty areas, the pursuit of traditional occupations such as hunting, fishing and trapping remained economically viable for a longer period, but increasingly restrictive

---

[77] Ibid.
[78] Ibid., p. 202.

regulations and a changing global economy brought about the demise of these economic pursuits. Transitions to other activities such as forestry, mining and tourism have been hampered by a variety of obstacles, including bureaucratic indifference and lack of training and capital required for new economic ventures. Thus, the full intent and benefits of the livelihood provisions of the treaties have not been implemented.

Socio-Economic Conditions

The results of the inability of First Nations to enter the new economy fully have been well-documented, although accurate statistics specific to Treaty First Nations in Saskatchewan are difficult to compile. While the majority of Canadians have prospered, most First Nations people are suffering the consequences of poverty. They face higher levels of unemployment – at least four times the national average. First Nations people have lower levels of education, which means those who are employed earn significantly less money. First Nations people have not been involved in developing businesses mainly because of the difficulties they face in accessing capital and investment dollars. This has translated into an economically marginalized population, which can be traced to the failure to fully implement the treaties:

> Indian livelihood was to be secured or enhanced by a treaty relationship, rather than diminished or encroached upon by it. In the immediate treaty-signing era, problems arose that reflect on the different understandings of the treaties and/or the failure to implement the treaties in good faith. [79]

The failure to implement the livelihood provisions of the treaties has had devastating consequences for First Nations during the past 100 years. The effects of new diseases, residential schools, racism, the *Indian Act* and the resulting oppression and disempowerment, and the introduction of the debilitating welfare system have all combined to cause harm to First Nations individuals, families and communities.

One of the cornerstones of the treaties between Canada and First Nations was the education provisions. Education, in the ways of the Europeans, was intended to prepare First Nations

---

[79] Ibid., p. 214.

children for the economy of the future. The failures associated with the attempts to implement this clause are well-documented. They range from the misguided efforts of the residential schools to the failed attempts of integrating First Nations children into the provincial school systems in the 1960s, to the continuing failure of too many educational institutions to provide First Nations with an adequate education that will allow them to complete high school and succeed in post-secondary education and the modern economy. The results of these unsuccessful efforts have been negative. The languages, values and belief systems of First Nations people have been seriously damaged and, in many instances, destroyed. Parenting skills were lost in the era of residential schools. The results are manifested in low self-esteem, a lack of trust, and feelings of powerlessness among many in the First Nations population.

A closer examination of the socio-economic conditions of First Nations people in Saskatchewan illustrates the impact of a lack of implementation of commitments made in the treaties. Looking again at education, while there is agreement between the treaty Parties that education was intended to prepare First Nations for the new economy, too many have not attained the educational levels needed to participate fully in today's economy. Levels of educational attainment for First Nations people are much lower than those found in the general population. This has resulted in much lower rates of participation in the labour force by First Nations people. That rate is only 52% on-reserve. This compares to the national participation rate of 67.5%. Of First Nations people in the labour force, about 28% of the on-reserve population are unemployed. That is about four times the national average of 7.2%. The "Aboriginal Peoples Survey 2001" points to the disparity in income levels between Aboriginal and non-Aboriginal people, with an average income of $15,700 for Aboriginal people and $25,400 for non-Aboriginal people. First Nations people who are unemployed or living on an income of $15,000 per year face tremendous, often overwhelming, challenges.

Workers with lower educational levels are more likely to be unemployed. When they do find work, their income levels are lower. Many give up searching for work, relying instead on social assistance. The feelings of despair and anger associated with a life of poverty come to the forefront. Many turn to alcohol or drugs in an attempt to cope. Young First Nations people may look to gangs or prostitution as escapes. The end result is often an encounter with the justice system, which translates into discouraging statistics: over 75% of youth in custody or on remand in 2003 were Aboriginal. A similar scenario applies to adult offenders, with over 80% of incarcerations being persons of Aboriginal ancestry. The impact of poverty and marginalization can be seen in the number of dysfunctional families, the high incidence of violence, the percentage of single parent families, alcohol and drug abuse and child prostitution. The social consequences have been severe.

In preparing this report, the Office of the Treaty Commissioner commissioned a summary of socio-economic conditions of First Nations People in Saskatchewan (included in Appendix 3). Data were drawn from the 2001 Census, Statistics Canada's 2005 Labour Force Survey and a 2005 Indian and Northern Affairs Canada comparison of socio-economic conditions in 1996 and 2001, as well as studies by Industry Canada. The summary concludes as follows:

> Overall the information, garnered largely from the 2001 Canadian census, provides a clear picture of the socio-economic conditions faced by the First Nations peoples of Saskatchewan. These indicators of employment and labour force activity, income levels, household characteristics, education, housing, health and entrepreneurship generally indicate that First Nations people endure socio-economic conditions far below those of the rest of society, with low incomes, low employment rates, poorer housing conditions and more health problems. On the other hand, there is much hope for improvement in evidence of rapidly improving labour market conditions, a very high rate of participation in the education system, a life expectancy converging on the standard for the rest of the population and increasing entrepreneurial success among First Nations people and businesses.[80]

All the current statistical data point to a frustrating socio-economic situation for most First Nations people, although certain educational and economic participation indicators show improvement. But the distance to close the socio-economic gap between First Nations people and non-Aboriginal people in Canada and Saskatchewan remains far too great:

---

[80] Saskatchewan Institute of Public Policy, *Socio-Economic Conditions of First Nations People in Saskatchewan*, study prepared for the Office of the Treaty Commissioner, June 2006 (included as Appendix 3).

- The life expectancy of Aboriginal men is roughly 7 years shorter than that of the average non-Aboriginal Canadian male. The life expectancy of Aboriginal women is approximately 6.5 years lower than that of the average non-Aboriginal Canadian female.

- Suicide is two to three times more common among Aboriginal people than among non-Aboriginal people. It is also five to six times more prevalent among Aboriginal youth than non-Aboriginal youth.

- The federal offender population in 1997, including those in the community, totalled about 23,200. Of this, about 2,900 (12%) were Aboriginal offenders. In comparison, Aboriginal people comprise about 3% of Canada's population.

- Approximately one-half of all Aboriginal children live in poverty.

- More than half of Aboriginal households in Regina and Saskatoon live below the poverty line.

- Approximately 28% of Aboriginal people over 15 years of age depend on social assistance.

- Approximately one half of the Aboriginal population between the ages of 15 and 24 in Canada live in the prairie provinces.[81]

These statistics point to the unequal benefits flowing from the treaties. The fact that Canadians generally have prospered while First Nations people have suffered the consequences of poverty and societal marginalization is a stark demonstration of the reality that the treaties have not been implemented.

---

[81] Commission on First Nations and Métis Peoples and Justice Reform, *Final Report, Volume 1: Legacy of Hope: An Agenda for Change.* (Regina, Saskatchewan, June 21, 2004), chapter 2.

The Socio-Economic Status Quo Is Unacceptable and Unsustainable

It is generally well accepted that the current socio-economic conditions of First Nations people are unacceptable. In a country such as Canada, which ranks at or near the top of the United Nations survey on socio-economic well-being among all countries, it is not tolerable to have a significant portion of the population living in conditions associated with impoverished developing countries. Those conditions of ill health, insufficient and unsafe housing, polluted water supplies, low education levels, high unemployment, poverty and family breakdown must be addressed.

As well as being unacceptable in a country as blessed as Canada, our society cannot sustain the socio-economic conditions of First Nations people. Due to the high, and growing, proportion of First Nations people, in no province is this truer than in Saskatchewan. A 2006 analysis of the benefits of increased employment among Aboriginal people in Saskatchewan, done by the Saskatchewan Institute of Public Policy for the Saskatchewan Department of First Nations and Métis Relations, estimated that an increase in Aboriginal people's participation rate in the labour market and employment rate to that of non-Aboriginal residents would lead to over 5,100 more Aboriginal people being employed, a 1.1% increase in the overall employment rate in the province. This analysis also estimated that the savings in social policy, justice and corrections fields from lowering the participation rates of Aboriginal people in these areas to those of non-Aboriginal people would be over $500 million per year.[82] The establishment of a process whereby implementation of the livelihood provisions becomes a reality is an essential part of the recovery of First Nations people in proud, self-sustaining communities, and an essential part of achieving full participation in Canadian society.

First Nations people have sought out many different solutions to the social and economic disadvantages they face. They have attempted to advance their educational attainment, to compete for jobs, to move from areas that are economically depressed and to adopt healthy lifestyles. But the barriers are often crushing. They must confront discrimination and

---

[82] Saskatchewan Institute of Public Policy, *Economic Benefits of Increased Aboriginal Employment*, study prepared for the Saskatchewan Department of First Nations and Métis Relations, October 2005 (unpublished).

racism. They come from lives of poverty to situations, particularly in urban centres in Western Canada, where continuing poverty and inadequate living conditions are combined with social dislocation. They most often do not have the skills necessary to enter the labour force. The resources and supports required to allow for a transition to the mainstream economy are often not accessible. The cycle of dependency continues.

Fortunately, there have been encouraging signs of change over the past decade. In 1996, the Royal Commission on Aboriginal Peoples called for a different approach:

> In dealing with the social and cultural concerns of Aboriginal people, we emphasize the need to place social issues in the context of political and economic relations with the rest of Canadian society. When adults have meaningful work and a respected role in society, families will be restored to their role of nurturing and protecting their members. When Aboriginal people have a more equitable share in the wealth of the land, and regain the authority to govern themselves, they will shake off the poverty and powerlessness that sap their emotional, intellectual and spiritual vitality.[83]

Since the Royal Commission on Aboriginal Peoples report, there have been changes in the federal government's approach. There have been attempts to negotiate self-government agreements, and to better understand treaties and the treaty relationship. Individual First Nations have also been developing their own constitutions and moving away from the *Indian Act* regime, with the support of Indian and Northern Affairs Canada. Economic development initiatives are being fostered through cooperative efforts between First Nations and Aboriginal Business Canada and Western Economic Diversification. First Nations are assuming increased responsibility for the delivery of social programs, such as Indian child and family services, wellness/health and housing. Serious attention is being paid to on-reserve water problems. Off-reserve partnerships between urban First Nations organizations and the federal government through the Urban Aboriginal Strategy are designed to improve the socio-economic conditions of First Nations people living in cities. First Nations continue to solidify their control over their own educational programs at all levels – early childhood, kindergarten-to-grade twelve and post-secondary. All of these measures will lead to improvement of the socio-economic conditions facing First Nations people, but progress has been agonizingly slow.

---

[83] Royal Commission on Aboriginal Peoples. *Gathering Strength*, Volume 3, Chapter 1.

The Royal Commission on Aboriginal Peoples recognized the slow pace of change as a factor that would have to be dealt with by First Nations.

> The social policy sectors in this volume are of vital concern to the life, welfare, identity and culture of Aboriginal nations. We anticipate that these will be among the first areas where Aboriginal governments will exercise authority. It will take time to put self-government agreements in place, however, and the pace of change will vary in different nations, depending on their degree of political development. We therefore see change proceeding on three fronts:
>
> 1. Negotiation to establish the scope of self-government and the institutional structures through which it will operate within the Canadian federation;
> 2. Transitional measures mandated under the proposed recognition and government act; and
> 3. Policy reform within the existing federal, provincial and territorial jurisdictions.
>
> The recommendations in this volume apply in any of these situations. They are based on the premise that Aboriginal people must have the authority to define their problems, establish goals, and mobilize and direct resources, whether these resources are found within their nations and communities or in federal, provincial and territorial governments' programs.[84]

Conclusion

In Saskatchewan, progress has been made on each of the three fronts identified by the Royal Commission on Aboriginal Peoples, but adequate resources to fully implement these and other measures have not been forthcoming. The provision of programs based on the socio-economic policies of the federal government present other limiting factors. They do not constitute a recognition of the livelihood provisions of the treaties. They do not create partnerships based on treaty. They do not meet the expectations of the Elders. As Cardinal and Hildebrandt have noted, "Throughout the presentations and the focus meetings, the Elders continued to emphasize the need to restore the self-sufficiency of First Nations and their peoples. In their view, that could only occur if the Parties implement the spirit and intent of their treaties."[85]

---

[84] Ibid., Chapter 7.
[85] Cardinal and Hildebrandt, *Treaty Elders of Saskatchewan*, p. 67.

Self-sufficiency, of course, requires First Nations people to share responsibility for taking advantage of the economic opportunities open to them; one is not self-sufficient if one expects others to provide prosperity without effort. As well, even in the best imaginable circumstances, not every First Nations person will become wealthy, or even middle class, just as not every non-First Nations person is. However, First Nations people need adequate education and access to economic opportunities, as promised to them in the treaties, in order to have the chance to become self-sufficient and achieve parity, as a group, with non-First Nations people.

It is most significant that education was specified in each of the numbered treaties. For the Crown and First Nations alike, one of the important benefits of the coming together of two peoples was the opportunity for both Parties to take advantage of new knowledge. First Nations did not regard this as a one-way process, but saw the advantages in sharing knowledge for the mutual benefit of the treaty Parties. The socio-economic gap must be met in part by improving educational opportunities available to Treaty First Nations students. The fulfillment of the treaty right to education is a critically important aspect of treaty implementation.

6. VIEWS ON TREATY IMPLEMENTATION

In order to ensure the analysis would have practical relevance to the Parties, the Office of the Treaty Commissioner hosted eight workshops[86] with First Nations people and federal officials between August 2005 and March 2006. The purpose of these workshops was to permit Elders and other First Nations people and federal government officials to speak freely and openly on issues arising from the treaties. Accordingly, the Office of the Treaty Commissioner is obliged to respect the confidence in which individuals at these workshops participated. Thus we cannot directly attribute statements or other information. Nor were these workshops intended to be a formal consultation as that term is becoming understood in law.

Two workshops were held with federal officials and six were held with First Nations groups. These workshops were as follows:

Federal Officials Workshops

- Federal Officials, Gatineau, Quebec, October 25, 2005
- Saskatchewan Federal Officials, Regina, Saskatchewan, February 1-2, 2006

First Nations Workshops

- Federation of Saskatchewan Indian Nations Youth Legislative Assembly, Yorkton, Saskatchewan, August 17-19, 2005
- Treaty 4 Gathering, Fort Qu'Appelle, Saskatchewan, September 13-14, 2005
- Northern Communities, La Ronge, Saskatchewan, November 23-24, 2005
- Treaty 6, North Battleford, Saskatchewan, January 24-25, 2006
- Federation of Saskatchewan Indian Nations Urban Conference, Regina, Saskatchewan, January 30-31, 2006
- Federation of Saskatchewan Indian Nations Officials, Saskatoon, Saskatchewan, February 22, 2006

---

[86] See Appendix 1 for a description of the methodology used.

In addition, one workshop was organized by the Federation of Saskatchewan Indian Nations at the Buffalo River Denesuline Nation Elders' Gathering in July 2005. Although this was not a formal workshop hosted by the Office of the Treaty Commissioner, it does form part of the information base used to develop this section. The First Nations workshops were held in rural and urban, southern and northern areas. They were organized so that Elders, youth and Federation of Saskatchewan Indian Nations officials all had a voice.

Predominant emotions in the Elders' workshops were an enormous sense of sorrow at the loss of land and culture and despair at the situation of First Nations communities today. Younger First Nations participants acknowledged the losses of the past, but also looked toward a brighter future. The word "frustration" best characterizes the tone of the workshops with federal officials – frustration at being without clear direction or defined mandate and frustration with the many barriers they seem to encounter.

Methodology

Comments and presentations made at most of the workshops were recorded and transcribed. Comments made in a First Nations language were translated into English and transcribed using the recordings as a basis for translation. In some cases, flipchart notes from the workshops were typed in order to make them usable. Information in this section was drawn from this workshop documentation.

The Office of the Treaty Commissioner met with Federation of Saskatchewan Indian Nations representatives and a small group of Elders to develop appropriate questions for use at the First Nations workshops. The questions were as follows:

- What are some of the concerns that people have about treaty rights?
- How would you make sure that treaties are being honoured and fulfilled?
- Who is responsible for fulfilling treaties? What kind of governing and funding arrangements are required?
- If the treaties were fulfilled today, how would it change the lives of First Nations people on reserve and in urban areas?

The Office of the Treaty Commissioner also worked closely with representatives of Indian and Northern Affairs Canada to develop questions for federal officials to consider during their workshops. The questions were as follows:

- What issues arise within your Department concerning First Nations and treaties?
- What concerns do you hear from First Nations and third parties?
- What do you need to make your role more effective?
- What are the key federal interests in dealing with First Nations issues? As Canada enters into dialogue with First Nations, what federal interests and objectives should be brought to that dialogue?

This section presents the findings of the workshops in five sections:

- *Contextual Themes* – broad themes that permeated and shaped all discussions. Contextual themes were always present as a backdrop regardless of the topic under discussion.
- *First Nations Concerns* – issues addressed primarily by First Nations groups.
- *Federal Concerns* – issues addressed primarily by federal government officials.
- *A Foundation for Treaty Implementation* – themes that are fundamental to treaty implementation. Addressing these themes will provide a foundation for future work.
- *Moving Forward* – specific actions that could be taken to move treaty implementation forward.

Contextual Themes

Most of the comments made during the consultations were framed within the context of two broad themes: First Nations people draw their understanding of the treaties from the knowledge of the Elders, and a long history of broken promises has created a profound distrust of the federal government. These two themes were always in the background. They shaped virtually all discussions at First Nations workshops and had an influence on discussions at federal workshops.

First Nations people draw their understanding of the treaties from the knowledge of the Elders – There are profound differences between the way "knowledge" is transmitted in Canadian and First Nations traditions. In the Canadian tradition, knowledge is passed from one generation to another through the written word and is stored in documents and libraries. In the First

Nations tradition, knowledge is passed from one generation to another through the spoken word and is stored in the hearts and minds of the Elders.

One First Nations workshop participant commented on the differences between First Nations and Canadian systems of knowledge. This speaker emphasized that both systems are valid and that oral history passed from one generation to another is just as reliable as written history. This same speaker also emphasized that a certain protocol must be followed when accessing the knowledge of the Elders – a protocol that recognizes the value of the Elders' knowledge and pays respect to the Elders themselves.

It was evident from Elders' comments that they want traditional ways of transmitting knowledge to continue. For example, they exhorted the young people to listen to the Elders and to learn from them, so the young people can share information learned from the Elders with future generations.

Broken promises have created an atmosphere of distrust – Earlier sections of this report describe a long history of dissention and discord between the Parties – a history of broken promises and misguided federal policies. Remarks made by First Nations people, particularly Elders, illustrate the results of this unhappy history. A sense of betrayal, a profound lack of trust in the government and, most of all, heartbreak and despair at the situation of First Nations people today permeate many of the Elders' remarks.

The Elders talked about a government that disrespected and actively attacked the traditional and cultural ways of First Nations people. They described a government that took advantage and stole land and resources that belonged to the First Nations people. One speaker noted that the government, which was supposed to help First Nations people, has instead created hardships for them.

The Elders talked about a federal government that breaks promises and regularly changes the concept of treaty rights to suit its convenience. Broken promises continue to this day; they are not a thing of the past. First Nations participants gave numerous examples of the way treaty rights have been changed and diminished by the government during the last two decades.

Some First Nations participants suggested it will be necessary to address and acknowledge the many wrongs and broken promises of both past and present before it is possible to move forward to a new relationship.

The federal government officials who participated in the workshops recognized that First Nations people do not trust the federal government and that this lack of trust is grounded in historical as well as present day events. Federal officials did not offer any suggestions about actions the federal government can take to address the wrongs of the past and restore trust.

First Nations Concerns

Two themes common in the First Nations workshops received little attention in the federal workshops. First Nations people said their treaty rights are being eroded; it is an ongoing problem – not just an historical problem. They also said revenue-sharing is needed for natural resources taken from traditional First Nations lands and that the *Natural Resources Transfer Agreement* of 1930 is a fundamental violation of the treaty relationship.

Treaty rights are continually being eroded – Erosion of treaty rights was a major theme at the First Nations workshops. Participants said the government is not keeping promises made in the treaties and erosion of treaty rights is an ongoing, present day problem as well as an historical problem. The phrase "the government is changing everything on us" was used by several speakers.

First Nations people gave numerous examples of ways in which their treaty rights are being eroded in the present day. Many of these examples related to health care. Participants described situations in which their health care costs were not fully covered and they had to pay for prescription drugs and ambulance services. In the North, the government's failure to provide transportation to the South for medical attention was a major issue. There were reports of people being required to pay for their own living expenses in the South and their flight home, and of people being denied treatment in the North and having to fly South at their own expense. There were also reports of seniors and new mothers being discharged from hospitals in the South with nowhere to go and no provision for their flight home.

Taxation was another example of the erosion of treaty rights. Participants said they have to pay taxes on many of the things they buy, and that businesses owned by First Nations people within their treaty areas are supposed to be exempt from taxation, but are sometimes not.

Other examples of the ongoing erosion of treaty rights relate to land use. Participants said that areas where First Nations people can hunt are restricted. They require a permit to hunt outside a specific area and have to go to court if they hunt without the permit. Similarly, First Nations people require a permit to build cabins in certain areas, which has not previously been the case.

Resource-access and revenue-sharing agreements are needed for natural resources taken from traditional First Nations land – Many of the Elders mourned the loss of their lands. They said their ancestors made a living from the land – the land provided everything they needed for a good life. Hunting, fishing and gathering sustained families and communities. But after the white man took their lands away – stole their lands many of the Elders said – they could not make a living on the reserve lands allocated to them and were reduced to poverty and dependency. As well as mourning the loss of their land, the Elders also grieved the damage that has been done to the land. They spoke about the disappearance of muskrat and other furbearing animals, about pollution of land and air, and about scars on the earth from construction and mining.

Elders and others who participated in the First Nations workshops said that loss of the bounty of the earth continues to this day. The oil, minerals, diamonds and gold that lie beneath the earth's surface are modern-day riches – riches that are lost to First Nations people even though all that was agreed to was the sharing of the land to the depth of a plough. First Nations representatives said over and over again that all of the profits from resource development go to the provincial government and to mining companies. They said that First Nations people derive no benefit from mining and other types of resource development. In fact, these activities cause further harm to First Nations communities because they damage the land and drive the animals away. Some First Nations representatives said that a revenue-sharing agreement is needed so that First Nations people benefit from resource development.

One of the fundamental issues raised was that of title. One participant asked, "Who has underlying title to the land where resource development is taking place?" This participant said the agency with underlying title has sovereignty and, thus, control of the land and its resources, and that for First Nations to accept less than underlying title to the land would be a violation of treaty. Issues relating to control of natural resources and revenue-sharing are complicated because, under the terms of the *Natural Resources Transfer Agreement*, the provincial government, not the federal government, controls natural resources in the province.

Federal Concerns

Four themes were discussed at federal workshops but received little attention at the meetings with First Nations. Federal officials said treaty implementation will require commitment and action by several federal government departments. Indian and Northern Affairs Canada cannot do it alone. Getting this type of government-wide collaboration may be difficult because some government departments are "stuck" in a particular operating mode and some do not accept any responsibility for treaty issues.

Federal officials said the design of some federal programs prevents First Nations' participation. For example, the Canadian Agricultural Income Stabilization Program recognizes only individual property rights, not collective property rights. In addition, the federal government needs to improve its ability to deal with First Nations, Métis and Inuit separately and not take a pan-Aboriginal approach in all situations.

Finally, some federal officials talked about the need for capacity building among First Nations if treaty implementation is to be effective. They saw capacity building as a First Nations issue, but there was limited recognition that the federal government may also need to do some capacity building.

Implementation of the treaties will require commitment and action by several federal government departments – Federal officials emphasized that Indian and Northern Affairs Canada alone cannot bear full responsibility for all aspects of treaty implementation. Several other federal government departments also have responsibilities relating to their particular mandates. For example, matters relating to First Nations health fall under the jurisdiction of Health Canada, matters relating to First Nations agriculture fall under Agriculture Canada, and so on. There is a tendency within the federal government for other departments to shrug off their responsibility and to view all matters relating to First Nations peoples and treaty implementation as the responsibility of Indian and Northern Affairs Canada.

The *Marshall* case is one situation in which a department other than Indian and Northern Affairs Canada assumed a major role in implementing treaty rights. The court decision provided clarity on First Nations' rights to fish in the Atlantic and the Department of Fisheries and Oceans was assigned responsibility for implementing the decision. Federal officials said that treaty implementation would be much easier if more federal government departments accepted responsibility for treaty rights as they relate to a particular departmental mandate. Accepting responsibility for implementation of treaty rights, however, will be a major paradigm shift for some federal government departments. Some departments have a certain way of operating and of relating to First Nations and they believe they are already doing what is required. Short of litigation, it will be very hard to move these departments away from their current position.

Some federal officials felt that, while Indian and Northern Affairs Canada is not responsible for all matters relating to treaty implementation, it is Indian and Northern Affairs Canada's job to inform other federal departments about their role and to advance the idea of shared responsibility. Federal officials repeatedly said that a federal policy on treaty implementation would provide common direction for federal government departments and make it easier for all departments to accept responsibility for treaty issues falling within their mandate.

Others suggest that getting departments other than Indian and Northern Affairs Canada to accept responsibility is only part of the answer. There is confusion even when other departments are involved in implementation of treaty rights. Various departments do not always know what the other is doing. There may be fragmentation of programming and departments may be working at cross-purposes or on parallel tracks. In addition, there is little coordination between federal and provincial governments, so the two levels may be duplicating programs or going in different directions. Changes in the operating procedures of federal departments would enable greater flexibility and promote cooperation between departments. These changes might include revised mandates that allow pooling of money and piggybacking of programs and services.

Fragmentation and lack of coordination among federal government departments creates problems for First Nations people too. Sometimes they have to deal with many different agencies on a particular issue and cannot get a definitive answer from any of them. As one Federation of Saskatchewan Indian Nations official said, "The buck doesn't stop anywhere."

The design of some federal government programs prevents First Nations' participation – One example of a program that precludes First Nations' participation is the Canadian Agricultural Income Stabilization Program administered by Agriculture Canada. Farmers must have title to their land to participate in this program. Many First Nations farmers are farming on reserve land, do not have title to the land, and so are ineligible for the Canadian

Agricultural Income Stabilization Program. In addition, the Canadian Agricultural Income Stabilization Program and other federal programs are accessed through individual income tax returns. Individuals who do not regularly submit income tax returns have no way of participating in these programs. Federal officials did not offer specific solutions to this issue, but noted that programs need to be designed to reflect First Nations' circumstances. Federal officials also acknowledged that a focus on programs does little to promote capacity building among First Nations: programs are generally of short duration – three years or less – and people are just starting to get up to speed when it ends.

The federal government needs to improve its capacity to deal with distinct Aboriginal groups – Federal civil servants stated the federal government needs to work on its ability and/or willingness to deal with distinct Aboriginal groups, rather than adopting a Canada-wide, pan-Aboriginal approach. The First Nations, Métis and Inuit are all distinct groups and there are regional differences within each of these groups. Federal officials also note that addressing the on-reserve/off-reserve split in many First Nations is an ongoing challenge. They asked whether there should be a difference in the way the federal government treats Treaty First Nations and non-Treaty First Nations in terms of service delivery and resource development.

Developing capacity to work with distinctive Aboriginal groups was a more significant issue at the federal workshops than at the First Nations workshops. However, some First Nations participants said that treaty people are being grouped together with other Aboriginal groups and all are being treated the same. Their fear is that distinctions between groups will be lost and treaty status will lose its meaning.

Capacity building is needed by First Nations and the federal government – Federal officials talked about the need for capacity building among First Nations if treaty implementation is to be effective. Some officials identified capacity building as a precondition of treaty implementation. For example, while transparent government is not always in place in all

First Nations settings, good governance would maximize treaty implementation. One federal representative pointed out that identifying capacity building and transparency of government as prerequisites for treaty implementation is based on the assumption these presently do not exist. He asked whether this assumption might not be a mindset among federal government officials and act as an impediment to treaty implementation.

Interestingly, federal government officials tended to see a lack of capacity as a First Nations issue, not a federal government issue. Despite acknowledging that the federal government does not have a policy on treaty implementation, that there is little coordination among government departments, and that the design of some government programs prevents First Nations participation, there was only limited recognition among federal officials that the government may, itself, have some capacity building to do.

A Foundation for Treaty Implementation

A number of themes fundamental to treaty implementation were mentioned at virtually every workshop. Addressing these themes would provide a solid foundation for future work. The socio-economic condition of First Nations people was one of these foundational themes. First Nations representatives, particularly Elders, contrasted the poverty and dysfunction of many communities today with the past when individuals, families and communities were strong and self-sufficient. The hope was that treaty implementation would lead to a brighter future. Federal officials said the government has a strong interest in improving socio-economic conditions in First Nations communities and that strategies to foster improvement need to be part of treaty implementation.

The spirit and intent of the treaties was discussed at every workshop. It was evident that First Nations people have a very clear and consistent understanding of the spirit and intent of the treaties. From their perspective, the treaties are nation-to-nation accords that have the status of covenants. The treaties are forever and cannot be extinguished. The treaties enable First Nations people to continue hunting and fishing as they always have, and include a promise that the government will take care of First Nations. Federal officials were much less clear on the spirit and intent of the treaties and referred not to the treaties themselves, but rather to court decisions.

The need to develop common understandings of treaties and treaty issues was another recurring theme. Individuals and organizations responsible for treaty implementation not only need a common understanding of what treaty implementation means, they need an understanding of each other's positions and perspectives. In addition, federal civil servants, First Nations youth and the general public lack a basic understanding of treaty issues. There is a need for education in all these groups.

The theme of accountability ran through many of the discussions in both First Nations and federal workshops. A belief that the federal government is accountable for upholding the promises made in the treaties permeated most discussion at First Nations workshops. Federal officials discussed monitoring as one aspect of accountability and said monitoring mechanisms would help ensure treaty implementation proceeds as planned and help the federal government monitor its own performance. First Nations people also identified the need for greater accountability of First Nations leaders to their people.

All Parties are concerned about the socio-economic conditions of First Nations people – All participants in the workshops, First Nations and federal representatives alike, spoke about the socio-economic conditions of First Nations people. They said that improving living conditions and quality of life must be a high priority.

The Elders described a past in which hunting and fishing and the wealth of the land sustained their communities and a present where poverty, drugs and alcohol are rampant. The Elders said they shed tears for future generations, should they continue on the same path. The Elders said they pray to the Creator for help in following a new path and once again living a good life.

Federal government officials, too, were concerned about the poor quality of life that many First Nations people experience. They said the government has a strong interest in improving socio-economic conditions in First Nations communities and strategies to foster improvement need to be a part of treaty implementation.

Most of the First Nations people who participated in the workshops said treaty implementation will mean a better life for them. This view was particularly prevalent among urban people. They said that if treaties are implemented, First Nations people would not have to struggle as much, they would have the resources to lead healthier lives, addictions and crime would decrease over time, and the socio-economic gap between First Nations people and the rest of the population would close. Some federal officials, however, did not share this perception. They said treaty implementation is not a magic wand and things will not suddenly get better for First Nations people when treaties are implemented.

First Nations people have a very clear understanding of the spirit and intent of the treaties, federal officials are less clear – The importance of honouring the spirit and intent of the treaties was emphasized by the Treaty Commissioner during the workshops.

The First Nations people, and particularly the Elders, were remarkably consistent in their understanding of the spirit and intent of the treaties. This understanding is as follows:

- The treaties are nation-to-nation constitutional accords that define the foundation of the First Nations' relationship with Canada. They are not contracts and should not be given narrow contractual interpretations. The treaties speak of co-existence, mutual benefit, mutual survival, mutual respect and make possible the distribution of constitutional authority in Canada.

- Some First Nations participants used the term "covenants" when referring to the treaties. Others said that there were three parties to the treaties: the First Nations people, the Queen, and the Creator. The treaties are sacred.

- The treaties are forever. "As long as the sun shines, the grass grows and the rivers flow," were words spoken many times by Elders. Elders spoke, too, of the government official who kicked a rock and said the treaties will endure "as long as that rock stands."

- The treaties say First Nations people will be able to keep on hunting and fishing as they always have without geographic limitation, without concern for borders and boundaries created by the government.

- The government promised it would take care of First Nations people and would provide them with a living and with education and medicine.

Federal government officials were not nearly as clear about the spirit and intent of the treaties and instead raised questions. For example:

- Federal officials questioned whether the treaties are forever. They asked, "Can land rights be extinguished? Have treaties run their course?"

- Federal officials asked whether fulfillment and implementation of treaties are the same thing. If the obligations implied in the treaties have been fulfilled, does that mean the treaties have been implemented?

When federal government officials were discussing the meaning of treaty implementation, they referred neither to the spirit in which the treaties were executed nor to the intent of those who signed the treaties, but rather to court decisions such as the *Marshall* case. The Supreme Court of Canada in the *Marshall* case reaffirmed the Mi'kmaq's treaty right to fish for a moderate living. Federal officials noted that, within the federal government, the phrase "moderate living" has become a standard, of sorts, that defines treaty rights.

When comparing First Nations and federal perspectives on the spirit and intent of the treaties, it can be said that First Nations people base their understandings on the intent of the Chiefs who negotiated the treaties, as understood from historical accounts that have been passed down through the generations. The federal government tends to look at the exact wording of treaties and at previous court decisions. This perspective is informed by a tradition of contractual law and a legal system based on adversarial relationships.

Common understandings of treaties and treaty issues are needed – Understanding treaties and the treaty relationship was discussed at virtually every workshop in a variety of different contexts. Three important themes were evident in these discussions.

- The meaning of treaty implementation is not clear. Workshop participants have numerous and varied understandings of the concept of treaty implementation. Often, discussions of treaty implementation contained more questions than answers. These questions include:

  - Are treaty implementation and self-government the same thing?

  - Is fulfillment of the obligations of the treaties and treaty implementation the same thing?

  - Does treaty implementation mean establishment of a relationship and processes that enable the Parties to work together or does it mean specific actions by one or both Parties?

  - Does treaty implementation mean holding the federal government accountable for its fiduciary responsibilities to First Nations people?

  - What is the relationship between treaty implementation and underlying title to land in this province?

  - Will treaty implementation be completed at some point in time or does it continue forever?

- There is a need to define and clarify some of the basic issues relating to treaty implementation so that everyone involved has a common understanding. A Federation of Saskatchewan Indian Nations representative said the positions of the two Parties is an issue that needs to be clarified. Federal officials expressed the hope that increased understanding between the Parties will create an informed relationship and common ground so First Nations and government officials can work together.

- The general public has little knowledge about treaties and treaty issues. This point was made by both First Nations and federal representatives. Government officials, apart from a few specialists whose work focuses on treaties, lack knowledge of the treaties. Even some First Nations people, typically young people, lack an understanding of treaty issues because they have not been well-informed. Some young First Nations people think that treaty means getting free medicine or education. They do not understand the full scope and intent of the treaties and why treaties were negotiated. Several participants said that education about treaties is needed for specific groups such as civil servants and First Nations youth, as well as for youth in general and members of the public.

Accountability is an issue that affects many dimensions of treaty implementation – The theme of accountability ran through many of the workshop discussions. Implicit in most of the First Nations workshops was a belief that the federal government is accountable for keeping the promises made in the treaties and for its fiduciary responsibilities to First Nations people.

Other aspects of accountability mentioned during the First Nations workshops included:

- Indian and Northern Affairs Canada is accountable to the First Nations people, not the other way around.

- The federal government is accountable for using the lands and resources of First Nations people in accordance with international standards of justice.

- First Nations governments need to be accountable to First Nations people.

Some of the topics addressed by federal officials also related to accountability.

- There was discussion about the need for transparent governance by First Nations. Implicit in this discussion was the idea that transparent governance would make it easier for First Nations to be accountable for money provided through treaty implementation.

- Federal officials all saw a role for the provincial government in treaty implementation. Some felt a mechanism needs to be found to hold the province accountable for fulfilling its obligations.

Monitoring to ensure that promises are kept and obligations fulfilled is one aspect of accountability discussed at length by both First Nations and federal officials. They emphasized that once processes for treaty implementation have been established, parallel monitoring processes need to be developed to ensure implementation proceeds in an appropriate manner. Suggestions for monitoring mechanisms included a treaty protection office, a treaty auditor general and an ombudsman to review concerns or issues brought forward by the Parties.

Federal government officials also talked about the need to monitor their own performance and measure whether they are meeting their goals. They suggest it may be necessary to develop new monitoring methods that reflect ongoing dialogue with First Nations people, and that the "traditional square, four-corner" government approach to performance evaluation will not work in this situation.

Moving Forward

Both First Nations and federal participants suggested specific actions that could be taken to move treaty implementation forward. One of the most significant would be development of a federal policy on treaty implementation. In the absence of such a policy, treaty rights are often determined through litigation, which, by its nature, is adversarial – the antithesis of a healthy treaty relationship. Another significant action to move treaty implementation forward would be clarification of the role of the provincial government in treaty implementation. Most of the treaties that affect Saskatchewan were made before the province was established, but today many matters that affect First Nations people fall under provincial jurisdiction.

A federal government policy on treaty implementation would reduce litigation and promote a consistent government-wide approach – The federal government does not have a policy that addresses treaty implementation nor has it defined a consistent approach across government. Present federal government approaches are driven by court decisions, by narrow policies relating to specific issues, or by program and service delivery priorities. Lack of a government-wide policy relating to treaty implementation was a major topic of discussion among federal officials and appeared to be a significant source of frustration. It was also mentioned at a First Nations workshop by a representative of the Federation of Saskatchewan Indian Nations.

The absence of policy leaves federal officials without broad or consistent direction. Federal officials do not know where they are going or the results they are expected to achieve. Reliance on litigation means that federal responses to treaty issues are often case-specific and piecemeal, rather than consistent and coordinated. As well, litigation creates an adversarial relationship between the Parties. There is a winner and a loser, and uncertainty on both sides until the court renders its judgment. Litigation is also very expensive and time consuming.

Several participants in both First Nations and federal workshops emphasized that Saskatchewan is an exception to the usual Canadian practice of defining treaty rights through litigation. The discussions in Saskatchewan in which the Office of the Treaty Commissioner, the Crown and First Nations are currently engaged was initiated to avoid litigation. Federal officials indicated that a clear and coherent policy regarding treaty implementation is a dream – a big dream – that would make them more effective when dealing with First Nations and treaty issues.

Federal government officials offered several ideas on elements to include in a federal treaty policy. The overall tone of the policy should reflect a greater commitment to First Nations issues generally and a greater willingness to reconcile. The policy should reflect and accommodate historic treaties and include a mechanism for resolving problems around them. It should also include mechanisms to ensure the provinces accept their responsibilities and to promote cooperation between federal government departments.

Federal officials agreed that it will take direction from the highest level – a court decision or a Cabinet mandate – to create a federal government-wide policy concerning treaty implementation and to ensure that it guides all government action. Some federal officials suggested that a Royal Proclamation II is needed to ensure implementation of the treaties.[87] Such a proclamation would be a modern-day parallel to the *Royal Proclamation of 1763*, which recognized the responsibility of the Crown to First Nations. Federal officials also suggested the possibility of a Treaty Recognition Act or treaty implementation legislation, saying such legislation could be a trigger to treaty implementation.

The idea of a Treaty Recognition Act received a cautious response from Federation of Saskatchewan Indian Nations officials. One representative emphasized that the treaties are covenants and asked how treaty implementation legislation would reflect the spirit and intent of the treaties. Others said legislation should not contain anything that would damage the inherent and treaty rights of First Nations peoples. They had questions about the role of the province, how provincial legislation would apply, and how a treaty implementation act can be designed so it does not get stuck in time. The Federation of

---

[87] Royal Commission on Aboriginal Peoples, *Gathering Strength*, Volume 2, chapter 2.

Saskatchewan Indian Nations officials said they would need to see concrete examples of the way treaty implementation legislation would work before commenting in detail and either accepting or rejecting the idea.

Some First Nations people saw a role for the provincial government in treaty implementation, others believe treaty implementation is the responsibility of the First Nations and the federal government alone, since the Parties to the original treaties were the First Nations, the Queen and the Creator. Virtually all federal government officials believe that the province has a role to play in treaty implementation, saying there should be three parties to treaty implementation: the federal government, the provincial government and the First Nations. The need to clarify the role of the province is a theme that runs through the comments of both First Nations people and federal government representatives. The province's role must be defined and a formal mechanism for provincial participation established.

A related topic of discussion was the *Natural Resources Transfer Agreement* of 1930. The agreement was mentioned and condemned in most consultations with First Nations people. First Nations participants said it is a fundamental breach of the treaty relationship. They also said that when this agreement was made there was no consultation, First Nations people were not treated as equals by the governments of the day and had no say in the agreement, which profoundly affects their lives. Some speakers said the *Natural Resources Transfer Agreement* should be revisited and renegotiated in order to implement treaties fairly.

Conclusion

The views shared by both First Nations and federal government participants in the Exploratory Treaty Table process provide the treaty Parties with a foundation on which they can construct a treaty implementation agenda. In cases in which one Party identified a concern not shared by the other Party, each Party will first need to understand why the other has a concern about the issue and seek to respond to that concern in a respectful fashion. In addition, when the Parties have divergent views on an issue or when an issue raises a fundamental conflict between the sovereignties and authority of the Parties, they will need to work together to find an honourable reconciliation of their conflicts or their sovereignty, drawing on the treaty promise of a brother-to-brother relationship. Reconciliation, an issue which will be addressed extensively in the next section, is in many ways at the heart of an agenda for treaty implementation and fulfillment of the treaty relationship.

7. HONOURING THE COVENANT

Treaties remain, as the *Statement of Treaty Issues* put it, a bridge to the future. The destination that lies at the other side of the bridge must be a future of "fulfillment." Part of this fulfillment involves the reconciliation of two sovereignties through a brother-to-brother relationship. Reconciliation was one of the underlying principles of the treaties at the time they were made. The gap between reconciliation as the initial animating principle of treaty making and reconciliation as a contemporary goal to address damaged relationships is the result of the failure to fulfill the treaty relationship from the time of the treaties until the present.

The etymology of the word "reconcile" is derived from the Latin *reconcilare*, which means "to bring together again." If the word is broken down even further it comes from *re* which means "again" plus *concilare* which means to "make friendly." Thus the word "reconcile" can literally mean "to make friendly again." Additionally, the word "reconciliation" comes from the same Latin roots *reconcilare*, with the added *sella* meaning "seat." Reconciliation can therefore literally mean "to sit together again in friendship."

The concept of reconciliation is not unique to European cultures. As Elder Pete Waskahat stated:

> We had our own First Nations' government; we had our own life teachings on education. Even when a person made mistakes in life, there were people that would counsel them. There was a process of reconciliation. It was done through the oral language. It was done through the Elders. There they talked about that person getting back into a balanced life..."[88]

First Nations teachings and ceremonies relating to the doctrines of *wâhkôhtowin* (the laws governing all relations) and *miyo-wîcêhtowin* (the laws concerning good relations) contain elements of reconciliation. Cardinal and Hildebrandt stated:

> The doctrine of "good relations" is an essential and integral component of the teachings of all the Treaty First Nations in Saskatchewan. It is perhaps best symbolized by the circle evident in the way many First Nations ceremonies are structured... The Elders told us that the circle

---

[88] Cardinal and Hildebrandt, *Treaty Elders of Saskatchewan*, p. 16.

represents a coming together or a bringing together of a nation. They state that, in coming together in this manner, the nation reaffirms its unity under the laws of the Creator. Under First Nations traditional teachings, this was one of the sacred ways in which the nation would continue to possess the capability to nurture, protect, care for, and heal its people... The Elders stated that it is for such reasons that the circle has come to be known variously as – a praying circle, talking circle, healing circle, and a circle of reconciliation... The teachings and ceremonies are the means given to First Nations to restore peace and harmony in times of personal and community conflict. These teachings also serve as the foundation upon which new relationships are to be created.[89]

The word "reconciliation" is especially significant in the context of treaty relationships. Reconciliation implies that the Parties have sat together in friendship in the past. This is, of course, true for the governmental treaty parties in Saskatchewan. They sat together in friendship when promises were made and obligations assumed in the treaties. Reconciliation would require that First Nations and the Crown once again sit together in friendship in the present. This would be the true fulfillment of the treaty relationship: people being brought together in a spirit of peace, friendship and respect.

Reconciliation is essential to treaty implementation. To understand the relationship between reconciliation and treaty implementation, it is useful to think of treaty implementation as having four main perspectives, reflecting different stages in the Crown's commitment to achieve reconciliation through the treaty relationship:

• The perspective of the Parties at the time of treaty making and their mutual wish to reconcile two systems of governance, law and use of land and resources, including areas of consensus and areas of divergent understandings.

• The perspective of post-treaty history in which the principle of reconciliation has not been consistently honoured, as the Crown has too often acted unilaterally and without regard for the spirit and intent of the treaties.

• The perspective of the present day, in which we see reconciliation once again identified as an organizing principle for the establishment of a renewed, harmonious and just treaty relationship between the treaty Parties.

---

[89] Ibid, p. 14, 15.

● The perspective of the future, in which treaty implementation is accomplished, the covenant is honoured, and the original spirit and intent of the treaties is fulfilled on an ongoing basis through the promised brother-to-brother relationship. This is a future in which the treaties take their rightful place in the Canadian state, and Treaty First Nations people take their rightful place in Canadian society.

Perspectives at the Time of Treaty Making

(a) The Spirit and Intent of the Treaties in First Nations Law

Canadian courts have recognized that unfairness can arise if the English language, with its common law bias, is too heavily relied upon to interpret treaties. In the 1990 case *R. v. Sioui* the Supreme Court of Canada observed that the treaty must be interpreted not according to the technical meaning of its content but in the sense that treaty would be naturally understood by the Indians:

> The factors underlying this rule were eloquently stated in *Jones v. Meehan*, 175 U.S. 1 (1899), a judgment of the United States Supreme Court, and are I think just as relevant to questions involving the existence of a treaty and the capacity of the parties as they are to the interpretation of a treaty (at pp. 10-11):
>
>> In construing any treaty between the United States and an Indian tribe, it must always . . . be borne in mind that the negotiations for the treaty are conducted, on the part of the United States, [...] by representatives skilled in diplomacy, masters of a written language, understanding the modes and forms of creating the various technical estates known to their law, and assisted by an interpreter employed by themselves; [...] and that the treaty must therefore be construed, not according to the technical meaning of its words to learned lawyers, but in the sense in which they would naturally be understood by the Indians.[90]

The language of the *Jones* decision makes it clear that the legal technicalities of the English language are not the proper basis, and certainly not the *sole* basis, upon which to interpret treaties, as they do not represent the true spirit and intent of the Parties. First Nations would most naturally understand their treaties not according to the technical meaning of the words of treaty texts to lawyers, but in their Indigenous languages. Thus, if we are to interpret treaties as the First Nations

---

[90] *R. v. Sioui,* [1990] 1 S.C.R. 1025·

would naturally have understood them at the time they were entered into, and indeed to the present day, the Parties must consider turning to First Nations languages and legal principles.

Developing solutions that account for both Parties' legal perspectives makes sense in the context of treaty interpretation and implementation, because these processes would involve the interaction of interests from both societies and the reconciliation of two legal and cultural orders. Including First Nations legal principles can counteract the powerful influence of Canadian laws in the development of *sui generis*[91] principles and help to ensure that this law is as impartial and free of bias as possible. Thus, the explicit reception of First Nations perspectives and principles in treaty interpretation more firmly establishes an autonomous body of law that bridges First Nation and Canadian legal cultures.[92] The *sui generis* doctrine allows for this *intermingling* of common law and First Nations legal principles. Such symmetry allows for the recognition of First Nations uniqueness, while building strong ties of cooperation and unity between First Nations peoples and other Canadians.

The numbered treaties were negotiated in different languages: Cree, Saulteaux, Dene, Assiniboine, as well as English. To the Cree and Saulteaux people, *Wâhkôhtowin* is viewed as the over-arching law governing all relations.[93] This law is said to flow from the Creator who placed all life on earth. Humans are a part of this order and are organized into families. Since humans exist within an over-arching natural law they are counselled to observe other living things for guidance in practising this law. A body of stories describes what people have learned from observing the natural world and is used to facilitate order.[94] The sun, moon, winds, clouds, rocks, fish, insects and animals all provide illustrations of *wâhkôhtowin*, which the First Nations incorporate within their understanding of natural law, or the body of laws given to them by the Creator. *Wâhkôhtowin* holds implications for individuals, families, governments and nations living under the treaties. Within larger treaty relationships, unrelated people were to apply *wâhkôhtowin* in accordance with the ideas found within the concepts of *miyo-wîcêhtowin, pâstâhowin, ohcinêwin* and *kwayaskâtotamowin*.

---

[91] Black's Law Dictionary defines *sui generis* as "of its own kind or class, i.e., the only one of its own kind." Black, Henry Campbell, *Black's Law Dictionary* (St. Paul, MN: West Publishing, 1979).

[92] Slattery, Brian, "Understanding Aboriginal Rights" (1987), 66 *Canadian Bar Review* 727 at 733; Slattery, Brian, "Making Sense of Aboriginal Rights" (2000), 79 *Canadian Bar Review* 196 at 200-204.

[93] O'Reilly-Scanlon, Kathleen, Kristine Crowe, Angelina Weenie, "Pathways to Understanding: Wahkotowin as a research methodology", (2004) 39 *McGill Journal of Education* 1.

[94] Elder Dolly Neapetung, in Cardinal and Hildebrandt, *Treaty Elders of Saskatchewan*, p. 6.

Miyo-wîcêhtowin is said to have originated in the laws and relationships that the Cree Nation has with their Creator:

> It asks, directs, admonishes or requires Cree peoples as individuals and as a nation to conduct themselves in a manner such that they create positive good relations in all relationships.[95]

> The root of *wîcehtowin* is wiceht which means to come along side or to support.[96]

Like most human societies that have struggled to live by their highest values, the Cree have not always managed to sustain the harmony they desired. There have been periods of conflict. Nevertheless, *miyo-wîcêhtowin* is an important legal principle for treaty implementation because it speaks to maintaining peace between people of different places and perspectives. The peace and order clauses in the treaties should be interpreted with this concept in mind.

The maintenance of mutual good relationships (*miyo-wîcêhtowin*) through positive support and assistance to maintain peace and order under the treaties is often represented by the circle in Cree law.[97] Circles are considered sacred and represent the bringing together of people.[98] They are meant to remind people of Mother Earth and their journey through life. Circles can be an important process and institution of treaty implementation because they embody relational decision making ideas.

Consequences of failing to abide by the promises in the treaties under Cree law are described as *pâstâhowin* and *ohcinêwin*.[99] *Pâstâhowin* is used to describe something that goes against natural law. If such an offence occurs, negative consequences, or *ohcinêwin*, will follow. *Pâstâhowin* and *ohcinêwin* can apply to any circumstance where the law is not followed, either by action or omission.

---

[95] Ibid., p. 14.
[96] Jobin, Shalene, *Guiding Philosophy and Governance Model of Bent Arrow Traditional Healing Society* (M.A.I.G. thesis, University of Victoria, 2005) [unpublished] at http://66.102.7.104/search?q=cache:pjbvzcj2LwMJ:web.uvic.ca/igov/research/pdfs/Bent%2520Arrow%2520G overnance-Final.pdf+miyo-wîcêhtowin&hl=en.
[97] Cardinal and Hildebrandt, *Treaty Elders of Saskatchewan*, pp. 14-15.
[98] Ibid.
[99] Ibid., p. 7; see also Brighton, Robert, *Grateful Prey: Rock Cree Human-Animal Relations* (Berkeley: University of California Press, 1993) at 104: "pastahow (verb) 'someone brings retribution on himself'."

A contemporary application of Cree linguistic concepts in Canadian law is found in Saskatchewan's Provincial Court. In 2001, a Cree speaking Judge was appointed to the bench and called to preside over a "Cree Court" in northern Saskatchewan. A majority of the people who appear before the court are Cree. All proceedings of the court are conducted in the Cree language and translators are provided to non-Cree speakers. This is not a Court of Cree law, but a Crown court using the Cree language. Canadian law applies in every respect within the court and people receive due process rights and substantive freedoms in conformity with the *Canadian Charter of Rights and Freedoms*.

At the same time, while Canadian law forms the basis of the Court's jurisdiction, its focus can be different from conventional Provincial Court proceedings. When legal proceedings are conducted in Cree, the dynamics of the legal process are different. Linguistically, people are brought into different relationships than are possible under normal English expression. Concepts like *wâhkôhtowin*, *pâstâhowin* and *ohcinêwin* come to life in a natural way when Cree people participate in the law in their own language. Furthermore, restorative concepts are more naturally applied within the Cree Court because of its cultural orientation. The Cree Court demonstrates how Cree concepts can be brought to bear in solving contemporary Canadian legal problems.

Although the Cree Court has not applied its energies and resources to treaty interpretation, it could evolve into a blended institution for both Canadian and Cree law. The operation of the Cree Court may provide insight into how Cree law might be used to interpret and implement treaties. It may also illustrate that the development of a body of inter-societal law to address the reconciliation of two legal systems is not an impossible goal, but something with practical application and value.

The treaties reconcile two sovereignties, two legal orders, two systems of economic use of land, and many cultures. Treaty implementation need not be confined to the rules set out by the Canadian courts. Indeed, to be legitimately undertaken it cannot be so confined. First Nations legal rules contain significant guidance about how to live together in peace and order within the Province of Saskatchewan, and also about achieving a true and complete understanding of what was reconciled, and how, in the treaties.

(b) Canadian Jurisprudence on Treaty Interpretation

Since Canada's approach to treaty issues is largely influenced by jurisprudence, it is useful to summarize the key principles of Canadian law on treaty interpretation. The most recent Supreme Court decision on treaty interpretation is *Mikisew Cree First Nation v. Canada*:[100]

> The interpretation of the treaty "must be realistic and reflect the intentions of both parties, not just that of the [First Nation]" (*Sioui*, at p. 1069). As a majority of the Court stated in *R. v. Marshall*, [1999] 3 S.C.R. 456, at para. 14:
>
>> The Indian parties did not, for all practical purposes, have the opportunity to create their own written record of the negotiations. Certain assumptions are therefore made about the Crown's approach to treaty making (honourable) which the Court acts upon in its approach to treaty interpretation (flexible) as to the existence of a treaty ... the completeness of any written record ... and the interpretation of treaty terms once found to exist. The bottom line is the Court's obligation is to "choose from among the various possible interpretations of the <u>common</u> intention [at the time the treaty was made] the one which best reconciles" the [First Nation] interests and those of the Crown. [Citations omitted.]

Under Canadian law, the principal task in interpreting a treaty is to determine the common intentions of the parties, but in doing so certain assumptions in favour of First Nations are made. This is legitimate, as First Nations were not literate in the English language in which treaties were recorded and it is in keeping with the principle of the honour of the Crown being always at stake. These factors permit a court to supplement or depart from the written text of a treaty, where the written treaty text is incomplete or inadequate as a record of the actual verbal treaty agreement.[101]

The 1996 Supreme Court of Canada decision in *R. v. Badger*[102] and the 1999 Supreme Court decision in *R. v. Marshall*[103] outline the guidelines that the Court has followed in interpreting the treaties:

---

[100] *Mikisew Cree First Nation v. Canada* [2005] 3 S.C.R. 388 at para. 28.
[101] *See R. v. Marshall,* [1999] 3 S.C.R. 456 at para. 35, per Binnie J.
[102] *R. v. Badger* [1996] 1 S.C.R. 771.
[103] *R. v. Marshall.*

1. A treaty represents an exchange of solemn promises between the Crown and Indians and the nature of this agreement is sacred.

2. The honour of the Crown is always at stake when dealing with Indian people, and it is always to be assumed that the Crown intends to fulfill its promises. The integrity of the Crown must be maintained when interpreting statutes or treaties that affect Aboriginal and treaty rights. The appearance of "sharp dealing" is not sanctioned.

3. When interpreting a treaty or document, any ambiguities or doubtful expressions in wording must be resolved in favour of the Indians. Any limitation that restricts Indian treaty rights must be narrowly construed.

4. The onus of proving the extinguishment of a treaty right lies with the Crown. Strict proof of the extinguishment is required, as is a clear and plain intention to do so.[104]

Commenting on a 1760 Mi'kmaq treaty in the 1999 *Marshall (No. 1)* case, the Supreme Court of Canada wrote, "The subtext of the Mi'kmaq treaties was reconciliation and mutual advantage."[105]

For our purposes, this serves as a good and concise summary of the underlying purpose of the treaties for both treaty Parties: reconciliation and mutual advantage. This suggests a general interpretive principle that is a secure foundation of any treaty implementation initiative.

Perspectives of Post Treaty History

(a) The Constitutional Context of Treaty Implementation

An examination of treaty implementation policies has to address developments in the legal status of treaties, particularly existing treaty rights. When Canada's Constitution was patriated and amended in the *Constitution Act, 1982*, a constitutional guarantee was made in the words of section 35(1) of that Act:

s. 35(1) The existing Aboriginal and treaty rights of the Aboriginal peoples of Canada are hereby recognized and affirmed.

---

[104] See Isaac, Thomas. *Aboriginal Law: Commentary Case and Materials. 3rd Edition.* (Saskatoon: Purich Publishing., 2004), p. 82.
[105] *R. v. Marshall* at para. 3.

The courts have given a large, liberal and purposive interpretation to that guarantee. This section explores some of the dimensions of that interpretation in laying the groundwork for treaty implementation.

More than 20 years after the guarantee was made by Canada's First Ministers, formalized by the Parliament of the United Kingdom, and then personally signed into law by Queen Elizabeth II on April 17, 1982, it is certainly clear that the "box" of existing treaty rights is far from empty. On that day, the Crown, in the person of the reigning sovereign, solemnly pledged its honour in giving effect to existing treaty rights. It is now for the subjects of the Crown, and Her Majesty's loyal governments, to meet the challenge of fulfilling our sovereign's word as it relates to the treaties. They have a positive duty to do so rather than continue to wait for the courts to direct them.

Nothing precludes the Parties from jointly determining the scope of the existing Aboriginal and treaty rights identified in section 35. A cooperative approach best represents the treaty relationship and avoids delaying resolution of issues and continuing uncertainty and lack of clarity.

It is also consistent with the Supreme Court of Canada's clear direction that the Parties work out their issues in a political forum rather than through litigation. The treaty Parties should state in any agreement that, without deciding the extent of the Aboriginal and treaty rights of the treaty Parties, they have agreed to record their shared understanding of what is required to implement the treaties in a modern context and to make commitments to one another accordingly. Such an agreement would fulfill Canada's duty to give meaning to section 35, or "fill the box," without usurping the role of the courts in making determinations of what constitutional law is.

(b) Divergent Views

Many terms of the treaties are clear when taken at face value, but an intention-based and contextual interpretation reveals important differences between the Parties. Even though there is consensus on a treaty issue, for example that hunting, fishing and trapping are treaty protected rights of First Nations, there can remain difficulties with many aspects of the exercise of those rights. Treaty implementation will necessarily include the attempt to secure consensus on the nature of harvesting rights and the necessary limits that might be imposed for conservation and safety reasons. Other clearly identified treaty issues include land entitlement, consultation and accommodation in relation to treaty hunting, fishing and other harvesting rights, the value of annuities, the present value of unpaid treaty benefits in relation to economic assistance, health and education. It is evident that even where the Parties agree on the existence of a treaty right, much work will be required to make the exercise of that right a reality.

While some treaty issues (such as traditional harvesting) do not involve matters of broad principle, there are other more difficult and fundamental issues in which the Parties have deeply divergent views. For example, the Crown maintains that First Nations rights to land, including First Nations title, were surrendered and thus extinguished by all the treaties that apply in Saskatchewan. Treaty First Nations hold a very different view. Similarly, Treaty First Nations assert their inherent sovereignty as peoples, while the Crown has not yet fully embraced the idea. Such issues have the potential to cause a serious rift between the Parties as they begin a treaty implementation process. Workshops have revealed the importance of issues such as title and sovereignty to Treaty First Nations Elders and others, and it would be a serious disservice to shy away from these issues just because they will be difficult to deal with.

Knowing that sooner or later the treaty implementation discussions will have to address such deeply held, divergent views can, to say the least, inhibit progress and perhaps cause an excess of caution in entering into the treaty implementation agenda. It is necessary to acknowledge the importance of these issues to each of the Parties. However, these are the issues where an honourable reconciliation is surely the answer. To achieve this, the Parties must begin by addressing common issues, thereby building momentum and creating mutual respect and trust that will carry them to an honourable reconciliation on difficult issues.

It is also necessary to acknowledge that neither party agreed to surrender its fundamental identity or world-view. The Crown did not agree to modify its system of Parliamentary democracy, the theoretical supremacy of the monarch as sovereign, the common law, statute law and the various conventions and usages that are the product of centuries of legal and constitutional evolution. Similarly, the Treaty First Nations did not agree to yield up or surrender their inherent rights as nations, their laws, their customs and traditions nor their spiritual connection to their lands. They did not agree to give up their spirituality, their oral tradition, their philosophies, their ethical systems, their traditional knowledge of the plants and animals of their territories, their technologies for living on their lands, and their ways of understanding their relationship with the Creator.

In short, both treaty Parties desired to continue to be who they were. Their treaty agreement was to coexist, with the mutual understanding that the agreement did not presume a static relationship but a dynamic one. Change and evolution was implicit in the treaties, yet that change was to occur within certain parameters of mutual respect. First Nations believe that Alexander Morris, the Treaty Commissioner in Treaty 4, specifically agreed to return on a yearly basis to discuss the treaty relationship, a practice they were familiar with in their relationship with the Hudson's Bay Company.[106] They expected a continuous review of the treaty relationship.

Certain fundamental matters were beyond the scope of the treaty negotiations. On these issues, we need to find a means to reconcile fundamental differences in a way that does not necessarily involve compromise of those things that are truly fundamental to each people's distinctiveness and systems of belief. In these instances, reconciliation may not mean a compromise but may involve finding a creative but mutually respectful way to acknowledge the incompatible views of the Parties, and then move on to making practical arrangements

---

[106] Ray, et al., *Bounty and Benevolence.*

both can live with. The Canadian political community confronts similar challenges on a regular basis and manages them through the vehicles of federalism and intergovernmental affairs. In order to define an agenda for treaty implementation, the Parties will need to acknowledge at the front end of the treaty implementation process that those issues exist and that the Parties need, eventually, to reconcile their differences.

i. Sovereignty, Self-Determination and Governance

First Nations have always maintained that they are sovereign and that by entering into treaties, the Crown recognized that sovereignty. The Elders use this language to the present day. Canada has traditionally maintained that only the Crown is sovereign. Sovereignty has been an uncomfortable topic for public discussion and debate in Canada. However, the protection of treaty rights under subsection 35(1) of the Constitution recognizes the government-to-government character of the treaties.

Subsection 35(1) focuses on "peoples," unlike rights that pertain to individuals under the *Charter of Rights and Freedoms*. The focus on peoples has potential international law consequences. Many First Nations regard themselves as peoples and thus as recipients of the right to exercise treaty making power as a sovereign state within international law.[107] The right to First Nations' self-determination is argued to exist within customary international law.[108] Article 1 of the *International Covenant on Civil and Political Rights* and Article 1 of the *International Covenant on Economic, Social and Cultural Rights* proclaim that all peoples have the right of self-determination:

> All peoples have the right of self-determination. By virtue of that right they freely determine their political status and freely pursue their economic, social and cultural development.

However, the courts have not been overly attentive to the international law implications of the word "peoples" in section 35(1). The word "Aboriginal" (in which First Nations are included) is mostly interpreted to the exclusion of the term "peoples" under section 35(1). The *Van der Peet*

---

[107] Barsh, Russel Lawrence, *International Context of Crown-Aboriginal Treaties in Canada: Final Report*. (Ottawa: Royal Commission on Aboriginal Peoples, 1994).

[108] Anaya, James, *Indigenous Peoples and International Law* (Oxford: Oxford University Press, 1996).

case narrowly defined rights in relation to Aboriginality, rather than qualifying and modifying Aboriginality by its relationship to the word "peoples."[109] Yet the term "peoples" holds the greatest significance for defining First Nations-Crown relationships because the word's content draws great meaning from international law, though in a *sui generis* way.[110]

The concept of "peoples" includes internal or external rights to self-determination,[111] depending on the circumstances of the people's treatment by the state. This issue was addressed extensively by the Supreme Court of Canada in the *Reference re. Secession of Quebec*. In its decision in this case, the Supreme Court noted that "international law expects that the right to self-determination will be exercised by peoples within the framework of existing sovereign states and consistently with the maintenance of the territorial integrity of those states. Where this is not possible, in the exceptional circumstances discussed below, a right of secession may arise."[112] A right to external self-determination arises in only the most extreme cases and, even then, under carefully defined circumstances.[113] One such circumstance that may exist in international law arises when a people is blocked from the meaningful exercise of its right to self-determination internally.[114] While the Supreme Court denied that such a circumstance existed for Quebec, its reasons for coming to that conclusion provide an impetus to governments to engage in serious, good-faith negotiations to implement the treaties with First Nations and fulfill the treaty relationship. Specifically, the Supreme Court stated:

> The population of Quebec cannot plausibly be said to be denied access to government. Quebecers occupy prominent positions within the Government of Canada. Residents of the province freely make political choices and pursue economic, social and cultural development within Quebec, across Canada, and throughout the world. The population of Quebec is equitably represented in legislative, executive and judicial institutions. In short, to reflect the phraseology of the international documents that address the right to self-determination of peoples, Canada is a "sovereign and independent state

---

[109] Borrows, John, "The Trickster: Integral to a Distinctive Culture," (1997) *Constitutional Forum* 29.

[110] The Supreme Court has written that international law is helpful by way of analogy when dealing with Aboriginal issues, though it is not determinative. See *Simon v. The Queen*, [1985] 2 S.C.R. 387 at para. 33: "While it may be helpful in some instances to analogize the principles of international treaty law to Indian treaties, these principles are not determinative."

[111] *Reference re. Secession of Quebec*, [1998] 2 S.C.R. 217 at para. 114: "The existence of the right of a people to self-determination is now so widely recognized in international conventions that the principle has acquired a status beyond "convention" and is considered a general principle of international law."

[112] Ibid., para. 122.

[113] Ibid., para. 126.

[114] Ibid., para. 134.

conducting itself in compliance with the principle of equal rights and self-determination of peoples and thus possessed of a government representing the whole people belonging to the territory without distinction."[115]

Such is not the case for Treaty First Nations, because they do not find themselves in equivalent circumstances to the population of Quebec.

The Supreme Court's discussion of the requirements of domestic constitutional law in the face of an expressed desire of a constituent unit of the federation to secede and become externally self-determining also provides important guidance to the treaty Parties. The Supreme Court noted that:

> The federalism principle, in conjunction with the democratic principle, dictates that the clear repudiation of the existing constitutional order and the clear expression of the desire to pursue secession by the population of a province would give rise to a reciprocal obligation on all parties to Confederation to negotiate constitutional changes to respond to that desire.[116]

Later in the Court's judgment, it added:

> Refusal of a party to conduct negotiations in a manner consistent with constitutional principles and values would seriously put at risk the legitimacy of that party's assertion of its rights, and perhaps the negotiation process as a whole. Those who quite legitimately insist upon the importance of upholding the rule of law cannot at the same time be oblivious to the need to act in conformity with constitutional principles and values, and so do their part to contribute to the maintenance and promotion of an environment in which the rule of law may flourish. ...
>
> To the extent that a breach of the constitutional duty to negotiate in accordance with the principles described above undermines the legitimacy of a party's actions, it may have important ramifications at the international level.[117]

Sovereignty was also discussed in the important Supreme Court decision in *Mitchell v. Minister of National Revenue*,[118] which involved an asserted Aboriginal right to take goods

[115] Ibid., para. 136.
[116] Ibid., para. 88.
[117] Ibid., paras. 95, 103.
[118] *Mitchell v. Minister of National Revenue*, [2001] 1 S.C.R. 911.

across the Canada-United States border for trade within Aboriginal communities. In this context, the relationship between Canadian sovereignty and Aboriginal rights was discussed by the Court. Chief Justice McLachlin introduced the analysis in this way:

> Long before Europeans explored and settled North America, Aboriginal peoples were occupying and using most of this vast expanse of land in organized, distinctive societies with their own social and political structures. The part of North America we now call Canada was first settled by the French and the British who, from the first days of exploration, claimed sovereignty over the land on behalf of their nations. English law, which ultimately came to govern Aboriginal rights, accepted that the Aboriginal peoples possessed pre-existing laws and interests, and recognized their continuance in the absence of extinguishment, by cession, conquest, or legislation: see, e.g., the *Royal Proclamation of 1763*, R.S.C. 1985, App. II, No. 1, and *R. v. Sparrow*, [1990] 1 S.C.R. 1075, at p. 1103. At the same time, however, the Crown asserted that sovereignty over the land, and ownership of its underlying title, vested in the Crown: *Sparrow, supra*. With this assertion arose an obligation to treat Aboriginal peoples fairly and honourably, and to protect them from exploitation, a duty characterized as "fiduciary" in *Guerin v. The Queen*, [1984] 2 S.C.R. 335.
>
> Accordingly, European settlement did not terminate the interests of Aboriginal peoples arising from their historical occupation and use of the land. To the contrary, Aboriginal interests and customary laws were presumed to survive the assertion of sovereignty, and were absorbed into the common law as rights, unless (1) they were incompatible with the Crown's assertion of sovereignty, (2) they were surrendered voluntarily via the treaty process, or (3) the government extinguished them: see B. Slattery, "Understanding Aboriginal Rights" (1987), 66 Can. Bar Rev. 727. Barring one of these exceptions, the practices, customs and traditions that defined the various Aboriginal societies as distinctive cultures continued as part of the law of Canada: see *Calder v. Attorney-General of British Columbia*, [1973] S.C.R. 313, and *Mabo v. Queensland* (1992), 175 C.L.R. 1, at p. 57 (per Brennan J.), pp. 81-82 (per Deane and Gaudron JJ.), and pp. 182-83 (per Toohey J.).[119]

However, in *Mitchell*, the majority declined the Crown's invitation to rule on a "sovereign incompatibility" approach to the Aboriginal right that was asserted:

> The Crown now contends that "sovereign incompatibility" is an implicit element of the *Van der Peet* test for identifying protected Aboriginal rights,

_____
[119] Ibid., paras 9-10.

or at least a necessary addition. In view of my conclusion that Chief Mitchell has not established that the Mohawks traditionally transported goods for trade across the present Canada-U.S. border, and hence has not proven his claim to an Aboriginal right, I need not consider the merits of this submission. Rather, I would prefer to refrain from comment on the extent, if any, to which colonial laws of sovereign succession are relevant to the definition of Aboriginal rights under s. 35(1) until such time as it is necessary for the Court to resolve this issue.[120]

A concurring judgment representing the views of two members of the Court observed:

> Section 35 does not warrant a claim to unlimited governmental powers or to complete sovereignty, such as independent states are commonly thought to possess. As with the federal and provincial governments, Aboriginal governments operate within a sphere of sovereignty defined by the constitution. In short, the Aboriginal right of self-government in section 35(1) involves circumscribed rather than unlimited powers.
>
> It is unnecessary, for present purposes, to come to any conclusion about these assertions. What is significant is that the Royal Commission itself sees Aboriginal peoples as full participants with non-Aboriginal peoples in a shared Canadian sovereignty. Aboriginal peoples do not stand in opposition to, nor are they subjugated by, Canadian sovereignty. They are part of it.[121]

That judgment went on:

> One of the defining characteristics of sovereign succession and therefore a limitation on the scope of Aboriginal rights, as already discussed, was the notion of incompatibility with the new sovereignty. Such incompatibility seems to have been accepted, for example, as a limitation on the powers of Aboriginal self-government in the 1993 working report of the Royal Commission on Aboriginal Peoples, *Partners in Confederation: Aboriginal Peoples, Self-Government and the Constitution, supra*, at p. 23:
>
>> ...Aboriginal nations did not lose their inherent rights when they entered into a confederal relationship with the Crown. Rather, they retained their ancient constitutions *so far as these were not inconsistent with the new relationship.* [Emphasis added.]
>
> Prior to *Calder, supra*, "sovereign incompatibility" was given excessive scope. The assertion of sovereign authority was confused with doctrines of feudal title to deny Aboriginal peoples any interest at all in their traditional lands or even in activities related to the use of those lands. To acknowledge

---

[120] Ibid., para. 64.
[121] Ibid., paras. 134-5.

that the doctrine of sovereign incompatibility was sometimes given excessive scope in the past is not to deny that it has any scope at all, but it is a doctrine that must be applied with caution.[122]

If Canadian law does not, in any way, permit the sovereignty of the Crown to be called into question, the idea that Aboriginal rights are inherent and predate the Crown's assertion of sovereignty provides an important context for a full understanding of the political reconciliation involved in treaty making. With the *Haida Nation* case, we no longer need to wonder whether the inherent rights of indigenous nations derive from their pre-existing sovereignty. But we have also learned from cases such as *Mitchell* that it is necessary to examine carefully the relationship between Aboriginal rights, including inherent rights of governance derived from pre-existing sovereignty, and the sovereignty of the Crown.

The vital issue is the contemporary meaning of the political reconciliation achieved by the treaties. It is clear that the pledging of mutual good faith and honour of the Parties negates any fear that recognizing First Nation sovereignty necessarily implies or leads to independence, separation and the endangering of our country. On the contrary, treaties that reconciled two orders of sovereignty must bind us more closely together, and the ties that bind us are all the more strong and vital if we recognize that Treaty First Nations and the Crown are inextricably linked by an act of treaty making that commits both to a path of sharing, mutual respect and mutual accommodation.

The purpose of the constitutional recognition and affirmation of existing Aboriginal and treaty rights has been judicially acknowledged as "reconciliation." We now have a contemporary legal and political theory that is acquiring its own robustness, founded on the sovereignty and honour of the Crown, the inherent rights of First Nations derived from their pre-existing sovereignty, the law governing Aboriginal rights, title and treaties and finally, the over-arching principle of reconciliation.

We have, then, the basis for the promise of a relationship in which the sovereignty of the Crown and the pre-existing and continuing sovereignty of First Nations are reconciled and

---

[122] Ibid., paras. 150-1.

accommodated, through treaty relations, without either sovereignty dominating the other and reducing it to an empty shell. While we do not have explicit judicial guidance on what this means in all its aspects, the sovereignty of each treaty party is modified and constrained in some ways by the making of treaties, without in any way calling into question Canada's integrity as a nation-state or the autonomy of Treaty First Nations in their spheres of self-government. As we will discuss more extensively below, this is consistent with the concept of treaty federalism and Canada's federalist tradition.

This recognition of the nexus among sovereignty, Aboriginal and treaty rights, reconciliation, and the treaties gives us tools to begin to build a new understanding of the relationship, in the present day, between the implementation of treaties and the negotiation of governance arrangements. It suggests that the negotiation of an inherent right of self-government (to use the terminology used in federal policy) is, in fact, related directly to the subject matter of what was addressed in the treaties.

In 1995, Canada introduced a formal policy, commonly referred to as the "Inherent Right Policy," that builds upon a federal government recognition that the inherent right of Aboriginal self-government is an existing Aboriginal right and mandates negotiations to give effect to that right. The policy framework proceeds from this basis:

> The Government of Canada recognizes the inherent right of self-government as an existing Aboriginal right under section 35 of the *Constitution Act, 1982.* It recognizes, as well, that the inherent right may find expression in treaties, and in the context of the Crown's relationship with Treaty First Nations. Recognition of the inherent right is based on the view that the Aboriginal peoples of Canada have the right to govern themselves in relation to matters that are internal to their communities, integral to their unique cultures, identities, traditions, languages and institutions, and with respect to their special relationship to their land and their resources.[123]

---

[123] Department of Indian Affairs and Northern Development, *The Government of Canada's Approach to Implementation of the Inherent Right and the Negotiation of Aboriginal Self-Government* (Ottawa: Public Works and Government Services Canada, 1995) http://www.ainc-inac.gc.ca/pr/pub/sg/plcy_e.html.

Thus, the policy acknowledges that there "may" be a linkage between treaties and the inherent right of self-government, but falls short of clarifying that the reconciliation of sovereign orders of governance was a critical aspect of the treaty relationship.

This speaks to one of the reasons for the present impasse about the Agreement-in-Principle and Tripartite-Agreement-in-Principle. The discussions should consider ways in which contemporary governance agreements can draw upon the Supreme Court's recognition of the relationship between the making of treaties and the reconciliation of the sovereignties of the treaty Parties, to rebuild the momentum and move toward treaty implementation and the fulfillment of the treaty relationship.

At present, the Agreement-in-Principle and the Tripartite-Agreement-in-Principle are only initialled. Their purpose is clear. To quote from section 2.1 of the Agreement-in-Principle:

> 2.1 The purpose of this Agreement-in-Principle is to serve as the basis for the negotiations of the Parties in the development of a Governance Agreement and a Tripartite Agreement.

The Agreement-in-Principle and Tripartite-Agreement-in-Principle both state explicitly that they themselves do not create binding legal obligations. Both pave the way for negotiations to achieve binding agreements that will in due course, after ratification and implementation, set out the jurisdiction of the two or three orders of government, as the case may be. Both establish an agenda for negotiation of binding agreements.

Among the issues to be considered is the eventual constitutional status of the Governance Agreement:

> 2.7 Prior to concluding a Governance Agreement, the Parties shall discuss and agree upon the constitutional status, if any, to be provided to it or any part of it.

The Agreement-in-Principle does contain references to the treaties in section 2.5:

> 2.5 The purpose of the Governance Agreement is to reflect and provide for a government-to-government relationship between First Nations and Canada, within the framework of the Canadian Constitution, that is

respectful of and builds on the Treaty relationship, while not re-
negotiating Treaties 4, 5, 6, 8 and 10.

This clause carefully avoids stating or implying that the treaty relationship is one that was established between sovereigns, or that reconciles two sovereign orders, or indeed that the subject of governance is related to the making of the treaties. Neither, though, does it deny the Parties the opportunity to include within the Governance Agreement an explicit treaty basis for them. It is immediately followed by this clause:

> 2.6 Subject to anything that may be agreed to pursuant to the commitment contained in section 2.7, the Governance Agreement is not intended to define the existence, content, scope or nature of the rights and benefits provided under the Treaties or of the inherent right of self government, and the Governance Agreement is without prejudice to differing positions on how these issues ought to be interpreted at law.

The Agreement-in-Principle, therefore, leaves it open to the Parties to negotiate treaty linkages as part of the negotiation of the Governance Agreement. It cannot be said, however, that these clauses contain a commitment to explore how linkages between the treaties and governance might be included in the Governance Agreement.

What is missing, both in the federal government's 1995 "Inherent Right Policy" and in the Agreement-in-Principle, is a commitment to define the relationship between the treaties and the overlapping sovereignties of the Parties and explicitly recognize that contemporary governance agreements where treaties have been made will necessarily build upon a pre-existing foundation of reconciliation. Another element missing from the Agreement-in-Principle is any express recognition by the Parties that the Crown is sovereign. It may be that the federal government regards this as self-evident, but it is perhaps no less self-evident to the Treaty First Nations that their governance rights are derived from their pre-existing sovereignty and that their political relationship with the Crown is based on a reconciliation achieved by the treaties. It may also be useful for the Parties to make reference, within a revised Agreement-in-Principle and Tripartite-Agreement-in-Principle, to the principles relating to the treaty relationship that have already been embraced in the *Statement of Treaty Issues* as well as others suggested in this report.

The broader treaty context of reconciliation should be an explicit foundation of the negotiation of a Governance Agreement between the Federation of Saskatchewan Indian Nations and the Crown in right of Canada. The Parties will need to give careful consideration to how a theme of political reconciliation through the treaties would advance their discussions. In the meantime, the Parties should consider expanding their agenda so that discussions on this issue can take place in the negotiation of the Governance Agreement. If some commitment at least to engage in negotiations on this issue is not forthcoming, the Treaty First Nations may not support the signing of the Agreement-in-Principle and Tripartite-Agreement-in-Principle and a great opportunity will be missed.

ii. Aboriginal Title

Another issue where no consensus exists is title to the land. The written texts of the treaties record the Crown's intention to take a surrender of what we now know as Aboriginal title, or to extinguish that title. Oral tradition records a consistent First Nation position that the treaties did not include a surrender of title, but an agreement to share the land.

Beyond general expressions about sharing, it is not entirely clear how Treaty First Nations reconcile their agreement to share their lands with the insistence that they retained their title without encumbrances. Neither is it clear how the Crown can reconcile the circumstances of nineteenth and early twentieth century treaty making with contemporary legal standards that require the free, informed and collective assent of First Nations people in order to surrender Aboriginal title.

An issue like title, on which the Parties appear to have diametrically opposed positions, may seem to make it impossible for treaty implementation to occur. The existence of such a fundamental and apparently intractable issue calls into question the very utility of a treaty implementation process. Will it be necessary for one Party to give up its long-held position and embrace a different position? What if there was such a gap in the Parties' intentions that no agreement was reached?

These issues make it essential for the Parties to reach a reconciliation of their opposing views through an honourable, respectful process of treaty implementation. As we have suggested, "reconciliation" need not mean coming to a consensus on all issues. It will require an honest evaluation of the legitimacy of each Party's views and introduction of practical ways of avoiding bringing remaining differences to an impasse due to irreconcilable positions.

From the Crown's point of view, the extinguishment of Aboriginal title was a central objective of its approach to making treaties. However, it was also regarded as a means to an end, namely the clearing of an obstacle to settlement of territories inhabited by indigenous nations. At the time of the treaties, the legal nature and consequences of Aboriginal title were not understood except in the most general of ways. Aboriginal title (or Indian title as it was then called) was understood primarily as a "burden" on the rights of the Crown, rather than a set of enforceable legal rights to land. The clearing away of the burden of Aboriginal title was regarded largely as a technicality that permitted settlement to occur. The limited discussion of Indian title in the treaty councils is testament to the fact that neither Party gave detailed thought to the idea that the surrender of an entire property regime, recognized in law, was being put on the table.

From the First Nations' point of view, consent was given to the settlement of their territories. First Nations strongly maintain they could never consent to sever their spiritual connection with the land. For First Nations, their relationship to the land was not limited to the legal regime common law regards as Aboriginal title; it was a deeper and more immutable relationship. They could agree to permit others to come and even to establish a new legal order in their territories, but they could not sever or extinguish their essential relationship with their lands. Many Elders recall that the treaties involved sharing of the land to the depth of a plough and no more.[124]

From both points of view, however, the use and benefit of First Nation territories were to be shared in the manner contemplated by the treaty. Neither party gave detailed consideration to the legal aspect of what we now know as Aboriginal title, which was only described as a legal matter in 1997 with the *Delgamuukw* decision. Even then, the Supreme Court sent the matter

---

[124] The late Elder Gordon Oakes from Nekaneet First Nation, Elder Richard Poorman from Kawacatoose First Nation, and others at the Exploratory Treaty Table.

back for a new trial.[125]   The result is that we still do not have a single judicial decision that describes the rights associated with Aboriginal title to a square millimetre of land in Canada.

The question of title to land now needs to be considered carefully by the treaty Parties and in such a manner that respective interests are brought together and reconciled, as opposed to being driven to an all-or-nothing conclusion. The Parties may be able to separate the *spiritual* aspects of "title" from *property* rights and seek a consensus that permits First Nations to reaffirm their inalienable spiritual connection to all of their territories, without contradicting the essential interest of both Parties to consent to and facilitate the use and ownership of lands in those territories. Treaty implementation, undertaken with care and building upon areas of consensus, can in fact permit the Parties to look at their respective interests and to reconcile and accommodate their differences. There is no reason why the "spiritual" and "property" aspects of land title cannot coexist without giving rise to uncertainties. Indeed, coming to agreements that affirm and reconcile the Parties' most fundamental interests is the essence of treaty implementation.

This has been recognized in New Zealand in innovative ways in the 1997 Deed of Settlement between the Ngäi Tahu *iwi* (tribe) of the South Island and the Crown. The mountain known in Maori as Aoraki and in English as Mount Cook was returned to Ngäi Tahu, and, in a gesture of huge significance, Ngäi Tahu gifted the mountain back to all the people of New Zealand for its continued inclusion within a national park. This example of extraordinary mutual generosity and creativity in negotiations is captured in the preamble to the section of the Deed of Settlement that addressed this arrangement:

a) In the spirit of co-operation, compromise and good faith which has brought about the Settlement, and in special recognition of the significance of Aoraki/Mount Cook to Ngäi Tahu Whänui, the Crown wishes to restore to Te Rünanga title to Aoraki/Mount Cook.

b) Te Rünanga in the same spirit wishes thereupon to make a gift to the Crown, on behalf of the people of New Zealand, of the title so restored in order that Aoraki/Mount Cook will remain and continue to be part of the National Park.

---

[125] *Delgamuukw v. British Columbia,* [1997] 3 S.C.R. 1010.

c) As further recognition of the significance to Aoraki/Mount Cook to Ngāi Tahu Whānui, this Deed also provides for a Statutory Acknowledgment, Deed of Recognition, Topūni and Statutory Advisor role for Te Rūnanga in relation to Aoraki/Mount Cook, and for the name of Mount Cook to be changed to Aoraki/ Mount Cook.[126]

Two sets of rights to an important national symbol were recognized and reconciled. We can therefore begin to see that the issue of "extinguishment" or "title," which appears absolute and irreconcilable, can, in fact, be seen as a more complex set of issues amenable to discussion, reconciliation and compromise, if the willingness exists to be open to new ideas and explore underlying interests which need to be acknowledged and respected.

The issue of "title" contains aspects that are spiritual in nature as well as aspects we may describe in terms of property rights. If we confuse the two, we will never reconcile the Parties' deepest ideals nor dispel their deepest fears. The idea of sharing a territory, the very underpinning of the Treaty First Nations' understanding of the treaties, implies that people other than the Treaty First Nations will acquire property rights in territories once held exclusively by the First Nations. The issue of property rights is thus one that – at least to some degree – is capable of discussion and reconciliation.

One must also remember that, even in European legal traditions, private property rights are not complete and absolute. Private holders of real property only hold an incomplete title as, ultimately, title is held by the Crown and is simply shared with the private property holder. Property rights that fall short of complete title, such as usufructary rights,[127] are also very familiar to those trained in the civil code legal tradition. To continue in this vein, property rights include the property rights of the Crown and the Treaty First Nations (the Parties to the treaties themselves) as well as the rights of private third parties whose titles are derived from Crown grants under the land regime governed by federal and provincial laws. As all of these forms of title are legitimate sources of rights, title must be understood in a way that allows all of them to exist and have meaning together.

---

[126] Office of Treaty Settlements, *Deed of Settlement – Te Rūnaunga O Ngāi Tahu and Her Majesty the Queen in Right of New Zealand, November 21, 1997* (Wellington: Office of Treaty Settlements, 1999), available at http://nz01.terabyte.co.nz/ots/DocumentLibrary/NgaiTahuDeed.pdf .

[127] The Concise Oxford Dictionary defines "usufruct" as the "right of enjoying the use and advantages of another's property short of destruction or waste of its substance," Oxford University Press, *The Concise Oxford Dictionary of Current English* (Oxford; Oxford University Press, 1982).

In a modern context, such concepts could be translated into co-jurisdiction over land. As former Yukon Premier and British Columbia Deputy Minister Tony Penikett recently suggested:

> Co-jurisdiction arrangements might be the best possible model for a true accommodation of Aboriginal ideas about land tenure and governance. Co-jurisdiction could mean the crafting of nation-to-nation protocols and institutions founded on government recognition of Aboriginal title, rather than its extinguishment.[128]

Elders maintain that the land in fact belongs to no one, it is a gift from the Creator which provides everything required for their survival and, in return, requiring their care and nurturing. Today, we are all custodians of that gift regardless of our ancestry. The perspective that we owe obligations to the land is one non-Aboriginal Canadians have only recently begun to embrace. We belong to the land; it does not belong to us.

People in Saskatchewan have a deep pride in the land that might be described as spiritual. The connection of First Nations to the land is different, however, as their roots go deeper. This in no way denies the legitimate feelings of attachment to land of all residents of our province; it is merely an observation of a deeper ancestral connection that only First Nations people have.

It is the distinction between "title" as a set of property rights and "title" as a symbol of a deep ancestral spiritual connection to the land that needs to be explored in treaty implementation discussions. The orderly reconciliation of property rights should in no way require the extinguishment of the spiritual connection to land. Reconciliation will be promoted by looking at ways in which the eternal and inalienable spiritual connection of First Nations to their territories can in fact be recognized and given tangible expression.

A new approach to sharing the benefits of the land will have to be worked out. The Royal Commission on Aboriginal Peoples wrote in its Final Report:

> The text of the post-1850 treaties clearly provides for the extinguishment of Aboriginal title. But the people of the treaty nations

---

[128] Penikett, Tony, *Reconciliation: First Nations Treaty Making in British Columbia* (Vancouver: Douglas & McIntyre, 2006), at p. 217.

reject that outcome. It is unlikely that any court decision could ever change their minds on this central issue. For this reason, the Commission proposes that the question of lands and resources be addressed on the basis that the continuing relationship between the parties requires both to accept a reasonable sharing of lands and resources as implicit in the treaty.[129]

Another fruitful and practical avenue for reconciliation of the title issue is resource access and revenue sharing, an issue the Federation of Saskatchewan Indian Nations has referred to on numerous occasions as one that should pave the way, along with symbolic acts, to reconcile the apparently divergent ideas about title.

(c) Common Views

Upon first encountering the great divergence between Treaty First Nations and the Crown on many treaty issues, a casual observer may feel despair at finding common ground. Indeed, there are many issues on which First Nations and the Crown have deeply different views and convictions. However, this observer may find the extent to which the treaty Parties agree on vital aspects of the treaty relationship surprising.

- Both First Nations and the Crown, for example, agree that the treaties are fundamental. The Crown could not legitimately initiate its plan to introduce settlement into First Nation territories without a treaty. Thus, both First Nations and the Crown agree the treaties legitimized the settlement of issues faced by both First Nations and newcomers.

- Both First Nations and the Crown agree that, by their very nature, the treaties cannot be terminated or dismantled. It was agreed they were to last as long as the sun shines, the grass grows and the rivers flow. Whatever they are, they are permanent features of our future as well as our past.

- Both First Nations and the Crown agree that the making of the treaties was an act of mutual recognition. The First Nations recognized the nationhood of the Crown and its legitimacy within First Nations territories; the Crown implicitly recognized the nationhood of the First Nations at the time of treaty, a point now explicitly recognized by the Supreme Court of Canada.

---

[129] Royal Commission on Aboriginal Peoples, *Gathering Strength*, Volume 2, p. 45.

- Both First Nations and the Crown agree that the treaties anticipated change in the lives of First Nations, but also that the change would respect the rights of First Nations to continue their traditional economic pursuits to the extent consistent with agreed-upon settlement by non-First Nations peoples.

- Both First Nations and the Crown agree that changes introduced by the making of treaties required the Crown to provide assistance to First Nations in the form of materials necessary for traditional harvesting, such as ammunition and twine, as well as agricultural assistance, health care and education. Thus, the treaties contemplated the preservation of the traditional economy as well as preparation for new forms of economic endeavours by Treaty First Nations.

- Both First Nations and the Crown agree the Parties contemplated that First Nations would have a land base for their exclusive use and benefit, protected from encroachment, on which First Nations could safely develop socially and economically, while continuing to use unoccupied land for traditional economic purposes.

- Both First Nations and the Crown agree that the purpose for including education provisions in the treaties was to empower Treaty First Nations peoples and to ensure they had tools to compete and succeed in changing economic and social circumstances.

- Both First Nations and the Crown agree the Parties agreed to annual treaty annuities, which at the time of treaty making were more than mere token amounts.

- Both First Nations and the Crown agree the Parties promised a mutually respectful relationship, in which their differences would be addressed lawfully and peacefully.

- Both First Nations and the Crown agree that the leadership structures of the First Nations were recognized by the medals, uniforms and cash payments to Chiefs and Headmen.

These areas of consensus can provide a basis for undertaking reconciliation and treaty implementation in those areas where the Parties have strong but divergent views. Equally important, though, will be approaching the future with a full understanding of what reconciliation means today, not only in law, but in political, socio-economic and spiritual aspects.

Perspectives of the Present Day: The Four Pillars of Reconciliation

The Office of the Treaty Commissioner believes that reconciliation is an ongoing principle for a renewed treaty relationship between the Parties.

(a) Political Reconciliation

Political reconciliation is implied in the *Haida Nation* case, which contains the important but also general acknowledgment that, "Treaties serve to reconcile pre-existing Aboriginal sovereignty with assumed Crown sovereignty."[130] There is a great deal in this passage, although there is also much ambiguity. The treaties serve to reconcile the sovereignty of *both* treaty Parties. This reference provides a profoundly important subtext for general questions about treaty implementation, in particular the linkage between treaty implementation, First Nations governance and Canadian federalism.

Two traditions of political reconciliation – treaty making and federalism – have ancient roots in both First Nations and European history. In terms of treaty making, First Nations in North America had their own well-established diplomatic protocols prior to contact with Europeans. The continued existence of wampum belts from those days is testament to this fact. Alliances among First Nations enabled the free flow of trade, safe passage, sharing of resources, military alliances and economic assistance in time of need. Such alliances were solemnized and nurtured through adoption, the exchanges of gifts and arranged marriages, methods similar to those used by the monarchies in feudal Europe. In European countries, treaty making can be traced at least to Roman times and the fundamental principle of *pacta sunt servanda* – "treaties should be honoured in good faith." Treaties were used to achieve military alliances, to promote peace, foster trade, provide for safe conduct, recognize the independence and boundaries of states and determine the terms of surrender following a war. In other words, treaty making and diplomacy served many of the same purposes in both Europe and North America.

These two ancient traditions came together when Europeans came to North America, resulting in an intermingling of two diplomatic traditions and cultures. A fine example is the Great Peace of Montreal in 1701. The last decades of the seventeenth century were marked by bloody conflicts among First Nations and between First Nations and New France, conflicts often referred to as the "Indian wars." Both Britain and France were seeking military alliances with

---

[130] *Haida Nation v. British Columbia* (Minister of Forests), [2004] 3 S.C.R. 511, at para. 42.

First Nations in America at the time. In response to an invitation of the Governor of New France, representatives from 40 First Nations travelled to Montreal in the winter and spring of 1701. They came by foot and by canoe from as far away as the Maritimes, the Great Lakes, James Bay and Illinois. It was a perilous journey, with many lives lost to weather and disease. By the summer, 1,300 ambassadors from these 40 First Nations had arrived in Montreal to defend their interests and to "bury the hatchet deep in the earth."[131] The negotiations resulted in a treaty between the Haudenasaunee (Iroquois confederacy) and members of the First Nation-French alliance, traditional enemies through most of the seventeenth century. It was a truly remarkable achievement. Delegates to the conference agreed to plant a "tree of peace upon the highest mountain," a reference to a general peace; to "eating from a common bowl," a reference to sharing lands for hunting and fishing; and to exchange prisoners. From the mixing of these two ancient diplomatic traditions in what is now Canada, treaties became the fundamental political relationship between First Nations and the Canadian state. In a sense, they are analogous to the terms of union through which the former British colonies – now provinces – joined Canada.

The origins of federalism in First Nations traditions are also evident long before the arrival of Europeans on their lands. First Nations in the Americas formed their own federal or confederal forms of political organization, from the Mi'kmaq confederacy of the Maritime region, to the Haudenasaunee (Iroquois) confederacy of the Great Lakes, to the Blackfoot confederacy of the West. These federal political forms ultimately influenced the design of the federal constitution of the United States of America. The origins of federalism in European traditions can be traced back to the works of Althusius, a Dutch philosopher in the 1600s who attempted to find a way to house diverse views within a religious order. This older thinking on federalism, with its focus on autonomy, mutual dependence, participatory and shared decision making, inclusion and institutional flexibility, appears similar in many ways to First Nations concepts.[132]

---

[131] Havard, Gillies, *The Great Peace of Montreal of 1701*. (Montreal & Kingston: McGill Queen's University Press, 2001, p. 4.

[132] Hueglin, Thomas O., "Exploring Concepts of Treaty Federalism: A Comparative Perspective", Research Program of the Royal Commission on Aboriginal Peoples, *For Seven Generations*. Ottawa: Libraxus CD-ROM.

These shared traditions of federalism may contain promise for accommodating the aspirations of First Nations within the Canadian state. First, federalism provides a fundamental respect for diversity. We see this reflected in the bilingual institutions of our country and in the recognition and affirmation of Aboriginal and treaty rights in our constitution. This could be extended to the cultures, languages, spiritualities, laws and ways of life of First Nations in Canada. Second, federalism can accommodate multiple identities and loyalties within a state, as well as different levels of government, some with shared sovereignty. The Royal Commission on Aboriginal Peoples concluded that:

> ... the inherent right of Aboriginal self-government is recognized and affirmed in section 35(1) of the *Constitution Act, 1982* as an Aboriginal and treaty-protected right. The inherent right is thus entrenched in the Canadian constitution, providing a basis for Aboriginal governments to function as one of three distinct orders of government in Canada.[133]

The Royal Commission on Aboriginal Peoples argued that Canadian federalism can accommodate a pooling of sovereignties – federal, provincial and First Nations. Third, intergovernmental relations within federal states are highly adaptive to change and capable of great innovation. For example, between 1983 and 1987, four federal-provincial-territorial First Ministers' Conferences were held with national Aboriginal leaders in Canada to address Aboriginal constitutional matters in an unprecedented, albeit unsuccessful, exercise in Canadian politics.[134] While this process was awkward and difficult, it did demonstrate the need for integrating First Nations into intergovernmental relations in Canada. Intergovernmental relations in Canada must include First Nations governments, so that federal-provincial-territorial-First Nations relations become normalized and institutionalized, while at the same time being effective and efficient.

If the sovereignties of the Parties, with their differing sources and attributes, were reconciled by the treaties, this implies that a process of political reconciliation must form an integral objective of a contemporary treaty implementation process. Surely it must therefore imply the clarification of the respective jurisdictions of the treaty partners over various matters, as well as the creation of

---

[133] Report of the Royal Commission on Aboriginal Peoples, *Gathering Strength*, Volume 1, Part 1, p. 213.
[134] Hawkes, David C., *Aboriginal Peoples and Constitutional Reform: What Have We Learned?* Kingston, Ontario: Institute of Intergovernmental Relations, 1989.

processes to manage interdependencies and resolve disputes in cases in which jurisdictions overlap. Presumably, it also implies an evolution in the fiduciary relationship between the Crown and First Nations, with the fiduciary relationship being reduced as First Nations' jurisdiction and autonomy is clarified by the Parties, and it being replaced with an intergovernmental, or brother-to-brother, relationship that respects First Nations' autonomy and authority.

The process of the political reconciliation of multiple sovereignties is nothing new for Canada. The very purpose of the federal arrangement we have lived with since 1867 was to reconcile the desire of formerly separate colonies to preserve their autonomy and distinctiveness with their desire to increase the welfare of all through the creation of a new, stronger entity called Canada. Federalism ensured that this new nation was an organic entity with its own areas of jurisdiction, rather than simply a forum for co-decision by provinces in a confederation. Federalism also ensured that the new nation would not erase the autonomy and distinctiveness of the pre-existing communities, by securing for them jurisdiction over matters of particular importance. The Supreme Court of Canada may have described this understanding of federalism in the *Reference re. Secession of Quebec* case:

> Federalism was a legal response to the underlying political and cultural realities that existed at Confederation and continue to exist today. At Confederation, political leaders told their respective communities that the Canadian union would be able to reconcile diversity with unity. It is pertinent, in the context of the present Reference, to mention the words of George-Étienne Cartier (cited in the *Parliamentary Debates on the subject of the Confederation* (1865), at p. 60):
>
> > Now, when we [are] united together, if union [is] attained, we [shall] form a political nationality with which neither the national origin, nor the religion of any individual, [will] interfere. It was lamented by some that we had this diversity of races, and hopes were expressed that this distinctive feature would cease. The idea of unity of races [is] utopian -- it [is] impossible. Distinctions of this kind [will] always exist. Dissimilarity, in fact, appear[s] to be the order of the physical world and of the moral world, as well as in the political world. But with regard to the objection based on this fact, to the effect that a great nation [can]not be formed because Lower Canada [is] in great part French and Catholic, and Upper Canada [is] British and Protestant, and the Lower Provinces [are] mixed, it [is] futile and worthless in the extreme. . . . In our own

> Federation we [will] have Catholic and Protestant, English, French, Irish and Scotch, and each by his efforts and his success [will] increase the prosperity and glory of the new Confederacy... [W]e [are] of different races, not for the purpose of warring against each other, but in order to compete and emulate for the general welfare.

> The federal-provincial division of powers was a legal recognition of the diversity that existed among the initial members of Confederation, and manifested a concern to accommodate that diversity within a single nation by granting significant powers to provincial governments. The *Constitution Act, 1867* was an act of nation-building. It was the first step in the transition from colonies separately dependent on the Imperial Parliament for their governance to a unified and independent political state in which different peoples could resolve their disagreements and work together toward common goals and a common interest. Federalism was the political mechanism by which diversity could be reconciled with unity.[135]

Elsewhere, the Supreme Court stated that:

> The principle of federalism recognizes the diversity of the component parts of Confederation, and the autonomy of provincial governments to develop their societies within their respective spheres of jurisdiction. The federal structure of our country also facilitates democratic participation by distributing power to the government thought to be most suited to achieving the particular societal objective having regard to this diversity.[136]

The Supreme Court of Canada also highlighted the importance of federalism to the creation of the new nation:

> The significance of the adoption of a federal form of government cannot be exaggerated. Without it, neither the agreement of the delegates from Canada East nor that of the delegates from the maritime colonies could have been obtained.[137]

One issue of particular importance to delegates from the colonies who met in Charlottetown in September of 1864 and then in Quebec in October of 1864 was the protection of minorities. For the francophone community of Quebec, protection of their language and culture was done both directly, by making French an official language in Quebec and in the new federation, and

---

[135] *Reference re. Secession of Quebec*, at para. 43.
[136] Ibid., para 58.
[137] Ibid., para. 37.

indirectly, through a federal structure that ensured that, among other matters, the new provinces retained jurisdiction over education, "property and civil rights in the province," and matters of "a merely local or private nature."[138] The protection of minority communities has thus been part of the discourse about Canadian federalism since federation was first contemplated and, indeed, since the passage of the *Quebec Act* in 1774. Clearly, the purposes of Canadian federalism described above are analogous to the purposes of the brother-to-brother relationship contemplated in the treaties between the Crown and First Nations, namely to reconcile multiple sovereignties through accommodation of competing desires for autonomy and interdependence. Since 1867, Canadian governments have managed the federal relationship in a way that seeks to respect both the autonomy of the provincial governments and their interdependence in the Canadian nation. It has not always been an easy relationship to manage, and some of the conflicts have been serious enough to cause Canadians to question whether the nation created in 1867 can survive the challenges. On the other hand, the necessity of balancing autonomy and interdependence in the collective interest of all has led to the gradual creation of norms, processes and mechanisms which have allowed Canada to grow and prosper. The number of intergovernmental meetings and conferences that occur each year is remarkable. Along with periodic First Ministers' Meetings and the meetings of the Council of the Federation (formerly the Annual Premiers' Conferences), there are provincial/territorial and federal/provincial/territorial meetings of Ministers and officials for virtually every government department. These meetings, and the intergovernmental committees and secretariats they have generated, are designed to share knowledge on public policy issues between jurisdictions and to address shared concerns that arise out of the interdependency of governments in Canada.

Other intergovernmental efforts have sought to establish over-arching norms by which intergovernmental relations operate in Canada. The most recent of these efforts is the Social Union Framework Agreement. This agreement sets out a framework for intergovernmental cooperation in the management of social policy. It addresses such issues as the mobility of citizens, public accountability and transparency, joint planning and intergovernmental collaboration, the use of federal spending power to establish and fund social programs in

---

[138] Ibid., para. 38.

areas of provincial jurisdiction, and avoidance and resolution of intergovernmental disputes. While the level of commitment of governments, particularly the federal government, to abide by the terms of the Social Union Framework Agreement has been a matter of some debate in intergovernmental circles, the agreement does demonstrate an effort on the part of governments to manage interdependency collaboratively, without destroying the autonomy of provincial governments.

Many people around the world see Canada as a model of an effective federal system, and we are justifiably proud of our accomplishments in building a modern, functioning federation together. To complete Canada's political development as a federation, we need to take the lessons we have learned as a political community in managing federal-provincial relations and apply them to fulfilling the treaty relationship between First Nations and the Crown. Ian Peach and Merrilee Rasmussen have described how the negotiators at the Canada/Federation of Saskatchewan Indian Nations/Saskatchewan Governance and Fiscal Relations Table sought to do precisely this in the Agreement-in-Principle and Tripartite-Agreement-in-Principle.

> ...as both political theory and the history of Canada's own struggle to become self determining from the 18th century to 1982 can tell us, the capacity for collective self determination of distinct political communities, through responsible government, is an essential condition of liberalism. ...
>
> First Nations self-determination is, at heart, the same project of building a self-governing polity out of societies subject to imperial authority that drove the development of responsible government in British North America over one and a half centuries ago and later drove the development of responsible government within the territories. Thus, Kymlicka is right to argue that, "Aboriginal rights would be more secure if they were viewed, not as competing with liberalism, but as an essential component of liberal political practice." [Will Kymlicka, "Liberalism, Individualism, and Minority Rights", Hutchinson and Green, Eds. Law and the Community (Toronto: Carswell, 1989), p. 187.] The principles of responsible government, along with the principles of federalism, thus provide the conceptual foundation for a new way of imagining First Nations governments within the Canadian political system.[139]

---

[139] Peach, Ian and Merrilee Rasmussen, "Federalism and the First Nations: Making Space for First Nations Self-Determination in the Federal Inherent Right Policy," paper presented to the conference, "First Nations, First Thoughts," Centre for Canadian Studies, University of Edinburgh, May 2005; http://www.cst.ed.ac.uk/2005conference/papers/Peach_Rasmussen_paper.pdf, accessed October 10, 2005, pp 4, 10.

Around the world, the right of self-determination of Aboriginal peoples within states often branches in two directions: (1) a drive for more autonomy for indigenous nations, and (2) a demand for greater participation in the decision making institutions of the state. These two branches of Aboriginal self-determination appear to fit very closely with the twin pillars of federalism – self-rule and shared-rule. In his cross-national survey of Aboriginal people and intergovernmental relations in both unitary and federal states, David Hawkes concludes that, "Treaties between states and Aboriginal peoples should be considered as federative instruments, binding the parties together in an association of autonomy and interdependence."[140]

In its work, the Royal Commission on Aboriginal Peoples deliberately focused on the self-rule pillar – the right of Aboriginal self-government and how it might be accommodated within Canada. What requires our attention now is the other pillar of federalism, shared-rule, and how First Nations can achieve greater participation in the decision making of the Canadian state. How should First Nations be reflected in the institutions of Canadian federalism? How can intergovernmental relations with First Nations become "normalized" and institutionalized, as we have achieved with federal-provincial relations? How can we develop effective and efficient intergovernmental relations among the federal, provincial and First Nations governments? Answering these questions is at the heart of political reconciliation.

In some ways, fulfilling the treaty relationship in this way would bring our political development full circle. One of the sources of federalist thought that influenced the design of the Canadian federation was the federal or confederal structure of North American First Nations, as previously mentioned. These federal and confederal arrangements were established through treaties between the federating Nations, treaties which subsequently influenced the process of treaty making between First Nations and the Crown in Canada. In turn, the history of Canadian federalism and of treaty making between First Nations and the Crown has led to development of the concept of "treaty federalism" as a way of understanding how the brother-to-brother relationship of the treaties can be implemented in a modern context. In effect, the most promising modern theories

---

[140] Hawkes, David C., "Indigenous Peoples: Self-Government and Intergovernmental Relations" *International Social Science Journal* Volume 53, issue 167 (March 2001), p. 159.

[141] See ibid, pp. 153-161 for a more extensive discussion of Indigenous self-government, intergovernmental relations, and treaty federalism.

on how to fulfill the promise of the treaty relationship draw on First Nations concepts, albeit as mediated through the history of the political development of newcomer society.[141]

This report was commissioned, in part, to assist the Parties in resolving an impasse over the relationship between First Nations governance and treaty implementation. When the Supreme Court recognizes that treaties serve to reconcile the sovereignties of both First Nations and the Crown, an evident linkage between governance and the making and implementation of treaties begins to come into focus.

(b) Legal Reconciliation

In the process of deciding many individual cases involving existing Aboriginal and treaty rights, the courts have revealed to us, in the bits and pieces that accompany the judicial process, a legal landscape that to a significant extent is yet to be fully disclosed. At the same time, the courts have expressed increasing frustration with the failure of the Crown to engage in negotiations to flesh out Aboriginal and treaty rights that have been recognized in many cases since at least 1763, and have received explicit constitutional protection since 1982.

Legal precedents are developed in the context of disputes that cannot be resolved outside the courts. The need for litigation on these matters represents a breakdown of the principles that ought to govern. In this sense, they are exceptions to the preferred method of addressing disagreements arising within a treaty relationship. Nonetheless, the treaties are part of the Canadian legal framework, and the courts remain available to address the legal aspects of the treaties.

Treaty and other jurisprudence are an important source, but not the only source, of interpretive and other principles applicable to the treaty relationship. The courts in recent years have increasingly urged the Crown and First Nations to address their differences through dialogue. Increasingly, the decisions of the Supreme Court of Canada encourage good faith negotiations to address questions of Aboriginal and treaty rights. Canadian law can be seen as a "floor" on which additional understandings can be built, but not an end in itself.

The legitimacy of Canadian law does not, in the eyes of many First Nations people, extend to the fundamental elements of the identity of First Nations or the treaty relationship they have with the Crown. Indeed, the nature of the relationship made by the treaties suggests it is not the courts who should determine how that relationship is implemented and completed, but the Parties themselves. The principles of law articulated by the courts do, however, provide an important framework and vital guidance on some fundamental aspects of the process.

The Supreme Court of Canada has recently addressed the way in which the treaties serve as tools of "reconciliation." In its November 2004 decision in *Haida Nation v. B.C.*, a case in which Aboriginal rights were asserted but not yet proven, the Supreme Court took the opportunity to survey the broad relationship between First Nation peoples and the Crown:

> In all its dealings with Aboriginal peoples, from the assertion of sovereignty to the resolution of claims *and the implementation of treaties*, the Crown must act honourably.
>
> *The honour of the Crown also infuses the processes of treaty making and treaty interpretation. In making and applying treaties,* the Crown must act with honour and integrity, avoiding even the appearance of 'sharp dealing.' ...
>
> *Treaties serve to reconcile pre-existing Aboriginal sovereignty with assumed Crown sovereignty* and to define Aboriginal rights guaranteed by s. 35 of the *Constitution Act, 1982.*
>
> Put simply, Canada's Aboriginal peoples were here when Europeans came, and were never conquered. *Many bands reconciled their claims with the sovereignty of the Crown through negotiated treaties.* Others, notably in British Columbia, have yet to do so. The potential rights embedded in these claims are protected by s. 35 of the *Constitution Act, 1982. The honour of the Crown requires that these rights be determined, recognized and respected.* This, in turn, requires the Crown, acting honourably, to participate in processes of negotiation.[142][Emphasis added.]

More recently, building upon these insights from the *Haida Nation* case in the *Mikisew Cree v. Canada* decision, the Supreme Court said that:

> The fundamental objective of the modern law of Aboriginal and treaty rights is the *reconciliation* of Aboriginal peoples and non-Aboriginal peoples and their respective claims, interests and ambitions. [Emphasis added.]

---

[142] *Haida Nation v. B.C. (Minister of Forests)*, paras. 17-25.

125

> Both the historical context and the inevitable tensions underlying
> implementation of Treaty 8 demand a *process* by which lands may be
> transferred from the one category (where the First Nations retain rights
> to hunt, fish and trap) to the other category (where they do not). The
> content of the process is dictated by the duty of the Crown to act
> honourably.[143] [Emphasis in the original judgment]

Thus, it is clear that the honour of the Crown has always been, is, and will always be at stake in the implementation of the treaties. It is important to emphasize that these are the words of our country's highest court, interpreting a guarantee found in our supreme law, the Constitution. They are not statements of mere policy or wishful thinking; they are statements that cannot be ignored.

The particular issue in *Mikisew* was whether the Crown had met its duty to consult a First Nation when taking up land in the traditional territory of a First Nation for a public purpose. In focusing upon the effects of Crown-approved developments upon the traditional treaty rights of hunting and fishing within that territory, the Court did not suggest that the ongoing process of treaty implementation be limited to managing the gradual encroachment of non-traditional development upon traditional Aboriginal economic pursuits. Indeed, read more broadly, the *Mikisew Cree* case makes it quite clear that the treaty relationship is an evolving and organic one. As the *Haida Nation* case says, "treaties serve to reconcile pre-existing Aboriginal sovereignty with the presumed sovereignty of the Crown."[144] The broad purposes of treaty implementation must include at least the ongoing reconciliation of the political aspirations of the Parties within a framework of mutual respect, consultation and accommodation.

First Nations certainly have the broad right to continue their traditional economic pursuits and to have that right respected through appropriate consultation and accommodation measures. Beyond this, as traditional game and fish habitats are affected by mining, forestry, tourism and other purposes for which the Numbered Treaties permit the Crown to "take up" land, First Nations have a right to have their economies evolve in such a way as to fairly participate in the benefits of development.

---

[143] *Mikisew Cree First Nation v. Canada* (Minister of Canadian Heritage), paras. 1, 33.
[144] *Haida Nation v. B.C.* (Minister of Forests), at para. 42.

In a very real way, the task of this report is to analyze these important judicial decisions and suggest how the treaty "process" mentioned in *Mikisew* be designed and put into place. While the reference in *Mikisew* is to a process of addressing the transfer of land subject to hunting, fishing and trapping to the category of land "taken up" for other purposes, it is clear from reviewing the *Haida Nation* and *Mikisew* cases as a whole that the Supreme Court has set the stage for the creation of a process of identifying and implementing existing treaty rights as a matter of legal obligation and as a matter of the honour of the Crown.

As the Supreme Court said in the *Haida Nation* case:

> Reconciliation is not a final legal remedy in the usual sense. Rather, it is a process flowing from rights guaranteed by s. 35(1) of the *Constitution Act, 1982*. This process of reconciliation flows from the Crown's duty of honourable dealing toward Aboriginal peoples, which arises in turn from the Crown's assertion of sovereignty over an Aboriginal people and de facto control of land and resources that were formerly in the control of that people. As stated in *Mitchell v. M.N.R.*, [2001] 1 S.C.R. 911, 2001 SCC 33, at para. 9, "[w]ith this assertion [sovereignty] arose an obligation to treat Aboriginal peoples fairly and honourably, and to protect them from exploitation . . ."[145]

As a legal matter, "reconciliation" is the objective of a treaty implementation process, as well as the touchstone for structuring and guiding the process itself. It is not yet fully clear what, in law, "reconciliation" implies. There is little doubt the legal content of reconciliation in various contexts will occupy much attention in coming years, as First Nations and other governments seek judicial guidance in various cases, but these cases will come to the attention of the courts only where the Parties are unable to work out their differences through a process of good faith negotiations.

In law, as both the *Haida* and *Mikisew* cases emphasize, reconciliation is a "process," and that process does not end with the making of a treaty. The process carries on through the implementation of that treaty and is guided by a duty of honourable dealing. The very nature of the treaties is to establish mutual rights and obligations. Fulfilling treaties is not a one-way street. Accordingly, the honour of Treaty First Nations is also at stake in the treaty implementation

---

[145] Ibid., para. 32.

process. As the Supreme Court of Canada has stated, "At all stages, good faith on both sides is required."[146]

These important statements of the Supreme Court of Canada are highlighted because they remind the Parties that the legal interpretation of various treaty rights must always cause one to consider the underlying relationship within which those rights exist. They remind one that the honour of the Crown and of the First Nations is always at stake. They remind one to consider what an honourable approach to the treaties might be, and that the treaties require ongoing dialogue and mutual understanding for the Parties' mutual benefit.

The Supreme Court has reminded us that the foundations of our Canadian society are reflected in its constitutional structure. While that structure is the subject of legal analysis, the Parties are free to act to give effect to that structure without the necessity of legal compulsion. Canada, as a state, has evolved co-operative institutions to give effect to its federal structure, and could hardly function without co-operative federalism. Similarly, Canada, as a state, must come to terms with the underlying realities of pre-existing First Nation societies, their rights and the relationships they made with the Canadian state in the treaties.

(c) Socio-Economic Reconciliation

Reconciliation has a *socio-economic* dimension as well. It is clear that as First Nations and the Crown came together, they brought different social and economic foundations, priorities and technologies to bear. The *Mikisew Cree* case makes it clear that reconciliation of the First Nations' economy (including reliance upon hunting and fishing) and the Canadian economy remains a key component of treaty implementation.

Looking at the treaties from an economic perspective, as was detailed in the 1998 *Statement of Treaty Issues*, it is clear they were intended to achieve the reconciliation of two sets of economic interests and two economic systems, one largely based on gathering and harvesting of game and fish, the other based on more intense settlement, agriculture, logging, mining and other activities. Reconciliation in the economic sense must also embrace the idea that First Nations expected the

---

[146] Ibid., para. 42.

treaties to ensure they would benefit from the development of their traditional territories by the influx of new people and technologies, to which they were giving their consent.

The treaties included promises that the Treaty First Nations were, through education and other assistance from the Crown, to learn the ways of agriculture and to participate in other economic opportunities created by the treaties. The treaties were to provide skills and tools required for the First Nations to fully participate in the new economy, with opportunities equal to those of the new society. In the northern part of the province, there was an expectation on the part of the Crown and the First Nations that a traditional form of economy would continue for a longer period. Regardless of these variations, it is fair to conclude that a reconciliation of the economic interests was not only contemplated in the making of the treaties but a central pillar to them.

The economic part of the treaty bargain remains largely unfulfilled, as Treaty First Nations have repeatedly said and as we have noted in previous sections. One side of the "economic reconciliation" coin was to preserve a full array of hunting, fishing and trapping rights on as-yet unoccupied land; the other was to secure for First Nations the capacity to participate in the new economy and to share in the new prosperity. In too many cases, First Nations people have been subjected to prosecution simply for attempting to make their living. Too many First Nations people have been dragged into court simply for trying to survive as they have always survived. In addition to the barriers to their traditional economic activities, the quality of First Nations education has often been substandard giving First Nations students inadequate skills to participate in the new society's economy.

First Nations have been caught in an economic squeeze that has impoverished reserve communities created pursuant to the treaties. This, in turn, has led to extensive unemployment, social malaise and out-migration. Economic reconciliation and the implementation of the treaty commitments to education, resource access and non-interference in First Nations' traditional economic activities are thus essential elements in any effort to fulfill the treaty relationship. Part of this effort must include a comprehensive, funded strategy to improve the socio-economic status of First Nations people.

(d) Spiritual Reconciliation

Reconciliation also has *spiritual* dimensions to Treaty First Nations. Spiritual reconciliation must be based on a truthful and heartfelt examination of what the treaties mean in terms of bringing harmony to relations between the Parties, and to relations with the natural world and the Creator. It must respect the fundamental view that the treaties are a covenant.

The spiritual aspect of the treaties cannot be forgotten or omitted from present day implementation of treaty promises. Spiritual reconciliation does not compromise the spirit and intent of the treaties, but rather honours the sacredness of the covenant.

This pillar is also necessary in order to honour the First Nations' cultures and spirituality, which have been greatly dishonoured in the past. The Office of the Treaty Commissioner has made it clear in previous sections that several government policies and actions have done great harm to First Nations people. The most devastating has been the attempt to suppress and destroy First Nations' spirituality. The federal government's attempts to "civilize and Christianize" First Nations by prohibiting their ceremonies and imposing the residential school system are flagrant examples of direct attacks on First Nations cultures and spirituality.

In contrast, the Elders present a much different view of the spiritual beliefs and traditions of the treaty Parties:

> Elders refer to the spiritual ceremonies conducted and spiritual symbols used by First Nations and the active participation of various Christian missionaries along with the Christian symbols utilized by the Crown in [the treaty] negotiations to assert that both parties anchored their goals and objectives on the values, and principles contained in the teachings of each of their own spiritual traditions.[147]

While steps have been taken in recent years by government and Christian denominations to acknowledge the damage their policies and actions have caused, many First Nations people and communities still live with the pain and dysfunction. Spiritual reconciliation would require, at

---

[147] Cardinal and Hildenbrandt, *Treaty Elders of Saskatchewan*, p. 7.

minimum, affirmation of the cultural and spiritual traditions of First Nations in Saskatchewan and clear actions designed to re-instil traditional values, languages and cultural ceremonies.

There may also be a spiritual dimension to the contemporary legal concept of the honour of the Crown. The Crown entered the treaties with full ceremony, pledging the Crown's honour to fulfill the promises made and understood on the occasion. The honour of the Crown is an idea that has taken root in the legal analysis of Aboriginal and treaty rights, but it can also be understood as the most serious and solemn pledging of the Crown's utmost good faith. It is not merely a legal technicality; it is nothing less than the pledging of the collective good faith of a society:

> The honour of the Crown is always at stake in its dealings with Aboriginal peoples: see for example *R. v. Badger*, [1996] 1 S.C.R. 771, at para. 41; *R. v. Marshall*, [1999] 3 S.C.R. 456. It is not a mere incantation, but rather a core precept that finds its application in concrete practices.[148]

If Canada breaches its honourable obligations, it will carry a feeling of dishonour. If, on the other hand, it honours the spirit and intent of the treaties, it can justly claim that, as a society, it has kept its faith and its word.

Perspectives of the Future

(a) Toward Fulfillment

There is now a consensus between the Parties that the treaties need to be made more prevalent in future relations between the Crown and Treaty First Nations in Saskatchewan. The Parties to the treaties need to fashion a process that enables them to identify the key principles defining their treaty relationship. The Parties have thus committed, in general terms, to embark upon a journey toward a better understanding of the treaties, with the objective of creating a process of treaty implementation. There is consensus the treaties need to be understood in a way that honours the fact that each Party brought its utmost good faith and good will to their making, and acknowledges that perhaps they will be even more important in the future than they have been in the past.

---

[148] *Haida Nation v. B.C. (Minister of Forests)* at para. 16.

The greatest challenge for all of us is to find in the treaties the road to fulfillment. It is thus to the future we must look, and in the future that the success of treaty implementation discussions will be judged. A treaty implementation process must include an acknowledgment of past mistakes, but also a willingness to move beyond this to reconciliation.

(b) Creating a Treaty Implementation Agenda

The Parties need to develop an agenda for treaty implementation. It is not enough to share principles and regretfully make statements of what ought to have been. The Parties need to look ahead to make progress on goals they appear to share. This means the Parties need to have a goal in mind. They also need to know how their journey might be broken down into manageable stages. And they need to start somewhere. This report will lay out the most important matters for the Parties to address as they begin their shared journey toward treaty implementation.

In undertaking this task, the Parties will need to draw upon their mutual good faith and the strength of their joint commitment to the ideals of treaty implementation. The Royal Commission on Aboriginal Peoples Final Report noted that the nature of the relationship between the Crown and Treaty First Nations has been seen as a partnership. However, the idea of partnership only partially describes the treaty relationship. As we have seen, the Treaty First Nations regard the making of treaty as the extension of family relations to the Crown, and have expressed this as the principle of brotherhood. This is a perspective that makes the bonds of treaties unalterable and everlasting. The treaty Parties, either explicitly or implicitly, formed a relationship of utmost loyalty and mutual respect, one that includes the honour of the Crown as an over-arching principle. These qualities will be in great demand as treaty implementation gathers momentum.

The task of implementing the treaties includes determining what *both* treaty Parties had in mind when they made the momentous agreements and how their intentions can be reconciled in the twenty-first century. To say that a treaty implementation process is necessary is, by definition, to say the treaties have not been implemented to date. Implementation means the carrying out or fulfillment of an agreed objective, whether it be a decision, agreement or plan.[149]

---

[149] The Concise Oxford Dictionary includes in its definition of the verb "implement," "complete (contract, etc.); fulfill (undertaking); put (decision, plan, etc.) into effect." *The Concise Oxford Dictionary of Current English.*

Any implementation process must begin with an understanding of what needs to be implemented. The term "implementation" is not normally used when the objective is not agreed upon. In such cases, it is customary to refer to the need for dispute resolution rather than implementation. This is true in the realm of commercial contracts and contemporary comprehensive claim agreements alike. It is also true of international trade agreements, such as the North American Free Trade Agreement, in which complex arbitration and other mechanisms to address disagreements between treaty parties are common. However, it is not clear whether there is a precise dividing line between "implementation" and "dispute resolution." Both processes require the parties to an agreement to discuss what they intended at the time the agreement was made, and to discuss how the agreement applies to new and often unforeseen situations. Implementation and dispute resolution are, in reality, parts of making a complex agreement work and making it relevant.

The Parties instructed the Office of the Treaty Commissioner "to explore options for treaty implementation." Treaty implementation is the term used to describe both the objective of renewing the treaty relationship and the process of reconciliation this objective requires. In the case of implementing the treaties, elements of both implementation and dispute resolution are present.

This report also uses the term "treaty implementation" in a broader sense; it embraces the need to carry out or fulfill agreed matters, but it also embraces the need to achieve consensus on issues before action can be taken. There are certainly aspects of the treaties where common ground allows implementation in the conventional sense, but there are also other issues in which common ground is lacking.

A successful process of treaty implementation can energize Treaty First Nations people and lead to notable differences in the everyday lives of Treaty First Nations people and in fact all residents of Saskatchewan. If it succeeds, our families and communities will be healthier. Our economies will be stronger. Our institutions will be accountable. We will have a Canadian society built on respect and honour.

Conclusion

When we consider the meaning of particular treaty terms, we must be careful to consider meaning from at least four perspectives. The first is the perspective of the time the treaty was made. This perspective gives us an insight into the intentions of the Parties, including those that might not have been clearly stated. The *Marshall* case is an excellent example of this point. The Parties to the treaty in question assumed, but did not record in the written treaty text (dating from 1760), that the Mi'kmaq would have the right to harvest game and fish to trade at the "truckhouses" mentioned in the treaty text. It was assumed, but not recorded, that the Mi'kmaq would have the right to a moderate livelihood, and in that connection could sell or barter game and fish they harvested. As the Supreme Court of Canada made clear in 1999, nearly 240 years after the treaty was made, an understanding of the Parties' intentions and unstated assumptions is essential to understanding the terms.

The second perspective is the post treaty experience. This period is replete with injustices to First Nations people. During this time, the divergent views and common views of treaties become evident. The injustice that resulted must be acknowledged and addressed, but must not be belaboured. In order for treaty implementation to occur, new goals must be set.

This brings us to the next two perspectives, which seek to give meaning to a treaty term today and, more importantly, tomorrow, when treaty implementation and fulfillment becomes a reality. This requires not only an understanding of the mutual intentions and unstated assumptions of the Parties at a particular moment in the past, but also a broader understanding of how a particular treaty term must be understood and given effect in a very different and continually changing world. Written words on old pieces of paper do not change. The rights and obligations recorded on that paper both live and evolve with changing times, circumstances and relationships. The Judicial Committee of the Privy Council observed in 1929 that "the British North America Act planted in Canada a living tree capable of growth and expansion within its natural limits."[150] Like the Canadian Constitution, the treaties should be thought of as "living trees."

---

[150] *Edwards v. Canada (Attorney General)* [1930] A.C. 124, per Lord Sankey.

The courts have provided a great deal of guidance in the effort to bring our understanding of the spirit and intent of the treaties into a modern context. Thanks to the courts, we now understand that the treaties were intended to reconcile the pre-existing sovereignty of the Treaty First Nations with the asserted sovereignty of the Crown. We now also know that a people's right to self-determination must be respected through a legitimate process of political negotiation, if those sovereignties are to be reconciled within a political community rather than being divided through separation. The courts themselves have repeatedly said we cannot leave the tasks of reconciliation, fulfillment and treaty implementation to the courts; the treaty Parties are duty-bound to accomplish these tasks through a process of discussion, based on mutual respect and mutual accommodation. The Crown in right of Canada, in particular, has a positive obligation to provide meaning and content to the Constitution's commitment to recognize and protect the "existing Aboriginal and treaty rights" of First Nations.

Giving effect to treaty terms means continuing to understand the underlying purpose of a treaty term, the underlying assumptions and mutual intentions of the treaty Parties, and relating those understandings to contemporary societal relationships. The world of "truckhouses" may seem as quaint and irrelevant as quill pens and powdered wigs. However, as the *Marshall* case and its aftermath revealed, the world of Mi'kmaq economic reliance on the natural resources of their territories is as relevant today as it was in 1760, when the Mi'kmaq and the Crown made their treaty.

Of course, the same is true for the Treaty First Nations of Saskatchewan. Is a "medicine chest" merely a box? Is the medal and uniform of a Chief merely so much metal and so much cloth? Is the payment of an annuity of $5.00 merely a token? Is the right to hunt an historical anachronism? The task of treaty implementation includes the task of answering questions such as these, which arise from a consideration of particular terms of each treaty within a broader context and meaning, ultimately leading the Parties to agreement on the true intent of each of the treaty terms.

Tying these themes together, the idea of reconciliation must be understood as a renewal of the spirit and intent of the treaties. It must address the political, legal, socio-economic and spiritual renewal of the treaty relationship as we now understand it. Reconciliation must mean that old breaches are aired, acknowledged and addressed, and then put behind the Parties, even if they are not and should not be forgotten. It also must mean that the treaties, which were themselves entered into as acts of political reconciliation, must be the template for a lasting societal reconciliation, as bridges to our reconciled future, in which each side knows what to expect of the other, as well as how to ensure compliance with those expectations. The Parties have a duty to build a practical, forward-looking relationship in order to see treaty implementation come to fruition. This will require a substantial effort by all the Parties, including the Government of Saskatchewan, to build policy frameworks that can make treaty implementation effective. The duty exists and must be acted upon.

Finally, treaty implementation must reflect a future in which treaties have found their rightful place in the Canadian state and First Nations peoples have found their rightful place in Canadian society. It must mean the development of a sense of harmony and deep acceptance of the treaties as instruments of reconciliation. This will take time.

8. THE DUTY TO IMPLEMENT THE COVENANT

In the previous section we discussed the *Reference re. Secession of Quebec* case as it pertained to sovereignty. It is a legal decision about a political issue, one that recognizes the limitations of the law and the courts as instruments to guide or supervise purely political processes. The decision is founded upon the Court's explicit and detailed examination of the fundamental principles underlying the Canadian Constitution, particularly the circumstances in which the duties to negotiate arise. It offers considerable assistance in addressing whether a duty to negotiate treaty implementation may exist, as well as the legal enforceability of such a duty. In this section we will return to that important *Reference re. Secession of Quebec* court decision for guidance on a process that should be used to reconcile divergent views about the treaties.[151]

The Court identified four fundamental principles of the Constitution, namely:

- Federalism
- Democracy
- Constitutionalism and the rule of law
- The protection of minorities.

In describing these principles, the Court stated:

> Although these underlying principles are not explicitly made part of the Constitution by any written provision, other than in some respects by the oblique reference in the preamble to the *Constitution Act, 1867*, it would be impossible to conceive of our constitutional structure without them. The principles dictate major elements of the architecture of the Constitution itself, and are as such its lifeblood.

> The principles assist in the interpretation of the text and the delineation of spheres of jurisdiction, the scope of rights and obligations, and the role of our political institutions. Equally important, observance of and respect for these principles is essential to the ongoing process of constitutional development and evolution of our Constitution as a "living tree", to invoke the famous description in *Edwards v. Attorney-General for Canada* [1930] A.C. 123

---

[151] The discussion of *Reference re. Secession of Quebec* under this heading is adapted from an unpublished paper prepared by Alan Pratt for the Treaty Rights Unit of the Assembly of First Nations in December 1999, entitled, "Treaties and Reconciliation: The Marshall Case and a Duty to Negotiate," which has been used with the permission of the author and the Assembly of First Nations.

(P.C), at p.136. As this Court indicated in *New Brunswick Broadcasting Co. v Nova Scotia (Speaker of the House of Assembly),* [1993] 1 S.C.R. 319, Canadians have long recognized the existence and importance of unwritten constitutional principles in our system of government.[152]

With respect to the **federalism** component, the Supreme Court stated:

> Federalism is the political mechanism by which diversity could be reconciled with unity....
>
> The principle of federalism recognizes the diversity of the component parts of Confederation, and the autonomy of provincial governments to develop their societies within their respective spheres of jurisdiction.[153]

The Court later makes the link between federalism and "the pursuit of collective goals":

> The principle of federalism facilitates the pursuit of collective goals by cultural and linguistic minorities which form the majority within a particular province.[154]

In explaining the role of **democracy** as a fundamental principle of Canada's Constitution, the Court commented:

> ...democracy is fundamentally connected to substantive goals, most importantly, the promotion of self-government. Democracy accommodates cultural and group identities: *Reference re Provincial Electoral Boundaries,* at p. 188. Put another way, a sovereign people exercises its right to self-government through the democratic process.[155]

In describing the two-headed principle of **constitutionalism and the rule of law**, the Court states that:

> Simply put, the constitutionalism principle requires that all government action comply with the Constitution. The rule of law principle requires that all government action must comply with the law, including the Constitution.[156]

The Court added three additional examples of this principle:

---

[152] *Reference re. Secession of Quebec*, paras. 51-52.
[153] Ibid., paras. 43, 58.
[154] Ibid., para. 59.
[155] Ibid., para. 64.
[156] Ibid., para. 72.

First, a constitution may provide an added safeguard for fundamental human rights and individual freedoms which might otherwise be susceptible to government interference. Although democratic government is generally solicitous of those rights, there are occasions when the majority will be tempted to ignore fundamental rights in order to accomplish collective goals more easily or effectively. Constitutional entrenchment ensures that those rights will be given due regard and protection. Second, a constitution may seek to ensure that vulnerable minority groups are endowed with the institutions and rights necessary to maintain and promote their identities against the assimilative pressures of the majority. And third, a constitution may provide for a division of political power that allocates political power amongst different levels of government. That purpose would be defeated if one of those democratically elected levels of government could usurp the powers of the other simply by exercising its legislative power to allocate additional political power to itself unilaterally.[157]

With respect to the **protection of minority rights**, the Court stated:

Undoubtedly, the three other constitutional principles inform the scope and operation of the specific provisions that protect the rights of minorities. We emphasize that the protection of minority rights is itself an independent principle underlying our constitutional order.[158]

In this connection, the constitutional guarantees of Aboriginal and treaty rights were specifically mentioned, possibly as a fifth underlying constitutional principle:

Consistent with this long tradition of respect for minorities, which is at least as old as Canada itself, the framers of the *Constitution Act, 1982* included in s. 35 explicit protection for existing Aboriginal and treaty rights, and in s. 25, a non-derogation clause in favour of the rights of Aboriginal peoples. The "promise" of s. 35, as it was termed in *R. v. Sparrow,* [1990] 1 S.C.R. 1075, at p. 1083, recognized not only the ancient occupation of land by Aboriginal peoples, but their contribution to the building of Canada, and the special commitments made to them by successive governments. The protection of these rights, so recently and arduously achieved, whether looked at in their own right or as part of the larger concern with minorities, reflects an important underlying constitutional value.[159]

These fundamental principles of constitutional law have a direct application to treaty implementation in a modern context.

---

[157] Ibid., para. 74.
[158] Ibid., para. 80.
[159] Ibid., para. 82·

The federalism principle has clear relevance to the treaties. In its 1996 Final Report, the Royal Commission on Aboriginal Peoples wrote:

> The treaties form a fundamental part of the constitution and for many Aboriginal peoples, play a role similar to that played by the *Constitution Act, 1867 (formerly the British North American Act)* in relation to the provinces. The terms of the Canadian federation are found not only in formal constitutional documents governing relations between the federal and provincial governments but also in treaties and other instruments establishing the basic links between Aboriginal peoples and the Crown. In brief, 'treaty federalism' is an integral part of the Canadian constitution.[160]

The principles of **federalism** are critical to an understanding of the treaty relationship as well as the Canadian constitution.

The principle of **democracy** exists to secure the legitimacy of representative institutions exercising the right to collective self-determination on behalf of self-determining individuals.

The principle of **constitutionalism and the rule of law** has particular relevance in light of the *Marshall (No. 1)*[161] decision, which clarifies that the Crown has not conducted itself in accordance with its legal and constitutional duties to respect the treaties.

The application of the principle of **protection of minorities**, including the protections of section 35, is self-evident.

The jurisprudence on treaty interpretation in cases such as *Marshall* shows that, despite the fact that existing treaty rights have been given constitutional protection by section 35(1) of the *Constitution Act, 1982*, the rights arising under the treaties are not what they may seem on the face of treaty documents. What was recorded in a treaty text may be incomplete and even misleading as a guide to the intentions of the parties.

The constitutionalism principle requires that all government action comply with the law and the constitution. To fulfill this most elementary expectation of constitutional law, the government

---

[160] Royal Commission on Aboriginal Peoples, *Gathering Strength*, Volume 2, Part 1, p. 194.
[161] *R. v. Marshall.*

must at minimum be able to know what legal rights, duties and corresponding constitutional constraints arise from the treaties.

The *Reference re. Secession of Quebec* makes it equally clear that duty to negotiate exists to ensure that our constitutional arrangements respect both the legality and legitimacy of a liberal democratic society.

When the treaties are shown to have been dishonoured or ignored by the Crown, and treaty rights are shown to have been elevated to constitutional status in theory yet ignored and marginalized in practice, surely there is a duty to engage in negotiations to place these rights in their proper place. Failure to do so would represent profound disrespect for the constitution, the rule of law and other fundamental principles that support our constitutional structure.

In the case of First Nations treaty rights, reconciliation is also a prominent theme in the jurisprudence. In decisions such as *Van der Peet, Gladstone* and *Delgamuukw,* the Supreme Court has stressed the theme of reconciliation between different groups of people with different rights. In *Van der Peet,* reconciliation is described as the rationale of the constitutional guarantee of existing Aboriginal and treaty rights in section 35(1) of the *Constitution Act, 1982:*

> ...what s. 35(1) does is provide the constitutional framework through which the fact that Aboriginals lived on the land in distinctive societies, with their own practices, traditions and cultures, is acknowledged and ***reconciled*** with the sovereignty of the Crown. The substantive rights which fall within the provision must be defined in light of this purpose; the Aboriginal rights recognized and affirmed by s. 35(1) must be directed towards the ***reconciliation*** of the pre-existence of Aboriginal societies with the sovereignty of the Crown. [162] [Emphasis added]

The treaties were negotiated agreements of a confederal nature and thus were inherently instruments of reconciliation when they were made. In *Reference re. Secession of Quebec,* the Supreme Court made it clear that a demand for secession is purely political and the resulting duty to negotiate is equally political. The task is to attempt to reconcile divergent interests, rights and duties, with no presumption this can be accomplished even if all parties approach the task in good faith.

---

[162] *R. v. Van der Peet,* [1996] 1 S.C.R. 507 para 193.

By contrast, in the context of the treaties, demand for implementation of *already legally protected* rights is based upon principles of constitutionalism and the rule of law and *must* be enforceable by the courts. The concluding words of the majority judgment in *Delgamuukw* state:

> Ultimately, it is through negotiated settlements, with good faith and give and take on all sides, **reinforced by the judgments of this Court,** that we will achieve what I stated in *Van der Peet, supra,* at para. 31, to be a basic purpose of s. 35(1) – "the reconciliation of the pre-existence of Aboriginal societies with the sovereignty of the Crown". Let us face it, we are all here to stay.[163] [Emphasis added]

Discussions to reconcile disparity between the words of treaty text and the true extent of the constitutional rights are inherently founded upon rights and obligations in the realm of *law* as well as *politics*.

The rulings of the courts have built a compelling case for the Government of Canada and the Treaty First Nations to establish a proper treaty implementation process. The courts will compel the Crown and the Treaty First Nations to negotiate in good faith. Both Parties will be constrained by the principles of the treaties and the treaty relationship. The objective of a treaty implementation process must be a real and lasting reconciliation.

There is a constitutional duty, which is both a legal and political duty, on the part of the Government of Canada, the Treaty First Nations and the Government of Saskatchewan to identify and implement all the treaty rights through a treaty process based on good faith discussions.

As previously noted, the Supreme Court of Canada in the *Haida Nation*[164] case has made it clear that treaties serve to reconcile First Nations' "pre-existing" sovereignty with the "assumed" sovereignty of the Crown. Thus, on an issue like sovereignty, something vital has been settled but new questions have arisen. It is going to be important for the treaty Parties to reach an understanding on *how* the treaties reconciled sovereignties, and further, what this reconciliation implies for future governance arrangements. These are political questions and require a principled,

---

[163] *Delgamuukw v. British Columbia.*
[164] *Haida Nation v. British Columbia (Minister of Forests)*, para 20.

careful political resolution, as the Supreme Court of Canada made clear in the *Reference re. Secession of Quebec.*

The Supreme Court simultaneously linked the pre-existing sovereignty of the First Nations to the reconciliation achieved in the treaties. As already mentioned, this judicial observation points the way to an examination of the treaty relationship as one of political reconciliation. It also suggests that treaty implementation can be the vehicle which puts discussion of sovereignty within a framework that emphasizes sharing, accommodation and mutuality as opposed to unilateralism and separation. There is even an existing theoretical basis for this framework of treaty implementation – treaty federalism.

Who Are the Treaty Parties?

The treaties affecting Saskatchewan were made by the Crown and the Treaty First Nations in the years before Saskatchewan became a province. Since 1905, the Province of Saskatchewan has possessed the same legislative authority as the original four provinces of Ontario, Quebec, New Brunswick and Nova Scotia. In 1930, Saskatchewan acquired administration and control of public lands and natural resources, subject, of course, to the requirements of the *Natural Resources Transfer Agreement* of that year.

The commitments made in the treaties bind the Crown, regardless of internal divisions in federal and provincial governments. In the federal structure of Canada, the federal government has inherited the duty to honour the treaties and the companion duties to implement them. In the words of Lord Denning of the English Court of Appeal, "No Parliament should do anything to lessen the worth of these guarantees. They should be honoured by the Crown in respect of Canada..."[165]

In a federal state, other levels of government have important roles to play. It is the Government of Canada, however, that has the constitutional responsibility to take leadership on treaty implementation. The role of the provincial government is controversial among First Nations.

---

[165] *R v. Secretary of State for Foreign and Commonwealth Affairs, Ex p. Indian Association of Alberta.*

They say, correctly, that they made treaties with the Crown.[166] If the Crown has chosen to complicate matters by dividing up authority to make laws among different layers of government, that is an internal matter to the Crown.   The Treaty First Nations often refer to their "bilateral" relationship with the Crown, and to the treaty implementation process as a "bilateral process" involving only the Treaty First Nations and the Crown in right of Canada.

This perspective, while undeniably valid, will do little to help the Parties develop the kinds of support and understanding a successful treaty implementation process will need. With the exception of Treaty 10, the treaties were made before the Province of Saskatchewan came into existence. Unlike most of the other provinces, Saskatchewan did not own public lands and natural resources when it was created. Not until 1930 was it put on the same basis as the original provinces, and British Columbia and Prince Edward Island. The creation of the province, the transfer of public land and natural resources to the provincial government, and the subsequent creation of rural and urban municipalities throughout the province have made it difficult to see how a purely bilateral treaty implementation process can succeed.

In theory the Crown is indivisible; in reality the Crown's authority is fragmented. In theory the Crown is sovereign, with absolute power; in reality, we live in a democratic state, in which theoretically absolute sovereign authority came under the rule of law centuries ago and is now exercised by a Parliament elected by popular support, by an executive branch of government drawn from that Parliament, overseen by an independent judiciary, and constrained by a complex web of written constitutional texts and unwritten principles and conventions.

It is time the provincial Crown's role in implementing the treaties in Saskatchewan was recognized. The province did not exist when the treaties were created, but that does not mean it does not have obligations today. Some constraints on the Crown's sovereignty, both provincial and federal, flow from legal obligations toward First Nations recognized by the courts.[167] The Supreme Court has

---

[166] See Miller, J.R., "'I will accept the Queen's hand': First Nations Leaders and the Image of the Crown in the Prairie Treaties," in *Reflections on Native-Newcomer Relations: Selected Essays* (Toronto: University of Toronto Press, 2004), 242-66.

[167] See Borrows, John, "Let Obligations Be Done" in Foster, Hamar, Heather Raven and Jeremy Webber, eds., *The Calder Case* (UBC Press, 2006) forthcoming.

been clear that Crown constraints are a part of the framework of subsection 35(1). As the Court observed in the leading case of *R. v. Sparrow*:

> Section 35 calls for a just settlement for Aboriginal peoples. It renounces the old rules of the game under which the Crown established courts of law and denied those courts the authority to question sovereign claims made by the Crown.[168]

Crown sovereignty, including provincial sovereignty, is constrained under subsection 35(1) by its obligations to Aboriginal peoples. The courts have jurisdiction to question the Crown's actions. Freedom is increased when the Crown is obliged to observe constitutional limitations on its power; section 35(1) falls within this tradition.[169]

The provincial Crown shares in the obligations existing toward First Nations, either directly or by virtue of its obligations to the federal government that allow it to fulfill its obligations to First Nations. The extent of provincial obligations that need to be met in treaty implementation will have to be determined through discussions, but the provincial government must certainly play a role in:

1. Recognition and respect for First Nations governance.

2. Assurance of minimal impairment of First Nations people's exercise of their inherent and treaty rights.

3. Provision of access to natural resources to First Nations and recognition of the priority of First Nations uses of resources over those of non-Aboriginal people.

4. Creation of opportunities for participation in the economy.

5. Compensation for previous interference with rights in circumstances in which the provincial government was a beneficiary.

6. Consultation and accommodation of First Nations rights and interests.

7. Protection of the *Charter* rights of First Nations people.

---

[168] *R. v. Sparrow* (1990), 70 D.L.R. (4th) 385 at 412, quoting Noel Lyon, "An Essay on Constitutional Interpretation" (1988), 26 Osgoode Hall L.J. 95.

[169] See Borrows, "Let Obligations Be Done."

These obligations apply to the Saskatchewan government in appropriate circumstances,[170] though one should not lose sight of the special federal constitutional responsibility under section 91(24) of the *Constitution Act, 1867*.[171] The federal Crown is the diplomatic partner, but the provincial Crown acquired certain responsibilities when its authority was split from the federal Crown. The listed obligations are part of subsection 35(1)'s "general guiding principle," which is to ensure the Crown fulfills its responsibility to act in a trust-like, non-adversarial manner when dealing with Aboriginal peoples.[172] These obligations must be generously understood and applied in *all* the Crown's dealings with First Nations peoples under the treaties.

On the First Nations side, there is also no single monolithic sovereign authority. First Nations' sovereignty lies with the Chiefs and Councils and the people, in individual First Nations communities and the broader nation. It is rooted in the sovereignty of the indigenous nations, the land, in natural law and in the Creator's will. Sovereignty is a complex concept but, for the practical purposes of undertaking treaty implementation discussions and making the accommodations necessary to make treaty implementation a success, "sovereignty" needs to be understood as residing in the will of First Nations people. They must play an integral role in mandating those speaking on their behalf and reviewing any agreements arrived at.

The First Nations people who entered into treaty relations with the Crown had political and social organizations that served them well. First Nations people were subject to the increasing regulation of the Government of Canada, first through identification of "Indian Bands" for whose benefits reserves were to be set apart, then through the application of the *Indian Act* to virtually every conceivable decision of the bands. Today, the First Nations in Saskatchewan, like those in other parts of Canada, are organized along the lines of "bands," but there are also Tribal

---

[170] *Paul v. British Columbia (Forest Appeals Commission)*, [2003] 2 S.C.R. 585 para. 24: "Section 35 therefore applies to both provinces and the federal government."

[171] *Constitution Act, 1867*, 30 & 31 Victoria, c. 3. Under section 91(24) the federal government has exclusive legislative authority in relation to "Indians and lands reserved for the Indians." These provisions should be interpreted in light of the human rights values in the Charter of Rights and Freedoms. See *R. v. Demers*, [2004] 2 S.C.R. 489, para. 85: "Since the promulgation of the Charter in 1982, the provisions set out therein have resulted in fructifying contact with the other elements of our Constitution. Thus, the human rights and freedoms expressed in the Charter, while they do not formally modify the scope of the powers in ss. 91 and 92 of the *Constitution Act*, 1867, do provide a new lens through which those powers should be viewed. In choosing one among several possible interpretations of powers that implicate human rights, the interpretation that best accords with the imperatives of the Charter should be adopted."

[172] *R. v. Sparrow*, p. 1108.

Councils and the Federation of Saskatchewan Indian Nations itself. In preparing for a treaty implementation process, First Nations must consider the type of political organization that will best enable First Nations to be effective.

All modern governments must address the question of how centralized or decentralized governmental functions ought to be. The principle of "subsidiarity," a principle used extensively in guiding the governance of the European Union (EU), dictates, in the context of the EU, that "the --Union shall act only if and insofar as the objectives of the intended action cannot be sufficiently achieved by the Member States, either at central level or at regional and local level, but can rather, by reason of the scale or effects of the proposed action, be better achieved at Union level."[173] Such a calculation, though generally less explicit, takes place both within governments and between governments in federal systems in deciding where authority for particular decisions lies.

This principle can also be of assistance to First Nations in deciding what level of First Nations government should have authority for different governmental functions. Internal First Nations governance arrangements would likely see some functions exercised at the first level of individual First Nations, some exercised at the second level of Tribal Councils, Agencies or Treaty areas, and some exercised at the third level of a province-wide government. Which functions are assigned to which level would be determined by balancing efficiency, the need for responsiveness to citizens, effectiveness and capacity.

A workable treaty implementation process is going to have to derive its legitimacy from the consent of the First Nations citizens who will be governed by its outcome. As part of securing consent, it will be important to consider the extent to which the process is able to respect the bilateral nature of the treaties, while at the same time finding ways to involve and eventually bind all of the different entities and perspectives.

The treaties are bilateral because they reconcile two sovereignties, two legal orders, two systems of economic use of land, and two cultures. Each side of the bilateral discussion must respect the

---

[173] Draft Treaty Establishing a Constitution for Europe, Article 9.

complexity within each of the two Parties. As the Royal Commission on Aboriginal Peoples put it in its Final Report:

> The treaties are correctly perceived by treaty nations as being bilateral in nature: the treaty nations are one party, and the Crown is the other. Treaty nations, in many cases, regard their relationship under treaty as one made between sovereigns. Certainly, they all regard their relationship as being between nations or peoples. Each of the treaties represents the coming together of two separate cultures, political systems, legal systems and systems of land tenure. The treaties are therefore, in this sense, fundamentally bilateral.
>
> Each side of the treaty implementation relationship, however, can be politically complex. Treaty nations, for example, can be made up of different clans, tribes or villages, recognized by their own laws and customs. In addition, in some places, traditional treaty nation political structures have been superseded by the establishment of band councils elected under the *Indian Act*, as well as by other entities, such as tribal councils and provincial, regional and national political associations, to represent some treaty nations for some purposes.
>
> Similarly, while 'the Crown' is in a very real sense a single party to a bilateral treaty relationship, Her Majesty the Queen is advised by many ministers of many governments and has no real authority independent of them. In Canada, Parliament has the primary legislative authority and the federal government executive responsibility for fulfilling the treaties, but many treaty issues involve matters within provincial jurisdiction and ownership, particularly lands and natural resources.
>
> The Crown in Canada today is a concept that both constrains governments from wrongful actions and acts more positively as an affirmative and honourable force that is required to uphold treaty relationships and treaty promises made on behalf of society as a whole.[174]

The success of a treaty implementation process will depend on how well the Parties can reconcile the need for a bilateral discussion with the complexity of the contemporary legal and political landscape, including the complexities of Canadian federalism.

The *Statement of Treaty Issues* observed:

> The parties acknowledge that there will also be a need to establish relations between First Nations governments and other levels of government. The Government of Canada and the Government of Saskatchewan need to work

---

[174] Royal Commission on Aboriginal Peoples, *Gathering Strength*, Volume 2, pp. 51-2.

in partnerships with the Treaty First Nations to find creative solutions that best serve the interests of all Saskatchewan residents. In this respect, the Government of Saskatchewan has a role in the renewal process that is described in this Statement. Saskatchewan, as a provincial government, has been given authority through the Constitution of Canada over people and territory. Treaty First Nations wish to exercise jurisdiction in many areas where Saskatchewan now exercises authority, such as education, child welfare, and justice. Clearly then, working out new arrangements must involve close contact and discussion with provincial authorities.[175]

In order to be successful, a treaty implementation process will require the cooperation and participation of the Government of Saskatchewan as an integral component of the Crown. It is going to be very important to the success of treaty implementation that the roles and responsibilities of all government agencies are clear and complementary. Thus, an examination of the meaning of the "Crown" will take the Parties into the creation of new intergovernmental relations and understandings. Both principle and pragmatic considerations will have to be taken into account. The role of the province is complex, because of the history of treaty making in what is now Saskatchewan and the views of First Nations people on the appropriate role of the provincial government in treaty implementation discussions. Nonetheless, because of the Government of Saskatchewan's role in making laws for the province on many issues of interest to First Nations peoples, their cooperation and involvement in discussions will be essential if treaty implementation is to be achieved. If all Parties keep this fact in mind and demonstrate goodwill in working out a process by which the Government of Saskatchewan can participate in treaty implementation discussions, agreement on the appropriate role of the province can be found. Some options for including the Government of Saskatchewan in treaty implementation discussions are set out in section 9.

Saskatchewan has assumed responsibility for numerous matters that affect First Nations people; in some cases provincial responsibility overlaps with federal.

---

[175] Office of the Treaty Commissioner, *Statement of Treaty Issues*, pp. 79-80.

Policy Direction Is Needed

To date, the Government of Canada has not formulated a policy to guide its officials in the implementation of treaties nor, to put it in terms that Canada might more comfortably embrace, to reconcile the divergent views on the treaties of the Crown and Treaty First Nations. It can be argued that the *Royal Proclamation of 1763* already contains such a policy, in that it committed the Crown to a process of acquiring First Nations lands with their informed, collective consent, This was clearly a major source of Crown policy which led to the making of the Numbered Treaties that apply within Saskatchewan. The Proclamation, however, did not suggest how the treaties, once made, should be honoured, fulfilled or implemented.

It can also be argued that Canada's current policy is one of deliberate avoidance of the issue. In the absence of such policy guidance with a particular focus on treaties, and seemingly by default, the courts have been given the task of determining the meaning of treaties. It is clear that existing laws and policies of the Government of Canada do not, in the eyes of Treaty First Nations, achieve the implementation of the treaties, nor do they achieve the reconciliation of the Parties' divergent views on the treaties.

The Treaty First Nations have declared their commitment to the implementation of the spirit and intent of the treaties as they understand them. However, Treaty First Nations have not developed the policies, instruments and institutions they would need to guide them in treaty implementation discussions. The legal and ethical values handed down by Elders can serve as foundational pillars of a Treaty First Nations approach. Since the Government of Saskatchewan has traditionally taken the position that it is not a party to the treaties, it has not developed the policies necessary to participate effectively in treaty implementation discussions.

It is a basic duty of each of the Parties to honour their treaty obligations. First, though, it will be necessary to identify those obligations and then to identify those that are unmet. Since the courts have made it clear in cases such as *Badger* and *Marshall* that the written texts of the treaties are not complete or accurate, the Parties have a fundamental duty to investigate what their treaty promises are. Similarly, the principle of the rule of law requires the Parties to know what treaty rights exist and how their respective laws and policies must adapt to those rights.

Treaties, by their nature, are agreements. One party to an agreement cannot undertake an investigation of its obligations without considering fully and fairly the views of the other party. This is especially true given the special relationship that exists between the Crown and First Nations, and the obligations of the Crown to deal honourably with First Nations in relation to their rights. While the honour of the Crown is always at stake in the fulfillment of treaty rights, it can also involve a fiduciary duty as stated by the Supreme Court of Canada.[176]

It is apparent that policies are needed to authorize the officials of both Parties to undertake a joint process of determining what the treaties mean and implementing the result of the consensus emerging from that determination. The policy must be enabling, not restrictive. It must authorize officials to undertake treaty implementation discussions in a respectful process. It must mandate serious exploration and negotiations. Each side must develop objectives and mandates for a process that will produce practical as well as principled outcomes.

Canadian Courts

The court process is the default process for determining treaty rights. It suffers because, among other institutional disadvantages, it is not designed to answer the large questions implicit in a treaty implementation process. It is designed to answer particular issues, such as whether a First Nation person has a defence to a penal charge or if lawful consent was given in a surrender of reserve land. Courts seldom have the occasion to consider a treaty relationship in a holistic fashion. They have repeatedly said these issues should be dealt with in a fair political process.

In a recent decision in *Marshall* and *Bernard,* Mr. Justice LeBel of the Supreme Court of Canada noted that it is not appropriate for issues such as Aboriginal title to be dealt with in summary conviction proceedings.[177] Similar considerations certainly apply when the issues of treaty

---

[176] *Ontario (Attorney General) v. Bear Island Foundation,* [1991] 2 S.C.R. 570.
[177] *R. v. Marshall; R. v. Bernard,* [2005] 2 S.C.R. 200 paras. 142-4.

implementation arise in summary proceedings, such as hunting and fishing prosecutions. How can a satisfactory and holistic examination of a treaty relationship be achieved when the issue before the court is whether a regulatory offence has been committed? To have these complex issues submitted to the courts instead of a process of discussion and principled reconciliation and accommodation is to abandon the principles of an honourable relationship. The courts, too, have begun in recent years to urge the Parties to engage in a respectful and honourable process of negotiation, with the courts serving to guide the Parties in understanding the legal dimensions of their respective rights and obligations.

To engage in treaty implementation discussions effectively, the scope of the agenda and the subject matters to be discussed will first need to be agreed upon. So will such matters as the type and status of any agreements emerging from the process, the role of courts or alternative dispute resolution processes in resolving rights and treaty interpretation questions arising in the course of discussions, and conflicts between the Parties at the negotiating table. Some of these matters could await a formal treaty implementation process, but it is difficult to see how officials could be given a meaningful mandate to engage in discussions without the most senior levels of government giving general guidance on such matters.

Federal Policy

Currently, the federal government has major, published policies on specific and comprehensive land claims and the inherent right to self-government. Each of these policies authorizes negotiations with First Nations, with the objective of reaching agreements. Implementation of these policies, however, is a matter of significant concern, as noted earlier in reference to the November 2003 observation of the Auditor General of Canada.

Northern leaders identified similar concerns in a March 24, 2004 letter to then Prime Minister Paul Martin. They commented that:

> There is a growing frustration with the Federal government's approach to implementation, and unmistakable signs that the original good will and hope generated with the signing of these agreements is being undermined. A

coherent Federal policy on implementation of land claims agreements is required, and should be developed co-operatively with Aboriginal peoples. Federal agencies, particularly Indian and Northern Affairs Canada, take the view that agreements are successfully implemented if federal contractual commitments have been discharged in a way that withstands legal challenge. This is a minimalist view that prevents agreements from delivering to us the full range of rights and benefits we negotiated. Federal agencies have lost sight of the objectives of these agreements. [178]

Beyond these difficulties with effective implementation of federal agreements with First Nations, the treaties are not the central focus of any of the federal government's policies. Each of these policies mentions the treaties in passing, but no more. No existing federal policy mandates discussion between the Crown in right of Canada and its treaty partners to examine and reconcile divergent views on treaties in order to implement the treaties and the treaty relationships in a comprehensive or holistic manner.

An example of the limitations of federal policy arose in the course of discussions at the Governance and Fiscal Relations Table. Negotiators for all three Parties were interested in jointly developing and jointly funding a socio-economic strategy for First Nations, in conjunction with self-government negotiations, as a way to achieve socio-economic parity for First Nations people. The negotiators often described the prospects for self-government in the absence of socio-economic parity as "governing misery." Such a strategy could have been a significant part of an effort to implement the treaty commitment to securing a livelihood for First Nations people. Federal officials, however, refused to agree to the negotiation of a socio-economic strategy as part of a self-government package, as it was beyond their mandate. In the absence of a more holistic federal mandate, such opportunities for policy innovation will continue to be lost.

The current lack of any federal treaty implementation policy that would permit federal officials to engage in substantive discussions is demonstrated by the "exploratory" nature of the discussions facilitated by the Office of the Treaty Commissioner. As the Office of the Treaty Commissioner noted in the 1998 *Statement of Treaty Issues*:

---

[178] Land Claims Agreement Coalition, letter to Prime Minister Paul Martin, March 24, 2004, as quoted in Penikett, Tony, *Reconciliation*, p. 183.

> At the beginning of the Exploratory Treaty Table discussions, Canada stated that, consistent with its commitment to working in partnership with Treaty First Nations in Saskatchewan, it would undertake not to create new policies or change its policies with respect to treaties in advance of the Exploratory Treaty Table discussions. Instead, it would outline Canada's current understandings regarding treaties in Saskatchewan and seek the views of Treaty First Nations regarding how best to achieve "a mutually acceptable process to interpret the treaties in contemporary terms, while giving full recognition to their original spirit and intent."

> Canada came to listen and to gather information to better understand the implications of moving forward and building on the treaty relationship in Canada.[179]

The Government of Canada, however, is aware that it can no longer simply "explore" the question of treaty implementation. It is now time to determine what it can and must do to act on its positive duty to implement the treaties in an honourable manner, and thereby fulfill all the elements of Canada's covenant with First Nations.

The Supreme Court has recently recognized in the *Mikisew Cree* case that treaty implementation is a *process*. Implicit in this is an acknowledgment that it is a fundamental mistake, as Treaty First Nations have always maintained, to think the treaties were one-time transactions. In the *Mikisew Cree* case, the Court concluded the process had broken down and the level of communication and respect that should characterize the treaty relationship had not been demonstrated by the Crown. In the very first paragraph of its reasons, the Court made an important observation that points out the need for a treaty implementation policy for the federal government as a whole:

> The multitude of smaller grievances created by the indifference of some government officials to Aboriginal people's concerns, and the lack of respect inherent in that indifference has been as destructive of the process of reconciliation as some of the larger and more explosive controversies. And so it is in this case.[180]

This observation succinctly states the need for policies to address the government's duties to First Nations people. It is going to have to become second nature for all government decision-makers to consider the rights and interests of Treaty First Nations at all times.

---

[179] Office of the Treaty Commissioner, *Statement of Treaty Issues*, p. 36.
[180] *Mikisew Cree First Nation v. Canada*, para. 1.

Similarly, the true path to reconciliation must include overcoming the indifference and lack of respect for First Nations to which the Supreme Court refers in *Mikisew*. Government officials are not free to conduct themselves in accordance with personal prejudices. Governments act through individuals, but those individuals are obliged to act in accordance with consistent and lawful policies and guidelines formulated by their superiors.

Until the *Haida Nation* case was decided in November 2004, government lawyers and officials believed that consultation with First Nations was only legally required where a clearly established Aboriginal or treaty right existed, and where a proposed government action would infringe such a right. This view was based on the government's interpretation of Supreme Court of Canada jurisprudence since the 1990 *Sparrow* case. Under this view, any doubt about the existence of such an asserted right or a disagreement on the scope of that right was reason enough to refuse to admit to a duty to consult. The *Haida Nation* decision revealed the error of that belief by making it clear the honour of the Crown demands good faith consultations whenever a contemplated government action *might* affect an *asserted* Aboriginal or treaty right, whether or not it had been formally proven.

In the 2005 *Mikisew Cree* case, however, federal Crown counsel argued that all consultation obligations with respect to a Numbered Treaty had been fulfilled at the time of making the treaty in 1899. This submission was consistent with the perspective held by many, and likely most, officials of the federal Crown that the treaties were one-time exchanges of rights and not templates of an ongoing relationship that requires both consultation and accommodation when circumstances warrant. Only with the Supreme Court's decision in 2005 has this overly narrow perspective been revealed to be erroneous in law. However, the conduct of Crown officials has been coloured by a widely held official view that the treaties do not matter in day-to-day government business, that they are old and settled business.

The process of treaty implementation, therefore, includes a process of increasing the awareness and altering the behaviour of government officials, who have been advised they need not consult with

Treaty First Nations in making the many decisions which may impact in some way the rights and interests of First Nations. Treaty implementation includes the making of large decisions at high levels. But it also includes changing of thought processes of government officials, enabling them to turn their minds to the potential impact of their work upon the rights and interests of the many Treaty First Nations.

For government, the immediate task is to digest the lessons of court decisions such as *Haida Nation* and *Mikisew Cree*, and to develop overall policies to guide officials both in the field and around negotiation tables. In principle, developing a treaty implementation policy is simple: the Crown must honour its existing treaty obligations. As the Royal Commission on Aboriginal Peoples observed in its 1996 Final Report, the interpretation of treaties is conceptually simple but practically complex:

> The commission's terms of reference required us to investigate and make concrete recommendations concerning
>
> > 5. The legal status, implementation and future evolution of Aboriginal treaties, including modern-day agreements.
> >
> > An investigation of the historic practices of treaty making may be undertaken by the Commission, as well as an analysis of treaty implementation and interpretation. The Commission may also want to consider mechanisms to ensure that all treaties are honoured in the future.
>
> We were also directed to propose specific solutions, rooted in domestic and international experience.
>
> This part of our mandate is in a sense the most simple to grasp. The treaties constitute promises, and the importance of keeping promises is deeply ingrained in all of us and indeed is common to all cultures and legal systems. Thus our task is, first, to identify the promises contained in the treaties. Then we must make recommendations for fulfilling any treaty promises that remain unfulfilled. This task, though simple to describe, takes us to the heart of our mandate and to the core elements of the relationship between Aboriginal and non-Aboriginal people in Canada.
>
> We begin this volume, which concerns the restructuring of the relationship between Aboriginal and non-Aboriginal people, with an examination of the

treaties because it has been through treaty making that relationships between Aboriginal and non-Aboriginal people have traditionally been formalized. In our view, treaties are the key to the future of these relationships as well. In this volume we address substantive issues such as governance, lands and resources, and economic development. Just as those issues were addressed traditionally in the nation-to-nation context of treaties, it is in the making of new treaties and implementation of the existing treaties that these issues can be addressed in a contemporary context.[181]

Federal policy today has acknowledged that the policies of the past were harmful and that the ongoing consequences of harmful policies demand reconciliation. In recent decades, federal policies have advanced a great deal in addressing such concepts as the inherent right of self-government and reconciliation in relation to residential schools. Since the withdrawal of the 1969 White Paper, federal government policy has increasingly emphasized First Nations' distinctive cultural and societal characteristics, their political autonomy within the Canadian federation, and the need for economic development so they can be full participants in the Canadian economy. Contemporary federal policy is based on the implicit recognition that past policies promoting cultural and social assimilation of First Nations people and fostering containment on reserves are no longer legitimate.

The failure of national political processes, however, has left us all with an unfinished agenda. The Royal Commission on Aboriginal Peoples made recommendations that, if implemented, would have dramatically altered the landscape for Aboriginal peoples in Canada. Despite some positive developments flowing from the Royal Commission on Aboriginal Peoples Final Report, it is difficult to discern any consistent or sustained policy development that would address the place of Aboriginal peoples within the Canadian federation since the defeat of the Charlottetown Accord in the referendum of 1992.

Meanwhile, by contrast, the courts have been busy. The 1982 constitutional guarantee of existing Aboriginal and treaty rights has frequently been the subject of judicial consideration, and it is to the courts that we increasingly look to understand the deeper significance of that guarantee. The 1982 guarantee refers to "rights," and the idea of "rights" has perhaps taken on a prominence that

---

[181] Royal Commission on Aboriginal Peoples, *Gathering Strength*, Volume 2, p. 10.

has limited other and more co-operative ways of addressing our unfinished agenda. However, the courts have also expanded the scope of analysis by increasingly addressing existing Aboriginal and treaty rights within a framework of reconciliation. This represents an evolution from a more traditional "rights" framework which, particularly within the litigation context, leans toward an analysis that produces hierarchies of rights and processes for determining when a right exists and is given effect, or when that right is found not to exist or is lawfully infringed.

Thus, the case law on Aboriginal and treaty rights has increasingly produced broad statements on the purpose of Aboriginal and treaty rights and their more recently attained constitutional status, but has not yielded clarity or predictability on the ground. We are left with a general constitutional guarantee and an increasingly complex body of law giving effect to that guarantee as it applies to particular rights, but no comprehensive process of identifying rights and working through how they can or cannot be exercised. This case-by-case approach is extremely difficult to access, is exceedingly demanding in terms of time and resources, satisfies no one, and creates uncertainty for everyone.

It is not, of course, the role of the courts to answer every legal question, nor to set out the parameters of negotiations required to reconcile varying perspectives on rights and relationships. In other contexts, the role of the courts in Canadian society is almost marginal. Only in relation to Aboriginal and treaty rights does it appear that the Government of Canada requires the assistance of judicial decisions before establishing basic policy and, even then, it establishes policy with a grave eye to the possibility of jeopardizing its legal interests. As we noted in previous sections, Canada has a positive duty to help define the meaning of section 35 of the Constitution, not simply leave the question to the courts.

While reconciliation has an increasingly important legal meaning in the context of treaties, we do not intend in any way to build our recommendations on the idea of legal imperatives. It is expected that the treaty Parties will disagree on many of the legal dimensions of their respective treaty rights and obligations, but will still choose to enter into a process of implementation of agreed upon points and reconciliation of their differences. The task of policy development in relation to treaty implementation must be to derive appropriate direction from unfinished political talks and broad statements by the courts, and to use them as inspiration to develop processes of reconciliation that are not necessarily founded on legal duties.

First Nations Policy

For First Nations, the challenge of developing a treaty implementation policy will have some important parallels to the challenge facing the Crown. Unlike the federal government, which has an interest in developing general guidelines for authorizing discussions and negotiations, each First Nation has the right to engage in a treaty implementation process according to its own priorities. In practice, though, it will be necessary for the Federation of Saskatchewan Indian Nations, Tribal Councils and individual First Nations to develop policies to clarify their roles and responsibilities and guide them in discussions, and to develop a set of particular objectives for the process.

As part of the necessary preparations to engage in treaty implementation discussions, the Treaty First Nations will have to consider how they are going to be represented, how they will ensure accountability and whether they wish to be organized along treaty area lines or some other fashion, both in the negotiations and in their subsequent governance. In making this decision, they will have to balance their rights with practicality and efficiency to ensure a workable result.

Arriving at the necessary decisions will require internal processes to discuss First Nations' understanding of the treaties and how they can be implemented in a modern context, how they can accommodate the sovereignties of First Nations and the Crown in a new treaty relationship, who has authority to speak on behalf of First Nations in discussions with the Crown, and how those with authority will be held accountable by First Nations people for their actions. The development of a treaty implementation policy should be done openly and jointly. First Nations will have to consult with their members, in particular with Elders from whom so much guidance is always received, and with their youth, for whose benefit the process is undertaken. They will have to ensure they have a meaningful mandate from their people to guide them in making accommodations for competing interests that are an inevitable part of negotiation. The most vital element of the development of a treaty implementation policy will be the empowerment of negotiating teams to engage in meaningful give and take, with the authority to bind their principals in the resulting negotiations.

Saskatchewan Policy

Like the federal government, the Government of Saskatchewan has established policies on Treaty Land Entitlement and the negotiation of First Nations' self-government agreements. And as with the federal government, each of these policies authorizes negotiations with First Nations with the objective of reaching negotiated agreements. The Government of Saskatchewan has traditionally taken the position that it was not a Party to the treaties, since the province did not exist at the time all but one of the treaties were negotiated, and consequently has no policy framework to mandate participation by the Crown in right of Saskatchewan in discussions to examine and implement the treaties and the treaty relationship.

This position of non-participation cannot be sustained if it becomes a barrier to treaty implementation. The process of treaty implementation, therefore, includes a process of increasing the awareness and altering the behaviour of government officials, who have been advised they have no role to play in implementing the treaties. As noted in the discussion of the need for federal government policy, treaty implementation includes the making of large decisions at high levels, but also the changing of thought processes of all government officials to enable them to turn their minds to the potential impact of their work upon the rights and interests of the many Treaty First Nations.

Conclusion

This report suggests that the treaties form a framework that already embodies the reconciliation principle. Within that framework, we have identified clear economic and political interests, as well as ways in which diverse interests may be reconciled. The development of policy must respond to the following realities:

- All First Nations have a right to a satisfactory treaty relationship with the Crown.

- "Historic" treaties need to be re-evaluated within contemporary policy terms in relation to a number of issues, including:

  - Lands and Resources
  - Education
  - Child and Family Services
  - Governance
  - Hunting, trapping, fishing and gathering
  - Economic development
  - Social and community development
  - Health
  - Sound fiscal relations and accountability
  - Justice
  - Housing.

- The Crown must find a way to engage in discussions of spiritual and other aspects of the historic treaties to produce a consensus on those matters.

- The Parties must determine the relationship that the results of today's discussions will have on the existing treaties.

Arriving at workable conclusions to address these realities will require each of the treaty Parties to make sometimes difficult policy decisions to guide them in discussions, and then to provide their officials with scope to adapt those policy decisions in a manner that will allow them to arrive at conclusions acceptable to all the Parties. It will also require them to work together to define a treaty implementation agenda that will be effective, will build commitment among the Parties to act, and is principled and respectful of the Parties' divergent views, as well as those matters on which they can easily agree.

In the next, and last, section of this report, we will set out recommendations for such an agenda. While it will sometimes challenge the creativity and commitment of the Parties, it is through this process that the treaty relationship will be fulfilled and the treaties implemented.

9. FULFILLING THE COVENANT: AN AGENDA FOR ACTION

In this report, we have articulated the reasons why treaty implementation remains an unfulfilled obligation for our society. We have also identified both the challenges and opportunities for treaty implementation within a number of contexts, and raised some of the issues that will form the substantive agenda for the Parties to address when they undertake treaty implementation discussions. The genuine commitment and effort of the Parties to address these issues in a mutually respectful way will lead to the development of better political, legal, social and spiritual relationships between the treaty Parties. The preceding sections have identified why Saskatchewan is both uniquely blessed and uniquely challenged to lead the country in implementing treaties. They have discussed the spirit and intent of the treaties and the meaning of treaty implementation. They have reflected on our shared history since the treaties were made, both the positives and the negatives, and the work of the Exploratory Treaty Table.

The preceding sections have concluded that treaty implementation is not complete. They have discussed the importance of reconciliation to our shared future. In short, the preceding sections have set out the imperatives for treaty implementation to demonstrate that all of us, First Nations and non-First Nations people alike, have a profound duty to reconstruct the treaty relationship and fulfill the promise the treaties held for our shared existence.

Identifying the First Step

The first step must be for the Parties to empower their representatives to act. To date, discussions have been impeded by an unwillingness on the part of federal officials to use this forum to address questions of treaty implementation. Unfortunately, there is an equal unwillingness on the part of First Nations leaders to go beyond the established rhetoric about treaty rights and provide their representatives with a meaningful mandate that could bring the Parties back to the "spirit and intent" of the treaties in a modern context.

Defining the Agenda of Treaty Implementation

Along with a commitment to engage in serious discussions, effective treaty implementation requires a plan. While the Parties share an understanding of the importance of the treaties, and of certain fundamental principles about the treaty relationship, they also have fundamentally different perspectives on their treaty relationship and their respective treaty rights and obligations. These differences arise from the original intentions of the Parties when they made the treaties and the Parties' subsequent conduct as it relates to the treaties in a modern context. The Province, for its part, has refused to engage in any formal discussions on treaties during the past ten years and in the preparation of this report, citing the absence of responsibility.

In meetings with Elders and with government officials, we came to the conclusion that there remain "two solitudes" in regards to the deep importance of the treaties themselves. This is ironic, as the treaties represented the coming together of two peoples in order to create a mutually beneficial relationship. Overcoming this requires dialogue, and dialogue needs an agenda.

The commitment to engage in dialogue must be genuine; at the same time, the Parties' expectations for progress must be real. An important part of the treaty relationship may be an agreement for mutual respect for deeply held and opposing views. While achieving consensus on all matters may be a desirable goal, we must not set expectations so high that the consequence of doing so will be to condemn the process to inevitable failure before it can begin. There are certain matters on which the Parties must be prepared to agree to disagree, and consequently find a means to manage their opposing views in a way that reflects the principles of a brother-to-brother relationship.

For First Nations, issues such as their inherent pre-existing sovereignty, their relationship to the land through the Creator and their conviction that the treaties are nation-to-nation agreements are fundamental. We have heard this from the Elders, in the communities and from the officials of the Federation of Saskatchewan Indian Nations. For the Crown, any acknowledgment of these matters is seen as fraught with potential legal prejudice to the interests of the Crown. The Crown has concerns about the sovereignty and integrity of the Canadian state and the system of public and private property rights that is the foundation of the Canadian economy.

We know that many Treaty First Nations people are concerned that any treaty-based discussions may result in changes to their treaty rights and treaty relationships with the Crown, and that such a result would contradict the principle that the treaties are immutable and eternal. There is also a concern that treaty implementation discussions with the Crown might "domesticate" treaties which Treaty First Nations view as being international in stature. These are serious concerns, but, given the opportunity to enter into substantive treaty implementation discussions with the Crown, the Treaty First Nations need to manage these matters.

The Parties must accept that treaty implementation is necessary and important and have a shared vision for treaty implementation, as well as a shared plan to achieve that vision. This report has provided a compelling case for the assertion that treaty implementation is necessary. It has also sought to increase understanding of the spirit and intent of the treaties as well as the views of the treaty Parties today, based on nearly ten years of discussions at the Exploratory Treaty Table, numerous workshops, and background research and analysis. In addition, it has attempted to identify current barriers to treaty implementation and consequent challenges to a modern process of treaty implementation in order to allow the Parties to prepare policy options and strategies to overcome barriers through discussion and mutual accommodation.

The Office of the Treaty Commissioner can recommend ways of achieving treaty implementation and reconciliation, and will do so in the remainder of this section, but it is necessary for the Parties to initiate treaty implementation and fulfill the treaty relationship.

The Parties are capable of generating momentum for an agenda of treaty implementation, by building upon the existing consensus achieved in the exploratory phase of treaty discussions and discussions at other tables. The policy environment is ready for success.

Contemporary federal policy is based on the implicit recognition that past policies which promoted cultural and social assimilation of First Nation peoples and fostered containment on reserves are no longer legitimate. This evolution in policy has been reflected in national political developments that in 1982 inserted a constitutional guarantee of existing Aboriginal and treaty rights, and in subsequent years attempted to build upon that guarantee. However, the incomplete national political processes have left us with an unfinished agenda.

In some ways, the courts have become the drivers of policy by default. It is not the role of the courts to answer every legal question, nor to set out parameters for negotiations to reconcile varying perspectives on rights and relationships. It is not our general approach in Canadian society to arrange our affairs according to judicial decisions. The courts exist to adjudicate on those relatively rare legal matters that cannot be dealt with in any other way. We do not generally wait for the courts to tell us how to behave in our families or in business or in any other field of endeavour.

While reconciliation has an increasingly important legal meaning in the context of treaties, it is to be expected that the treaty Parties will disagree about many of the legal dimensions of their respective treaty rights and obligations. Nonetheless, there are compelling reasons for them to choose to enter into a process of reconciliation. Contemporary law and policy require that we find an honourable reconciliation between First Nations peoples and the Crown. The treaties form a framework that already embodies the reconciliation principle, a conclusion the courts have embraced and the Parties would accept as a general principle. Reconciliation under the treaties is an idea that must address at least three disparate but related subjects:

- First, the very act of entering into the treaties was one that reconciled certain differences of the Parties and gave them a shared future characterized by mutual respect, mutual recognition and mutual advantage.

- Second, achieving an understanding of the broader spirit and intent of the mutual promises of the treaties requires a reconciliation of the Parties' understandings as they existed at the time the treaties were made. Those understandings must guide, but not enslave, the Parties as they define their contemporary relationship.

- Third, where there are variances between the treaty Parties about the contemporary meaning and force of the treaties, an ongoing reconciliation of their various positions and understandings is required, but always within the framework of mutual respect, mutual recognition and mutual advantage.

A plan to guide any collective endeavour needs to contain certain elements: a vision of an ideal state, a statement of the mission of those responsible for achieving the vision, a set of principles to guide how the mission will be undertaken, a set of operational guidelines and perspectives, a set of goals to define the specific outcomes that need to be achieved, a plan of action, and a system of evaluation and accountability to achieve the goals. This is the framework used to organize the recommendations which follow.

Recommendation 1 – Vision

The vision for treaty implementation is that the treaties find their rightful place in the Canadian state and Treaty First Nations find their rightful place in Canadian society.

Recommendation 2 – Mission

The mission for treaty implementation is to implement the treaties and the treaty relationship in a way that respects their spirit and intent, and brings certainty and clarity in a modern context.

Recommendation 3 – Principles

Treaty implementation is to be based upon the following foundational principles, which direct and govern the interaction between the Parties:

a) Treaty making incorporated the customs of the respective Parties and created a fundamental political relationship between Treaty First Nations and the Crown. Treaties gave shape to this relationship, creating obligations and expectations on both sides.

b) The treaty relationship is perpetual and unalterable.

c) The treaties are political agreements that are properly dealt with in a political forum.

d) The treaty relationship is one in which the Parties expect to resolve differences through mutual discussion and decision.

e) The treaty making process between the Parties involved the exchange of solemn promises, based on respect for the spiritual and traditional values of the other. The Crown and Treaty First Nations entered into the agreements freely and of their own accord as the best possible means of advancing their respective interests.

f) The treaty relationship acknowledges the solemnity of the treaties.

g) The treaty relationship embodies mutual benefit, mutual respect, reciprocity and mutual responsibility.

h) Treaty implementation is a shared responsibility.

i) The act of treaty making was indicative of mutual recognition of the authority vested in the Treaty Commissioners on behalf of the Crown and in the Chiefs and Headmen on behalf of their First Nations to enter into treaties.

j) In entering into these agreements, both the representatives of the Crown and the Treaty First Nations recognized each other's authority and capacity to enter into treaties on behalf of their respective people.

k) The treaty making process contains within it the treaty principle of maintaining the honour of the Crown and the honour of Treaty First Nations in maintaining the treaty relationship. Equally important was the conduct and behaviour of the Parties to honour and respect the commitments made in treaties.

l) The treaty relationship embodies the honour of the Crown and the honour of the Treaty First Nations and supports the trust-like, non-adversarial, brother-to-brother relationship.

m) The treaty making process was a means of building lasting and meaningful alliances between the Parties that would foster the future well-being of the people they represented.

n) The treaties were foundational agreements entered into to provide the Parties with the means of achieving survival and stability, anchored on the principle of mutual benefit.

o) The treaties were designed to provide equal opportunity between First Nations and newcomers.

p) The treaties were designed to provide the First Nations with the education required to integrate them into the economy of the newcomers; they were not designed to assimilate them culturally, linguistically or spiritually.

q) The treaties were to provide for peace and good order between the Parties and among the First Nations.

r) The relationship between the Treaty First Nations and the Crown is one in which the Parties have both benefits and responsibilities with respect to one another. The treaties created mutual obligations that were to be respected by the Parties.

s) The Parties share a common commitment to reinvigorate the treaty relationship and to build on their partnership to address the well-being of both Parties in a respectful and supportive way.

t) Canada and Treaty First Nations can enter into arrangements whereby Treaty First Nations exercise jurisdiction and governance over their lands and people, building upon the foundation of their treaty relationship with Canada. These agreements should not alter the treaties; rather they should implement the treaty partnership in a contemporary way while respecting the principles of treaty making.

u) The Parties recognize that the participation of the Government of Saskatchewan is required for there to be significant progress on the implementation of Treaty First Nations' jurisdiction and governance within Saskatchewan, and they believe that the principles of the treaty relationship are beneficial for all people in Saskatchewan.

Recommendation 4 – Goals

> The Parties adopt the following four goals for treaty implementation in Saskatchewan:

> Goal 1 – Political
> > That the Parties renew the treaty relationship.

> Goal 2 – Legal
> > That Canada and First Nations give meaning and content in a Saskatchewan context to section 35 of the *Constitution Act, 1982* with a view to bringing certainty and clarity to the promises of the past.

> Goal 3 – Socio-economic
> > That First Nations people achieve socio-economic parity with other Canadians.

> Goal 4 – Spiritual
> > That the Parties fulfill their covenant by coming to agreement on a common understanding of the spirit and intent of the treaties in a modern context.

These goals are, in effect, the distillation of what the Office of the Treaty Commissioner has heard through this process and over the past ten years. For the Crown, it is time to apply the creativity, knowledge and intelligence of all those government officials who genuinely desire to improve the relationship between the Crown and First Nations. It is time to accept that a new relationship must be built upon honesty, frankness about the mistakes of the past and a solemn conviction not to repeat them in future. It is also time to accept that any enterprise as extensive and demanding of creativity as implementing the treaties and fulfilling the treaty relationship entails some risk; while risk can be managed, it cannot be eliminated. For the Treaty First Nations, it is time to embrace the Canadian federation as their home, where they can live with pride, dignity and prosperity.

The Office of the Treaty Commissioner regards the objectives of treaty implementation in terms of the original spirit and intent of the treaties themselves, as applied to the contemporary circumstances of the treaty Parties.

Recommendation 5 – Objectives

The Parties adopt the following objectives for treaty implementation in Saskatchewan.

- To implement the Treaty First Nations' right to livelihood.

- To fundamentally restructure the relationship between the Parties.

- To reconcile the Parties from political, legal, socio-economic and spiritual perspectives.

- To revitalize the treaty relationship.

- To recognize that the treaty relationship is perpetual and unalterable in its principles.

- To reverse the damage done by the non-implementation of the spirit and intent of the treaties.

- To reverse the damage done by the assimilation policy inherent in the *Indian Act*.

- To provide the Treaty First Nations with equality of opportunity.

- To recognize that equality of benefit may require differential treatment.

- To ensure that the Treaty First Nations have healthy families and communities.

- To ensure that the Treaty First Nations create economic development and diversification opportunities.

- To clarify the respective jurisdictions of the Parties.

- To establish certainty in the treaty relationship.

- To implement the Treaty First Nations' right of governance.

- To ensure there is accountability by both Parties in a brother-to-brother relationship.

Recommendation 6 – Operational Guidelines and Perspectives

The Parties adopt the following operational guidelines and perspectives for treaty implementation in Saskatchewan.

- That the brother-to-brother treaty relationship implies a fundamentally political relationship that can only be revitalized at the political level, through a political commitment to fulfill the Parties' obligations to the treaties in a modern context.

- That the spirit and intent of treaty implementation has not been achieved.

- That the implementation strategies of the past have provided many important lessons, and have provided a greater common understanding upon which the Parties can build.

- That the modern context is vastly different from the time when the treaties were made.

- That the modern context, in part, means bringing certainty and clarity to the rights and obligations of each party in the treaty relationship.

- That the largely unproductive, frustrating and stalled treaty implementation strategies of the past are damaging to First Nations people and indeed to all Canadians.

- That the principles that underlie the *Indian Act* are the antithesis of the principles that underlie treaty implementation.

- That the past has been a problem, but it is time to turn the page on the past and move on to revitalize the treaty relationship.

- That we now have a greater legal understanding of the treaty relationship upon which the Parties can build.

- That the treaty relationship is a trust relationship based on a non-adversarial brother-to-brother relationship that must proceed on an interest-based approach.

- That accountability by both Parties is one of the salient features of the brother-to-brother relationship in a modern context.

- That treaty implementation is a developmental and incremental process that must proceed with urgency while remaining realistic and conscious of the largely sequential and iterative nature of such a process.

- That it is time for the exploratory process to end and discussions to begin to explicitly address the need to implement the treaties and fulfill the treaty relationship, while at the same time identifying new avenues for reaching a shared understanding of the principles that will take the discussions forward.

These operational guidelines and perspectives provide a number of starting points or baselines for future work. Although it is not absolutely necessary to agree on all aspects of these guidelines and perspectives, the Parties should be able to work through them quickly and adopt them as a foundation for the plan of action that follows.

A Plan of Action

To achieve the goals of treaty implementation and the vision described above, it is necessary to begin fulfilling the covenant, to revitalize the treaty relationship, to develop a treaty implementation process and to start building upon a contemporary understanding of the spirit and intent of the treaties. These efforts can build upon:

- The work at the Exploratory Treaty Table.
- The Agreement-in-Principle and the Tripartite-Agreement-in-Principle discussions.
- The years of work by the Royal Commission on Aboriginal Peoples.
- The summary that encompasses the body of this report.
- The input provided by people in the many discussions held by the Office of the Treaty Commissioner during preparation of this report.

Building on the accomplishments of the past, the Parties must develop a plan of action that leads to the accomplishment of the Vision, Mission, Principles, Goals, and Objectives, as based on the Operational Guidelines and Perspectives. The recommended plan of action features the following five strategic initiatives:

Strategic Initiative 1 – Acknowledgment of the Importance of Treaties, Treaty Implementation and First Nations Culture

This strategic initiative represents both the first outcome of the treaty implementation process and the Parties' commitment to recognizing their treaty obligations and revitalizing the treaty implementation process. It is intended to be a noncontroversial, high profile, inspirational and political commitment to the treaties and treaty implementation process.

Strategic Initiative 2 – Structures and Mechanisms

The second initiative is designed to establish the structures and mechanisms needed for the ongoing efforts intended to achieve treaty implementation. These structures and mechanisms serve to:

- Establish a forum for discussion – the Table for Treaty Implementation.
- Define the role for Saskatchewan.
- Identify a senior representative from all Parties.
- Establish powerful internal decision making and capacity building processes within each of the Parties.
- Re-mandate an Office of the Treaty Commissioner whose role, among other things, is to advocate for treaties, facilitate discussions, monitor progress and hold the Parties accountable.

Strategic Initiative 3 – Opportunities for Early Progress

In this initiative, three high priority areas on which the Parties should focus their first efforts are identified: education, child and family services and the Dakota/Lakota adhesion.

Strategic Initiative 4 – Treaty Implementation Framework Agreement

The fourth initiative outlines five components for an overall Treaty Implementation Framework Agreement, which would set out the general areas for long-term action by the Parties. The five components are: adopting a strategic plan, bringing meaning to section 35 of the Constitution, working toward socio-economic parity, addressing self-government and sharing responsibility.

Strategic Initiative 5 – Accountability

This strategic initiative addresses the need for accountability of the treaty implementation process to First Nations people and all Canadian citizens. It is recommended that the Parties establish an evaluation and accountability plan which focuses on outcomes, requires reporting to the Parties and their legislative assemblies, and mandates the Office of the Treaty Commissioner to publicly report on progress.

The following pages elaborate on each of these strategic initiatives.

Strategic Initiative 1: Acknowledgment of the Importance of Treaties, Treaty Implementation and First Nations Culture

The first component of the plan of action is an acknowledgment by the Parties of the importance of the treaties to the future of Canada. The constitutional context exists through the recognition and affirmation of existing treaty rights, but the Government of Canada has relied on the courts to require it to act. It has sent officials to the various exploratory tables without a mandate, or at least without a mandate that has an opportunity to build toward a solution. As we learned from our discussions with the federal officials, there is a contradiction between their responsibility for the administration of the *Indian Act* and a policy stance that would honour the spirit and intent of treaties.

Although at the political level First Nations have broadly accepted the treaties as foundational for the future, they have not yet organized themselves adequately for treaty implementation discussions. They have not yet created the necessary structures to accomplish their objectives, they have not communicated with their communities about objectives for treaty implementation, and they have not sought a meaningful mandate from their citizens to guide discussions. Most importantly, they have not developed a sufficient understanding of what, in practice, they wish to be the outcome of the treaty implementation process.

The treaty implementation plan of action requires both Parties to clearly articulate their political commitment to the treaties in a substantive, meaningful, realistic and concrete way.

Recommendation 7 – Obligation to Treaties and the Treaty Relationship

The Parties sign a Joint Declaration on the treaty relationship, which would acknowledge that the treaties created an obligation on both Parties to maintain a treaty relationship between the Crown and First Nations people, and that the treaty relationship requires a continuing dialogue between the First Nations and Canada in order to address differences in treaty interpretation and implementation. The signatories to this Joint Declaration should be the Crown as represented by the Governor General of Canada and the First Nations as represented by the Chief of the Federation of Saskatchewan Indian Nations.

Recommendation 8 – Shared Responsibility

The Parties make a joint declaration on their shared responsibility for treaty implementation, either as part of the Joint Declaration on the treaty relationship or separately signed as a supplement to it.

Recommendation 9 – Affirmation of First Nations People

The Parties and Saskatchewan prepare a formal joint statement describing, affirming and acknowledging the place of the cultural, linguistic and spiritual traditions of the First Nations in Saskatchewan, and prepare an action plan to secure their rightful place in modern Canadian society. Elders must have a prominent role in the development of this statement.

Strategic Initiative 2: Structures and Mechanisms

To meet their goals, the Parties will need to establish the structures, mechanisms and resources needed to give meaning to their treaty implementation commitment and put that commitment into operation. Over the years, there have been many structures and mechanisms aimed at providing a forum for addressing First Nations socio-economic conditions and treaty issues. These include the Indian Claims Commission, treaty renovation, Treaty Land Entitlement negotiations and the Treaty Land Entitlement Framework Agreement, the Office of the Treaty Commissioner, the Exploratory Treaty Table, the Governance and Fiscal Relations negotiations, and the Indian Residential Schools

Agreement. It is fair to ask, though, whether these structures and mechanisms are articulated clearly enough and sufficiently empowered by the Parties to provide an opportunity for finding a solution or whether new structures and mechanisms need to be developed. Some effort will have to go into the design, mandating and resourcing of new structures and mechanisms in order for them to be effective. As well, accountability systems will need to be in place to ensure adequate oversight of the discussions and encourage success.

i. Structuring the Discussions

While it is up to the Parties to design a structure for discussions that will encourage effective negotiations and lead to implementation of the treaties and fulfillment of the treaty relationship, we wish to provide the Parties with recommendations we believe could be effective.

Recommendation 10 – Table for Treaty Implementation

The Parties establish a Table for Treaty Implementation that oversees treaty discussions in Saskatchewan.

This would include the previous work of the Exploratory Treaty Table, the Governance and Fiscal Relations Table and the Common Table. Membership of the Table for Treaty Implementation would include representatives of the Crown (including Canada and Saskatchewan), the Federation of Saskatchewan Indian Nations, the Office of the Treaty Commissioner and Treaty First Nations Elders. The purpose of the Table for Treaty Implementation would be to coordinate, provide leadership and act as a clearing house for treaty implementation discussions related to treaties in Saskatchewan.

Recommendation 11 – Role for Saskatchewan

The Parties come to agreement between themselves and with the Government of Saskatchewan on the role of the provincial government in treaty implementation discussions.

As the Crown signed the treaties as a single party, the best way to respect the bilateral nature of the treaties may be for the Government of Saskatchewan to be represented along with the Government of Canada as a single delegation representing the Crown. However, to ensure that the divergent interests of the federal and provincial governments can be addressed and resolved, there would need to be a separate bi-lateral federal-provincial table to clarify respective roles and responsibilities and come to an agreement on how the Crown delegation will present its views. If this "parallel bilateral" arrangement was unacceptable to one of the Parties, the Parties could establish a bilateral treaty implementation table and a tripartite treaty relationship table, and assign different issues to the different tables depending on whether they could be resolved bilaterally between the Federation of Saskatchewan Indian Nations and the Government of Canada or whether they require the agreement of the Government of Saskatchewan as well.

Recommendation 12 – Senior Representatives

The Parties and Saskatchewan each appoint a senior representative to lead the treaty implementation process.

In each case, this representative would be responsible to the Chief or Minister for managing discussions on treaty implementation and fulfillment of the treaty relationship in Saskatchewan. As part of their mandate, senior representatives would also be responsible for ensuring regular, adequate consultation with First Nations people and other Canadians.

To be effective all three Parties need to create better, more focused and higher-profile internal processes to ensure representatives have a clear and meaningful mandate. In this way, they can enter discussions confident that their political masters are committed to implementing the decisions made at the table.

Recommendation 13 – Canada – Policy Processes

The Government of Canada create a Cabinet Committee on Treaty Implementation and a committee of senior officials, including central agency officials, to develop a "treaty implementation policy" and mandate that will guide their representatives during treaty implementation discussions and monitor progress.

Recommendation 14 – Canada – Treaty Education

The Government of Canada engage in a process of education for government officials to improve their understanding of their role in facilitating treaty implementation.

Recommendation 15 – Saskatchewan – Policy Processes

The Government of Saskatchewan create a Cabinet Committee on Treaty Implementation and a committee of senior officials, including central agency officials, to develop a "treaty implementation policy" and mandate that will guide their representatives during treaty implementation discussions and monitor progress.

Recommendation 16 – Saskatchewan – Treaty Education

The Government of Saskatchewan engage in a process of education for government officials to improve their understanding of their role in facilitating treaty implementation.

Recommendation 17 – Federation of Saskatchewan Indian Nations – Policy Processes

The Federation of Saskatchewan Indian Nations create a Treaty Implementation Commission to develop a "treaty implementation policy" and mandate that will guide their representatives during treaty implementation discussions and monitor progress.

Recommendation 18 – Federation of Saskatchewan Indian Nations – Treaty Education

The Federation of Saskatchewan Indian Nations engage in a process of education for their officials to improve their understanding of their role in facilitating treaty implementation.

ii. Role of the Treaty Commissioner

The existing mandate of the Office of the Treaty Commissioner comes to an end in the spring of 2007, after a decade of solid accomplishments in support of an improved understanding of the treaties and the requirements of treaty implementation.

Recommendation 19 – Office of the Treaty Commissioner

The Parties re-mandate the Office of the Treaty Commissioner as part of a new "made-in-Saskatchewan" treaty implementation process. This Office should be empowered to:

a) Be a neutral and independent office.

b) Advocate for the treaties, the treaty relationship and treaty implementation.

c) Facilitate discussions at the Table for Treaty Implementation.

d) Establish, foster and participate in treaty celebrations, commemorations and other acts of renewal.

e) Enhance public education and understanding of treaties, the treaty relationship and treaty implementation.

f) Foster treaty implementation by engaging the Parties in discussions aimed at resolving different views on the following matters as well as others the Parties may identify: education; child welfare; shelter; health; justice; treaty annuities; hunting, fishing, trapping and gathering; and lands and resources.

g) Conduct research and prepare reports, which will contribute to the resolution of treaty implementation and other matters within its mandate.

h) Establish and implement dispute resolution mechanisms.

i) Monitor and audit agreements and the independent actions of the Parties with respect to the treaties, the treaty relationship and treaty implementation.

j) Make recommendations to the Parties.

With a renewed mandate, the Office of the Treaty Commissioner will play an important role in the treaty implementation process. The most important tasks would be to facilitate discussions between the Parties, identify shared principles on which to base the treaty relationship, define treaty implementation in the modern context, monitor the plan of action for treaty implementation, identify areas of agreement and matters on which the Parties have differing interpretations of the treaties, and report on progress. The Office of the Treaty Commissioner would stand outside the fray of disputes between the Parties, but retain an intense interest in the reconciliation of any differences. At the same time it would offer its services to remind the Parties of the principles the treaties embody.

In another sense, the Office of the Treaty Commissioner may be seen as an advocate – not an advocate for one position or another, but an advocate for the treaty relationship and the principles of honourable and respectful dealing. The Office of the Treaty Commissioner should also support public education and advocacy for treaty implementation. The Parties also need to consider how to increase and institutionalize a role for Elders in treaty implementation discussions.

Disputes and differences will arise. It would not be the role of the Office of the Treaty Commissioner to prevent the Parties from having disagreements, nor would that be possible. It would, however, be the role of the Office to continue to remind the Parties of the imperative of reconciliation and to offer practical advice on ways to resolve disagreements. As processes are renewed, the Office of the Treaty Commissioner should provide additional support through independent research and analysis of treaty issues, mediation of conflicts, public education, public advocacy and independent reporting to the Parties and the public on progress being made in achieving the goals of treaty implementation.

Strategic Initiative 3: Opportunities for Early Progress

To ensure they build momentum toward treaty implementation and fulfillment of the treaty relationship, the Parties must look for opportunities to make early progress and achieve initial successes. We see three potential opportunities for early success. The first is in the area of education, where a significant body of work generated at both the Exploratory Treaty Table and the Governance and Fiscal Relations Table already exists.

Recommendation 20 – Education Action Plan

The Parties and Saskatchewan develop an action plan for:

a) Strengthening First Nations control of First Nations education.

b) Enhancing the quality of First Nations education by:

- The establishment of shared standards for the education of First Nations children in both First Nations and provincial education systems.

- The expansion of support systems at primary, secondary and tertiary levels.

- The support of innovative development in mathematics and science education, distance learning, special education, gifted education, alternative education and accountability.

Recommendation 21 – Child and Family Services System

The Parties and Saskatchewan establish a province-wide First Nations child and family services system that would operate both on and off reserves and address the need for mutual recognition of standards and interjurisdictional protocols.

Recommendation 22 – Dakota/Lakota Adhesion Claim

The Parties focus their attention on resolving the matter of the Dakota/Lakota adhesion to treaty.

Strategic Initiative 4: Treaty Implementation Framework Agreement

For many years, the Parties have been working to address several specific treaty issues within the original mandates of the Office of the Treaty Commissioner and the Exploratory Treaty Table, and to build a foundation for further progress. In reflecting on the progress of the past, the work of the *Statement of Treaty Issues* and the Treaty Land Entitlement Framework Agreement stand out as significant milestones. The Treaty Land Entitlement Framework Agreement provided an overall framework for the detailed implementation that followed. The framework concept can also be applied to overall treaty implementation. It has been discussed by the Parties and holds the promise of addressing issues at a larger conceptual level and facilitating more detailed discussions, clarifications and administration.

Recommendation 23 – Treaty Implementation Framework Agreement

The Parties work toward a Treaty Implementation Framework Agreement, which would be an over-arching, comprehensive umbrella agreement with the following components:

a) As a starting point for discussion, the Parties agree upon a vision, a mission, principles, goals for treaty implementation and operational guidelines and perspectives (such as those set out in recommendations 1 through 6).

b) That section 35 of the *Constitution Act, 1982* be given content and meaning in a Saskatchewan context through a negotiated effort to define and implement the inherent and treaty rights of First Nations peoples in Saskatchewan.

- That the Parties to the treaties have an agreed-upon working definition of the content of treaty rights in a modern, Saskatchewan-specific context that allows for effective implementation of the treaties.

- That outstanding land claims issues are resolved through negotiation.

- That agreements are reached to allow for the orderly exercise of First Nations' rights to hunt, fish, trap and gather renewable resources.

- That First Nations' access to non-renewable resources and revenues from resource exploitation are settled through negotiation.

- That First Nations' right to govern themselves is recognized as an inherent right contained within section 35 of the Constitution.

- That the Parties create improved processes to address past injustices.

- That public education programs be established to increase awareness of the treaties. These programs should strive to emphasize the treaty relationship in all its complexity, but with a strong emphasis on the positive contribution of the treaties to a harmonious Canadian society.

c) That First Nations peoples achieve socio-economic parity with other Canadians.

- That First Nations peoples have access to primary, secondary and post-secondary education that is both culturally relevant and adequate to ensure their full participation in modern Canadian society.

- That First Nations peoples are provided with the support needed to build self-sustaining economies on First Nations lands and to participate in the provincial economy as employers, partners and employees.

- That the over-representation of the First Nations people in the justice system and their reliance on social assistance are addressed by equal access to education, health and employment.

d) That the right of First Nations to be self-governing is realized within the Canadian federation.

- That First Nations have the jurisdiction and authority to govern their members on matters internal to those Nations, integral to their cultures, and essential to their operation as a government.

- That First Nations have institutions of governance and administration that are recognized by their members/citizens as culturally appropriate, legitimate and effective.

- That First Nations governments have the capacity to effectively operate their institutions and exercise their jurisdictions.

- That First Nations governments are accountable to their members/citizens for their decisions.

e) That responsibility for ensuring a mutually respectful, brother-to-brother relationship be shared by the treaty Parties.

- That the *Indian Act* relationship of legislated dependency is replaced by an intergovernmental relationship of equals.

- That the Parties and Saskatchewan involved in the brother-to-brother relationship are accountable to one another and their electorates for the effective implementation and ongoing management of the relationship.

- That the Parties and Saskatchewan work to include First Nations in their intergovernmental relations, so that federal-provincial-First Nations relations become normalized and institutionalized, while at the same time remaining effective and efficient.

- That intergovernmental mechanisms for policy coordination, mutual recognition of laws and standards, and dispute avoidance and resolution are established.

- That all governments involved in the brother-to-brother relationship are committed to providing one another with advance notice of a policy or program change that will likely have a significant impact on the policies and programs of other governments, and consult with potentially affected governments on the implementation of these changes.

- That the Crown's fiduciary obligation to First Nations peoples is reduced and modified incrementally, as is appropriate in response to First Nations' exercise of self-government.

- That certainty and clarity on the meaning of treaties and the treaty relationship in a modern context are achieved.

During discussions of this nature, success relies to a great extent on the creation of relationships of trust. Given the history of Crown-First Nations relations, there is great distrust between the Parties that will have to be overcome to achieve treaty implementation. The Parties must be conscious of this reality. An important element of the action plan must be actions that build trust between the officials of each Party.

Strategic Initiative 5: Accountability

During discussions and meetings with communities and officials, a recurring theme was the call for accountability – accountability of the federal government to live up to the spirit and intent of the treaties; accountability of the Parties to come to the table prepared and with an end point in mind; accountability for the various representatives at the table to demonstrate some success; accountability of First Nations leadership to adhere more closely to democratic principles of good government; accountability of members of the bureaucracies in the federal government, the Federation of Saskatchewan Indian Nations and the provincial government to become more aware of the treaties and their impact on program design and delivery in all areas.

Recommendation 24 – Accountability Characteristics

The Parties and Saskatchewan design an evaluation and accountability plan for treaty implementation. The characteristics of the accountability plan include:

- A focus on the outcomes of the treaty implementation process.

- Reporting of outcomes by the Parties to the other Parties, to the Office of the Treaty Commissioner and to the public through the Parliament of Canada, the Federation of Saskatchewan Indian Nations legislative assembly and the Saskatchewan legislature.

- A public report of outcomes on progress of treaty implementation by the Office of the Treaty Commissioner to the Parties and Saskatchewan.

Conclusion

These recommendations cannot all be implemented at once, and certainly not instantly. A timeline is necessary to guide the Parties and allow for an evaluation of their progress in treaty implementation discussions.

Recommendation 25 – Funding Agreement

That the Government of Canada and the Federation of Saskatchewan Indian Nations work in cooperation to establish a joint five year work plan and the required funding arrangements to allow the Parties to fully engage in the recommended comprehensive treaty implementation process.

Recommendation 26 – Implementation

The Parties and Saskatchewan implement the recommendations in this document between now and March 2012, according to the following timeline:

April 2007 – the Parties agree to re-establish a mandate for the Office of the Treaty Commissioner (recommendation 19).

June 2007 – the Parties and Saskatchewan begin creating internal processes to develop "treaty implementation policies" and mandates for treaty implementation discussions, and establish capacity building processes to prepare for treaty implementation (recommendations 10 to 18).

January 2008 – the Governor General of Canada and the Chief of the Federation of Saskatchewan Indian Nations sign a Joint Declaration affirming their mutual commitment to the treaty relationship, to sharing responsibility and to revitalizing First Nations communities and cultures (recommendations 7-9).

- *The Parties and Saskatchewan come to an agreement clarifying the role of the Government of Saskatchewan in treaty implementation discussions (recommendation 11).*

- *The Parties each appoint a senior representative to lead treaty implementation discussions on their behalf (recommendation 12).*

September 2008 – the Parties and Saskatchewan begin the establishment of an education action plan (recommendation 20).

January 2009 – the Parties resolve the Dakota/Lakota adhesion to treaty (recommendation 22).

September 2009 – the Parties and the Government of Saskatchewan begin the establishment of the province-wide First Nations child and family services system (recommendation 21).

March 2010 – the Parties sign a Treaty Implementation Framework Agreement (recommendation 23).

- *The Parties and the Government of Saskatchewan sign an evaluation and accountability plan for treaty implementation.*

March 2012 – the first phase of the treaty implementation is completed.

As we have seen, shortly after the making of the earliest treaties in what is now Saskatchewan, the treaty relationship quickly deteriorated into a paternalistic relationship based on the colonial culture of the day, under which First Nations were subjugated by government decisions and policy. That was not the intent of either of the treaty Parties. For the relationship to change, the Parties will need to sit down without recriminations, without blame and with the original spirit of mutual respect and sharing. In doing so, the Parties should develop common understandings so as to return to the original spirit and intent of the treaties. They also need to develop a shared commitment to acknowledge the role of treaties; a plan for treaty implementation; and a shared set of structures, mechanisms and resources that will favour success rather than failure.

At the beginning of this report, we noted it would identify the many reasons why, as a Canadian society, we must act to implement the treaties; that it would define what treaty implementation would be, set out an agenda and a plan of action for treaty implementation, propose processes to achieve the plan and identify short-term achievable results to generate momentum for full implementation of the treaties. We have addressed all of these tasks.

The treaties created a relationship with rights and obligations on both sides. We are all treaty people. The reality is that the treaties have not been implemented as they ought to have been. Let us accept that fact and move on in the name of justice and honour to embrace the treaty relationship, implement the treaties and fulfill the covenant in the name of the children yet to come.

"My dream is that our peoples will one day be clearly recognized as Nations."[182]

The late Elder Gordon Oakes, 1997.

"Today you see many things are being controlled for us. This should never have happened, it should have been followed as the Elders have said in the way that the treaties were concluded."[183]

The late Elder Norman Sunchild, 1997.

---

[182] The late Elder Gordon Oakes, Nekaneet First Nation, Treaty 4, Treaty Elders Forum, 1997.
[183] The late Elder Norman Sunchild, Thunderchild First Nation, Treaty 6, Treaty Elders Forum, 1997.

BIBLIOGRAPHY

Books and Articles

"Top 100: Saskatchewan's Top 100 Companies of 2006," *Saskatchewan Business Magazine*, Vol. 27, issue 4 (Aug. 2006): 17-25.

Anaya, James, *Indigenous Peoples and International Law* (Oxford: Oxford University Press, 1996).

Black, Henry Campbell, *Black's Law Dictionary* (St. Paul, MN: West Publishing, 1979).

Borrows, John, "The Trickster: Integral to a Distinctive Culture," (1997) *Constitutional Forum* 29.

Brighton, Robert, *Grateful Prey: Rock Cree Human-Animal Relations* (Berkeley: University of California Press, 1993).

Cardinal, Harold and Walter Hildebrandt, *Treaty Elders of Saskatchewan* (Calgary: University of Calgary Press, 2000).

Carter, Sarah, *Lost Harvests: Prairie Indian Reserve Farmers and Government Policy*, (Montreal and Kingston: McGill University Press, 1990).

Christensen, Deanna, *Ahtahkakoop* (Shell Lake: Ahtahkakoop Publishing, 2000).

Havard, Gilles, *The Great Peace of Montreal of 1701* (Montreal: McGill-Queen's University Press, 2001).

Hawkes, David C., "Indigenous Peoples: Self-Government and Intergovernmental Relations," *International Social Science Journal* Volume 53, issue 167 (March 2001), 153.

Howe, Eric, "Saskatchewan with an Aboriginal Majority; Education and Entrepreneurship" *SIPP Public Policy Paper 44* (Regina: Saskatchewan Institute of Public Policy, 2006).

Isaac, Thomas. *Aboriginal Law: Commentary Case and Materials* (3rd Edition) (Saskatoon: Purich Publishing, 2004).

Miller, J.R., *Shingwauk's Vision* (Toronto: University of Toronto Press, 1996).

-----, *Skyscrapers Hide the Heavens: A History of Indian-White Relations in Canada* (3rd edition) (Toronto: University of Toronto Press, 2000).

-----, *Reflections on Native-Newcomer Relations: Selected Essays* (Toronto: University of Toronto Press, 2004).

Milloy, J.S., *A National Crime: The Canadian Government and the Residential School System, 1879 to 1986* (Winnipeg: University of Manitoba Press, 1999).

Morris, Alexander. *The Treaties of Canada with Indians of Manitoba and the North-West Territories* (Toronto: Belfords, Clark and co, 1880).

Opekokew, Delia and Pratt, Alan, "The Treaty Right to Education in Saskatchewan" (1992), 12 *Windsor Yearbook of Access to Justice* 3.

O'Reilly-Scanlon, Kathleen, Crowe, Kristine, and Weenie, Angela, "Pathways to Understanding: Wâhkôhtowin as a research methodology," (2004) 39 *McGill Journal of Education* 1.

Oxford University Press, *The Concise Oxford Dictionary of Current English* (Oxford; Oxford University Press, 1982).

Peach, Ian and Rasmussen, Merrilee, "Federalism and the First Nations: Making Space for First Nations Self-Determination in the Federal Inherent Right Policy", paper presented to the conference, "First Nations, First Thoughts", Centre for Canadian Studies, University of Edinburgh, May 2005; http://www.cst.ed.ac.uk/2005conference/papers/Peach_Rasmussen_paper.pdf, accessed October 10, 2005.

Penikett, Tony, *Reconciliation: First Nations Treaty Making in British Columbia* (Vancouver: Douglas & McIntyre, 2006).

Pettipas, Katherine, *Severing the Ties that Bind: Government Repression of Indigenous Religious Ceremonies on the Prairies* (Winnipeg: University of Manitoba Press, 1994).

Price, Richard, *Legacy: Indian Treaty Relationships* (Edmonton: Plains Publishing, 1991).

Ray, Arthur J, Jim Miller, and Frank Tough, *Bounty and Benevolence* (Montreal & Kingston: McGill-Queen's University Press, 2000).

St. Germain, Jill, "'Feed or Fight': Rationing the Sioux and the Cree, 1868-1885," *Native Studies Review*, 16, no. 1 (2005): 71.

Slattery, Brian, "Understanding Aboriginal Rights" (1987), 66 *Canadian Bar Review* 727.

-----, "Making Sense of Aboriginal Rights" (2000), 79 *Canadian Bar Review* 196.

Tobias, John L., "Protection, Civilization, Assimilation: An Outline History of Canada's Indian Policy," in J. R. Miller, ed., *Sweet Promises: A Reader on Indian-White Relations in Canada* (Toronto: University of Toronto Press, 1991), 139-40.

Weaver, Sally, *Making Canadian Indian Policy: The Hidden Agenda, 1968-70* (Toronto: University of Toronto Press, 1981).

Unpublished Works

Borrows, John, "Let Obligations Be Done" in Hamar Foster, Heather Raven and Jeremy Webber, eds., *The Calder Case* (Vancouver: UBC Press, 2006) forthcoming.

Jobin, Shalene, *Guiding Philosophy and Governance Model of Bent Arrow Traditional Healing Society* (M.A.I.G. thesis, University of Victoria, 2005) [unpublished] at http://66.102.7.104/search?q=cache:pjbvzcj2LwMJ:web.uvic.ca/igov/research/pdfs/Bent%2520Arrow%2520Governance-Final.pdf+miyo-wîcêhtowin&hl=en.

Leslie, John F., *Assimilation, Integration or Termination? The Development of Canadian Indian Policy, 1943-1963* (Ph.D. dissertation, Carleton University, 1999).

Pratt, Alan, "Treaties and Reconciliation: The *Marshall* Case and a Duty to Negotiate," paper prepared for the Treaty Rights Unit of the Assembly of First Nations, December, 1999.

Saskatchewan Institute of Public Policy, *Economic Benefits of Increased Aboriginal Employment*, study prepared for the Saskatchewan Department of First Nations and Métis Relations, October 2005.

-----, *Socio-Economic Conditions of First Nations People in Saskatchewan*, study prepared for the Office of the Treaty Commissioner, June, 2006 (included as Appendix 3).

Reports and Government Documents

Consensus Report on the Constitution, August 28, 1992 (the Charlottetown Accord), http://www.thecanadianencyclopedia.com/index.cfm?PgNm=TCE&Params=A1ARTA0010099, accessed December 8, 2006.

First Nations – Federal Crown Political Accord on the Recognition and Implementation of First Nations Governments, May 31, 2005, http://www.afn.ca/cmslib/general/PolAcc.pdf, accessed December 8, 2006.

Auditor General for Canada, *2003 Report of the Auditor General of Canada to the House of Commons* (Ottawa: Auditor General for Canada, 2003).

-----, 2005 Report of the Auditor General of Canada to the House of Commons (Ottawa: Auditor General for Canada, 2005).

Barsh, Russel Lawrence, *International Context of Crown-Aboriginal Treaties in Canada: Final Report* (Ottawa: Royal Commission on Aboriginal Peoples, 1994).

Canada, Treaty No. 6 (1876).

Commission on First Nations and Métis Peoples and Justice Reform, *Final Report, Volume 1: Legacy of Hope: An Agenda for Change* (Regina: Commission on First Nations and Métis Peoples and Justice Reform, 2004).

Department of Indian Affairs and Northern Development, *The Government of Canada's Approach to Implementation of the Inherent Right and the Negotiation of Aboriginal Self-Government* (Ottawa: Public Works and Government Services Canada, 1995).

-----, *Gathering Strength: Canada's Aboriginal Action Plan* (Ottawa: Minister of Public Works and Government Services Canada, 1997).

European Union, draft *Treaty Establishing a Constitution for Europe.*

Giokas, John, "The *Indian Act*: Evolution, Overview and Options for Amendment and Transition", March 22, 1995, published by Royal Commission on Aboriginal Peoples on CD-ROM *For Seven Generations* (Ottawa: 1996).

Hawthorn, H.B., ed., *A Survey of the Contemporary Indians of Canada: Economic, Political, Educational Needs and Policies* (Ottawa: Department of Indian Affairs, 1966-7).

Hueglin, Thomas O., "Exploring Concepts of Treaty Federalism: A Comparative Perspective", Research Program of the Royal Commission on Aboriginal Peoples, *For Seven Generations*. Ottawa: Libraxus CD-ROM.

Martin-McGuire, Peggy, *First Nations Land Surrenders on the Prairies 1896-1911* (Ottawa: Indian Claims Commission, 1998).

Oberle, Frank, *Treaty 8 Renovation Discussion Paper*, January 31, 1986 (unpublished).

Office of the Treaty Commissioner, *Statement of Treaty Issues: Treaties as a Bridge to the Future* (Saskatoon, Saskatchewan: October, 1998).

Office of Treaty Settlements, *Deed of Settlement – Te Rūnaunga O Ngāi Tahu and Her Majesty the Queen in Right of New Zealand, November 21, 1997* (Wellington: Office of Treaty Settlements, 1999).

Royal Commission on Aboriginal Peoples, *Gathering Strength: Final Report of the Royal Commission on Aboriginal Peoples.* (Ottawa: Queen's Printer, 1996).

Special Committee of the House of Commons on Indian Self-Government, *Report of the Special Committee of the House of Commons on Indian Self-Government* (Ottawa: Queen's Printer, 1983).

Special Joint Committee of the Senate and the House of Commons on the *Indian Act, Minutes of Proceedings and Evidence of the Special Joint Committee of the Senate and the House of Commons on the Indian Act* (Ottawa: Queen's Printer, 1947).

Standing Senate Committee on Aboriginal Peoples, *Forging New Relationships: Aboriginal Governance in Canada* (Ottawa: Queen's Printer, 2000).

Statistics Canada, "Profile of Citizenship, Immigration, Birthplace, Generation Status, Ethnic Origin, Visible Minorities and Aboriginal Peoples, for Canada, Provinces, Territories, Census Divisions and Census Subdivisions," *2001 Census of Population* (Ottawa: Statistics Canada, 2003).

Wright, Cliff, *Report and Recommendations on Treaty Land Entitlement* (Office of the Treaty Commissioner, Saskatoon; May, 1990).

Legislation

Canada, *Constitution Act*, 1867, 30 & 31 Victoria, c. 3.

Canada, *Indian Act*, R.S.C. 1985, I-5, s. 87.

Canada, *Saskatchewan Treaty Land Entitlement Act*, S.C. 1993, c. 11.

Canada, *Specific Claims Resolution Act*, S.C. 2003, c. 23.

Saskatchewan, *The Treaty Land Entitlement Implementation Act* R.S.S., c. T-20.1.

Cases

Chippewas of Sarnia Band v. Canada (2000), 51 O.R. (3d) 641 (C.A.).

Delgamuukw v. British Columbia, [1997] 3 S.C.R. 1010.

Dreaver et al. v. the King (1935), 5 C.N.L.C. 92 (Exchequer Court of Canada).

Edwards v. Canada (Attorney General) [1930] A.C. 124.

Haida Nation v. British Columbia (Minister of Forests), [2004] 3 S.C.R. 511.

Mikisew Cree First Nation v. Canada [2005] 3 S.C.R. 388.

Mitchell v. Minister of National Revenue [2001] 1 S.C.R. 911.

Ontario (Attorney General) v. Bear Island Foundation, [1991] 2 S.C.R. 570.

Paul v. British Columbia (Forest Appeals Commission), [2003] 2 S.C.R. 585.

R. v. Badger [1996] 1 S.C.R. 771.

R. v. Demers, [2004] 2 S.C.R. 489.

R. v. Horseman, [1990] 1 S.C.R. 901.

R. v. Marshall [1999] 3 S.C.R. 456.

R. v. Marshall; R. v. Bernard, [2005] 2 S.C.R. 200.

R v. Secretary of State for Foreign and Commonwealth Affairs, Ex p. Indian Association of Alberta, [1982] 1 Q.B. 892.

R. v. Sioui [1990] 1 S.C.R. 1025.

R. v. Sparrow [1990], 70 D.L.R. (4th) 385.

R. v. Van der Peet, [1996] 1 S.C.R. 507.

Reference re Secession of Quebec, [1998] 2 S.C.R. 217.

Simon v. The Queen, [1985] 2 S.C.R. 387.

APPENDIX 1. TREATY IMPLEMENTATION DISCUSSION WORKSHOPS METHODOLOGY

The Office of the Treaty Commissioner and the Exploratory Treaty Table are part of a broader "made-in-Saskatchewan" process created by the Federation of Saskatchewan Indian Nations and the Government of Canada to discuss treaties as well as First Nations governance and jurisdiction. The Treaty Table, with the coordination and facilitation of the Office of the Treaty Commissioner, produced several reports intended to inform negotiations taking place at a Governance and Fiscal Relations Table. The three parties at the Governance and Fiscal Relations Table – the Federation of Saskatchewan Indian Nations, Canada and Saskatchewan – negotiated a draft Agreement-in-Principle and Tripartite-Agreement-in-Principle in July 2003. However, as a result of a Federation of Saskatchewan Indian Nations review in 2004, self-government negotiations were suspended. At issue was a poor linkage between the governance arrangements and the treaty relationship. The parties began to consider using the Office of the Treaty Commissioner and the Treaty Table as a forum to move discussions forward.

The parties began preliminary treaty implementation discussions at the Treaty Table in the fall of 2004. In February 2005, the Office of the Treaty Commissioner suggested that the Treaty Table continue to explore the requirements and implications of treaty implementation and produce a report and recommendations. The Parties and the Office of the Treaty Commissioner agreed that the Office of the Treaty Commissioner would produce the report, independently, but with input from the Federation of Saskatchewan Indian Nations and Canada.

In a letter to the Treaty Commissioner dated July 18, 2005, the Chief of the Federation of Saskatchewan Indian Nations and the Minister of Indian Affairs stated:

> ...it is the will of the parties to direct the Office of the Treaty Commissioner to explore options for treaty implementation and to produce a report. The report could provide an in-depth analysis of

195

> concepts and principles of treaty implementation, in both the historic and modern context. It could also, to the extent possible, provide recommendations and options to the parties for future direction in the evolution of treaty policy. Subject to the will of the parties, this report could inform the further negotiation and development of the governance arrangements at the Governance and Fiscal Relations Table.

The letter went on to say:

> The Office of the Treaty Commissioner, in conjunction with the parties at the Treaty Table, can decide on appropriate formats for completing the work. ...

> The parties will commence the work by meeting with the Treaty Commissioner to frame the general questions that will guide the preparation of the report. A work plan will be created by the Treaty Commissioner...and be submitted to the parties prior to the commencement of the work.

All work related to the treaty implementation discussions flowed from instructions provided by the Minister and the Chief. A partnership approach was used to design and implement the treaty implementation discussion work plan. In meetings between the Office of the Treaty Commissioner and the Parties, several key issues were agreed upon, including the following:

- The work plan for treaty implementation discussions would be coordinated jointly between the Federation of Saskatchewan Indian Nations and the Office of the Treaty Commissioner.

- The work plan and budget would be jointly developed and administered by the Federation of Saskatchewan Indian Nations and the Office of the Treaty Commissioner.

- The Federation of Saskatchewan Indian Nations would be responsible for coordinating at least five community forums with First Nation representatives.

- The Office of the Treaty Commissioner would facilitate all community forums with First Nation representatives.

- Canada would be responsible for coordinating meetings with various federal departments.

- The Office of the Treaty Commissioner would facilitate the meetings with federal officials.

The Federation of Saskatchewan Indian Nations and Canada worked together to develop terms of reference and, with input from the Office of the Treaty Commissioner, identify the funding required to undertake the work. The terms of reference outlined the process, the roles and responsibilities of the Office of the Treaty Commissioner and the Parties, and the questions to be answered in the Treaty Implementation Report.

According to the terms of reference, the Federation of Saskatchewan Indian Nations' roles and responsibilities included the following:

• Coordinate at least five community forums and undertake any cultural protocols required to initiate treaty implementation discussions and meetings with First Nations leadership.

• Identify First Nations participants at the community forums.

• Invite the Office of the Treaty Commissioner and Canada to attend the forums.

• Review and provide comments on any reports developed by the Office of the Treaty Commissioner.

Canada's roles and responsibilities included the following:

• Coordinate meetings with various departments within the Federal Government.

• Invite the Office of the Treaty Commissioner and the Federation of Saskatchewan Indian Nations to attend the meetings.

• Review and provide comments on any reports developed by the Office of the Treaty Commissioner.

Finally, the Office of the Treaty Commissioner's roles and responsibilities included the following:

• Facilitate all community forums organized by the Federation of Saskatchewan Indian Nations.

• Develop discussion questions and appropriate public presentation to engage participants in the treaty implementation discussions.

- That discussions could include consideration of the following questions:
  - What does treaty implementation mean to the Parties?
  - Have treaties or elements of the treaties been implemented?
  - What are each Party's criteria for treaty implementation?
  - What are the mechanisms for treaty implementation?

- Work with Canada to engage federal government departments in the discussions.

- Work with Federation of Saskatchewan Indian Nations and assist with undertaking necessary cultural protocols within the First Nations community.

- Provide an interim report to the Federation of Saskatchewan Indian Nations and Canada on progress being made.

- Refer draft reports to the Exploratory Treaty Table for comments and input.

- Analyze and respond to comments from the Federation of Saskatchewan Indian Nations and Canada on the report.

- Prepare a draft final report for review and comment by the Federation of Saskatchewan Indian Nations and Canada with the objective of submitting a final report to the Parties within a specified timeframe.

Between August 2005 and March 2006, eight treaty implementation discussion workshops were held. Workshops with Treaty First Nations were organized by the Federation of Saskatchewan Indian Nations, who ensured that proper cultural protocols were followed prior to and during the discussions. Canada also played a lead role in organizing workshops with federal officials from Ottawa, Gatineau and Regina. The Office of the Treaty Commissioner developed background papers and workshop guides and provided overall facilitation.

During the first phase of the process, workshops were held with the following Treaty First Nations and Crown representatives:

- The Federation of Saskatchewan Indian Nations Youth Legislative Assembly in Yorkton in August 2005.

- Cree, Saulteaux and Nakota Elders at the Treaty 4 Gathering in Fort Qu'Appelle in September 2005.

- Senior federal officials in Gatineau, Quebec in October 2005.

- Dene, Swampy Cree and Woodland Cree in La Ronge in November 2005 from Treaties 5, 6 and 8.

- Treaty 6 Plains Cree in North Battleford in January 2006.

- The Federation of Saskatchewan Indian Nations Urban Conference in Regina in January 2006.

- The Saskatchewan Council of Senior Federal Officials in Regina in February 2006.

- Federation of Saskatchewan Indian Nations senior officials in Saskatoon in March 2006.

The first two treaty implementation discussion workshops were held based on the terms of reference and questions identified therein. Both workshops began with Federation of Saskatchewan Indian Nations officials providing background information and the Treaty Commissioner explaining the process and timeframes. Workshop participants then had an opportunity to provide their feedback.

The Elders at the Treaty 4 Gathering discussed treaties, treaty rights and the treaty relationship, but also stated they were uncertain what information the Office of the Treaty Commissioner was actually seeking. They felt the questions should be revised to be more specific. Based on this advice, the Office of the Treaty Commissioner met with the Federation of Saskatchewan Indian Nations and a small group of Elders to develop appropriate questions for use at the First Nations workshops. The following questions were developed:

- What are some of the concerns that people have about treaty rights?

- How would you make sure that treaties are being honoured and fulfilled?

- Who is responsible for fulfilling treaties? What kind of governing and funding arrangements are required?

- If the treaties were fulfilled today, how would it change the lives of First Nations people on reserve and in urban areas?

The Office of the Treaty Commissioner also worked closely with officials from Indian and Northern Affairs Canada to develop questions for federal officials to consider during their workshops. Questions included the following:

- What issues arise within your Department concerning First Nations and treaties?

- What concerns do you hear from First Nations and third parties?

- What do you need to make your role more effective?

- What are key federal interests in dealing with First Nations issues? As Canada enters into dialogue with First Nations, what federal interests and objectives should be brought to that dialogue?

The remaining workshops were conducted using these questions to guide the discussions. The Office of the Treaty Commissioner and the Federation of Saskatchewan Indian Nations also identified other needs and adjusted the work plan accordingly. It was agreed that the remaining First Nations forums would include plenary sessions, which would require overall facilitation, as well as small group discussions, which would each require a facilitator, a translator and a recorder. The Federation of Saskatchewan Indian Nations recorded the small group discussions and provided translation and transcripts to the Office of the Treaty Commissioner for use in writing the report. The Office of the Treaty Commissioner recorded the plenary discussions, which were also transcribed for use in writing the report.

During this time, the Office of the Treaty Commissioner met on several occasions with provincial officials, who declined to formally participate in the process. Provincial officials maintained their view that treaties and, therefore, treaty implementation issues were the exclusive jurisdiction of the Federal Crown. They also stated that, in the absence of a provincial policy on treaties, they did not have a mandate to engage in any treaty implementation discussions or present their views.

Based on the information, views, concerns and recommendations received from First Nations and federal government workshop participants, as well as case law and published reports, including both legal and academic analyses of treaty and Aboriginal rights, the Office of the Treaty Commissioner produced an interim report and presented it to the parties on March 31, 2006. The parties reviewed the report and met with the Office of the Treaty Commissioner to provide their comments and feedback. Written comments were also provided.

The Office of the Treaty Commissioner believes the treaty implementation discussion process was a success. Accordingly, best practices can be identified, including the following:

1. Commitment from the Parties at the most senior level – the Minister of Indian Affairs and the Chief of the Federation of Saskatchewan Indian Nations – set the stage and demonstrated the serious nature of the work.

2. The Minister and the Chief clearly stated their expectations.

3. The Parties and the Office of the Treaty Commissioner adopted a partnership approach in developing and implementing the treaty implementation discussion work plan.

4. The parties and the Office of the Treaty Commissioner clearly understood their roles and responsibilities.

5. Questions to guide the discussions were jointly developed and revised when necessary.

6. Appropriate funding to undertake the work was provided by Canada to the Federation of Saskatchewan Indian Nations and the Office of the Treaty Commissioner.

7. Elders' views and advice were sought and followed.

8. Flexibility was adopted during the process and the work plan was adjusted as needed.

9. Prior to the First Nation forums, Federation of Saskatchewan Indian Nations officials met with First Nations leadership and explained the process, which enabled them to identify and invite participants that were knowledgeable and willing to offer their views.

10. Prior to the federal meetings, Indian and Northern Affairs Canada officials met with federal officials from various departments and explained the process, which enabled them to identify and invite participants that were knowledgeable and willing to offer their views.

11. First Nations cultural protocols were respected.

12. Discussions occurred in First Nations languages, when required, and translators were present.

13. Discussions occurred in plenary sessions and in small groups.

14. All discussions were led by facilitators.

15. All discussions were recorded, translated (when required) and transcribed.

16. Timelines were extended, when required.

17. Finally, the Parties reviewed drafts of the report and provided their feedback and advice to the Office of the Treaty Commissioner – the report was not written in a vacuum.

In the letter of transmittal included with the Interim Report to the Parties, Treaty Commissioner Judge David Arnot stated, "This report sets an agenda, and thus it should be seen as an outline of the next steps for the Parties as they complete the road map for reconciliation and treaty implementation."

APPENDIX 2. SELECTED RECOMMENDATIONS FROM THE FINAL REPORT OF THE ROYAL COMMISSION ON ABORIGINAL PEOPLES IN RELATION TO TREATY IMPLEMENTATION

With regard to fostering public education and awareness, the Commission recommends that:

2.21 Federal, provincial ... governments provide programs of public education about the treaties to promote public understanding of the following concepts:

(a) Treaties were made ... by [First Nations] on a nation-to-nation basis, and those nations continue to exist and deserve respect as nations.

(b) Historical treaties were meant by all parties to be sacred and enduring and to be spiritual as well as legal undertakings.

(c) Treaties with [First] Nations are fundamental components of the Constitution of Canada, analogous to the terms of union whereby provinces joined Confederation.

(d) Fulfillment of the treaties, including the spirit and intent of the historical treaties, is a test of Canada's honour and of its place of respect in the family of nations.

(e) Treaties embody the principles of the relationship between the Crown and [First] Nations that made them ...

With respect to the historical treaties, the Commission recommends that:

2.21 The Parties implement the historical treaties from the perspectives of both justice and reconciliation:

(a) Justice requires the fulfillment of the agreed terms of the treaties, as recorded in the treaty text and supplemented by oral evidence.

(b) Reconciliation requires the establishment of proper principles to govern the continuing treaty relationship...

Treaty Implementation: Fulfilling the Covenant

Appendix 2. Selected Recommendations from the Final Report of the Royal Commission on Aboriginal Peoples in Relation to Treaty Implementation

2.2.3 The federal government establishes a continuing bilateral process to implement and renew the Crown's relationship with and obligations to the treaty nations under the historical treaties, in accordance with the treaties' spirit and intent.

2.2.4 The spirit and intent of the historical treaties be implemented in accordance with the following fundamental principles:

(a) The specific content of the rights and obligations of the Parties to the treaties is determined for all purposes in a just and liberal way, by reference to oral as well as written sources.

(b) The Crown is in a trust-like and non-adversarial fiduciary relationship with the treaty nations.

(c) The Crown's conflicting duties to the treaty nations and to Canadians generally is reconciled in the spirit of the treaty partnership.

(d) There is a presumption in respect of the historic treaties that:

- treaty nations did not intend to consent to the blanket extinguishment of their Aboriginal rights and title by entering into the treaty relationship;

- treaty nations intended to share the territory and jurisdiction and management over it, as opposed to ceding the territory, even where the text of an historical treaty makes reference to a blanket extinguishment of land rights; and

- treaty nations did not intend to give up their inherent right of governance by entering into a treaty relationship, and the act of treaty making is regarded as an affirmation rather than a denial of that right...

In relation to all treaties, the Commission recommends that:

2.2.5 Once the spirit and intent of specific treaties have been recognized and incorporated into the agreed understanding of the treaty, all laws, policies and practices that have a bearing on the terms of the treaty are made to reflect this understanding.

2.2.11 The following matters be open for discussion in treaty implementation and renewal and treaty making processes:

- governance, including justice systems, long term financial arrangements including fiscal transfers and other inter-governmental arrangements;

- lands and resources;

- economic rights, including treaty annuities and hunting, fishing and trapping rights;

- issues included in specific treaties (for example, education, health and taxation); and

- other issues relevant to treaty relationships identified by either treaty party.

With respect to establishing a new treaty process, the Commission recommends that:

2.2.7 The federal government prepare a Royal Proclamation for the consideration of Her Majesty the Queen that would:

(a) supplement the Royal Proclamation of 1763; and

(b) set out, for the consideration of all Aboriginal and treaty nations in Canada, the fundamental principles of
    (i) the bilateral nation-to-nation relationship;
    (ii) the treaty implementation and renewal process; and
    (iii) the treaty making process.

2.2.8 The federal government introduce companion treaty legislation in Parliament that:

(a) provides for the implementation of existing treaty rights, including the treaty rights to hunt, fish and trap;

(b) affirms liberal rules of interpretation for historical treaties, having regard to
    (i) the context of treaty negotiations;
    (ii) the spirit and intent of each treaty; and
    (iii) the special relationship between the treaty Parties;

(c) makes oral and secondary evidence admissible in the courts when they are making determinations with respect to historical treaty rights;

(d) recognizes and affirms the land rights and jurisdiction of Aboriginal nations as essential components of treaty processes;

(e) declares the commitment of the Parliament and Government of Canada to the implementation and renewal of each treaty in accordance with the spirit and intent of the treaty and the relationship embodied in it;

(f) commits the Government of Canada to treaty processes that clarify, implement ... the spirit and intent of each treaty and the relationship embodied in it;

(h) commits the Government of Canada to treaty processes based on and guided by the nation-to-nation structure of the new relationship, implying
  (i) all parties demonstrating a spirit of openness, a clear political will and a commitment to fair, balanced and equitable negotiations; and
  (ii) no party controlling the access to, the scope of, or the funding for the negotiating process; and

(i) authorizes the establishment, in consultation with treaty nations, of the institutions this Commission recommends as necessary to fulfill the treaty processes.

2.2.10 The Royal Proclamation and companion legislation in relation to treaties accomplish the following:

(a) declare that entry into ... treaty implementation and renewal processes by ... treaty nations is voluntary;

(b) use clear, non-derogation language to ensure that the Royal Proclamation and legislation do not derogate from existing Aboriginal and treaty rights;

(c) provide for short- and medium-term initiatives to support treaty implementation ... since those processes will take time to complete; and

(d) provide adequate long-term resources so that ... treaty implementation and renewal processes can achieve their objectives.

2.2.12 The Royal Proclamation and companion legislation in relation to treaties provide for one or more of the following outcomes:

(a) protocol agreements between treaty nations and the Crown that provide for the implementation and renewal of existing treaties, but do not themselves have the status of a treaty;

(e) other instruments to implement treaties, including legislation and regulations of the treaty Parties.

2.2.13 The Royal Proclamation and companion legislation in relation to treaties:

(a) establish a Crown Treaty Office with a new Department of [First Nations] Relations; and

(b) direct that Office to be the lead Crown agency participating in nation-to-nation treaty processes.

With regard to provincial ... responsibilities, the Commission recommends that:

2.2.9 The governments of the provinces ... introduce legislation, parallel to the federal companion legislation, that:

(a) enables them to meet their treaty obligations;

(b) enables them to participate in treaty implementation and renewal processes...and

(c) establishes the institutions required to participate in those treaty processes, to the extent of their jurisdiction.

2.2.14 Each province establishes a Crown Treaty Office to enable it to participate in treaty processes.

Regarding the creation of treaty institutions, the Commission recommends that:

2.2.15 The governments of Canada, relevant provinces ... and treaty nations establish treaty commissions as permanent, independent and neutral bodies to facilitate and oversee negotiations in treaty processes.

2.2.16 The following be the essential features of treaty commissions:

- Commissioners to be appointed in equal numbers from lists prepared by the Parties, with an independent chair being selected by those appointees.

- Commissions to have permanent administrative and research staff, with full independence from government and from ... treaty nations.

- Staff of the commissions to act as a secretariat for treaty processes.

- Services of the commissions to go beyond simple facilitation. Where the Parties require specialized fact finding of a technical nature, commissions to have the power to hire the necessary experts.

- Commissions to monitor and guide the conduct of the Parties in the treaty process to ensure that fair and proper standards of conduct and negotiation are maintained.

- Commissions to conduct inquiries and provide research, analysis and recommendations on issues in dispute in relation to historical ... treaties, as requested jointly by the Parties.

- Commissions to supervise and facilitate cost sharing by the Parties.

- Commissions to provide mediation services to the Parties as jointly requested.

- Commissions to provide remedies for abuses of process.

- Commissions to provide binding or non-binding arbitration of particular matters and other dispute resolution services, at the request of the Parties, consistent with the political nature of the treaty process.[184]

---

[184] Royal Commission on Aboriginal Peoples, *Gathering Strength*, Volume 2, Part Two, pp.1025-31.

APPENDIX 3. SOCIO-ECONOMIC CONDITIONS OF FIRST NATIONS PEOPLE IN SASKATCHEWAN

Introduction

While much has been said about specific socio-economic conditions among First Nations people, a rigorous, comprehensive documentation of data on socio-economic status is a rare find. In this appendix, a number of socio-metric measures are considered, drawn from legitimate sources, especially the 2001 Census of Canada and the special Aboriginal Peoples Survey component of that Census. The data has been organized under key subject headings and, as much as possible, compared to equivalent data for the population as a whole in the jurisdiction under comparison to allow a greater context for understanding the data. This survey will examine a number of measures of economic conditions, including employment, incomes and incidence of poverty and a number of other social indicators such as educational experience, cultural indicators and overall indicators of population health.

Employment and Labour Force Activity

The 2001 Census provided a comprehensive review of labour force activity for First Nations people in Saskatchewan and for the population as a whole, allowing easy comparison of measures of labour force attachment between the two populations, as shown in Table 1.

NOTE : For census data, "First Nations" will be used to refer to those survey respondents who responded with "North American Indian" only for cultural identity on census forms, excluding any groups who may have identified themselves by more than one cultural orientation.

Table 1: Labour Force Activity for First Nations[185] Respondents and the Total Non-Aboriginal Population, Saskatchewan, 2001 Census

	First Nations	Non-Aboriginal Population	Difference
Total Population over 15 Years (number)	41,200	673,930	n.a.
Labour Force Participation Rate (% of Population over 15)	44.4%	69.2%	(24.8) ppt
Employment Rate (% of Population over 15)	30.3%	69.2%	(38.9) ppt
Unemployment Rate (% of Labour Force)	31.7%	4.9%	26.8 ppt

Source: Statistics Canada, Selected Labour Force Characteristics, Aboriginal Origin, 20% sample data, 2001 Census.

In this case, it can be seen that there were 41,200 people over the age of 15 in Saskatchewan who identified themselves as "North American Indian" in the 2001 Census, without any other ethnicity identified. This represented approximately 5.4 percent of the province's total population over 15 years of age. Of this total population, the First Nations participation rate (percentage of the population in the labour force) was 44.4 percent, less than two-thirds the rate of the non-Aboriginal population, which was 24.8 percentage points higher at 69.2 percent of the total population. The corollary was that, in 2001, more than half (55.6 percent) of the First Nations adult population was not in the labour force, as compared to just over 30 percent of the adult non-Aboriginal population.

The Census also revealed that in 2001 there were 12,480 First Nations people employed, which represented 30.3 percent of the population over 15 years of age. This compares with an employment rate of 65.9 percent among the non-Aboriginal population. First Nations people were only about two-thirds as likely as non-Aboriginals to be in the labour force and only about half as likely to be employed.

---

[185] For census data, "First Nations" will be used to refer to those survey respondents who responded by "North American Indian" only for cultural identity on census survey forms, excluding any groups who may have identified themselves by more than one cultural orientation.

The 2001 unemployment rate (the percentage of the labour force unemployed) was 31.7 percent for First Nations people, while the equivalent rate for non-Aboriginal people was 4.9 percent in Saskatchewan. This suggests that even among those in the labour force, First Nations people were almost six and a half times more likely to be unemployed as non-Aboriginal workers.

The 2001 Census also provided data on the industry of employment of the 18,280 First Nations people who were in the labour force in Saskatchewan. The data is presented in Table 2 with comparisons to the non-Aboriginal adult population in Saskatchewan. It shows the employed First Nations population was more highly represented in the service sector than in the goods-producing sectors, as a greater proportion of First Nations workers were employed in each of "Educational Services," Health Care and Social Assistance," "Arts, Entertainment and Recreation" and "Public Administration" than non-Aboriginal workers.

In goods production, only "Construction" attracted a higher proportion of First Nations workers than was the case for non-Aboriginal workers. In all other industries, the proportion of non-Aboriginal workers employed exceeded the rate for First Nations workers, who were particularly under-represented in the Retail industry and in Agriculture, Forestry, Fishing and Hunting. It should be noted, however, that 13.4 percent of First Nations workers responded that the choices of industries listed were not applicable in their case, while only 1.0 percent of the non-Aboriginal employed responded to that effect. This might suggest some inconsistency in interpreting the data on industrial distribution of employment on the part of First Nations respondents, as compared to non-Aboriginal respondents.

Table 2: Percentage of Total Employment by Industry for First Nations[186] Respondents and the Total Non-Aboriginal Population, Saskatchewan, 2001 Census

Industry	First Nations (percent)	Non-Aboriginal Population (percent)	Difference (percentage points)
Agriculture, Forestry, Fishing and Hunting	4.4%	15.0%	(10.6) ppt
Mining and Oil & Gas	2.0%	2.8%	(0.8) ppt
Utilities	0.8%	1.0%	(0.2) ppt
Construction	7.7%	5.1%	2.6 ppt
Manufacturing	3.1%	5.8%	(2.7) ppt
Retail	5.3%	10.7%	(5.4) ppt
Transportation and Warehousing	3.0%	4.8%	(1.8) ppt
Information and Cultural Industries	0.5%	2.2%	(1.7) ppt
Finance and Insurance	0.8%	3.8%	(2.0) ppt
Real Estate and Rental and Leasing	0.6%	1.3%	(0.7) ppt
Professional, Scientific and Technical Services	0.7%	3.3%	(2.6)ppt
Management	0.0%	0.05	(0.05) ppt
Waste Management	3.4%	2.6%	0.8 ppt
Educational Services	10.8%	7.0%	3.8 ppt
Health Care and Social Assistance	12.0%	10.8%	1.2 ppt
Arts, Entertainment and Recreation	4.6%	1.6%	3.0 ppt
Accommodation and Food Services	6.1%	6.7%	(0.6) ppt
Other Services	2.6%	4.9%	(2.3) ppt
Public Administration	17.4%	5.5%	11.9 ppt
Industry – Not Applicable	13.4%	1.0%	12.4 ppt

Source: Statistics Canada, Selected Labour Force Characteristics, Aboriginal Identity, 20% sample data, 2001 Census.

---

[186] For census data, "First Nations" will be used to refer to those survey respondents who responded by "North American Indian" only for cultural identity on census survey forms, excluding any groups who may have identified themselves by more than one cultural orientation.

More current labour force data has been collected through Statistics Canada's monthly Labour Force Survey, which added a specific "Aboriginal Identity" component in 2005.

Although the survey group identifies all Aboriginal peoples and is, therefore, not identical to the Census data cited above, an update on conditions may be evidenced from the alternate data set. The data from the latest Labour Force Survey is included in Table 3 below and identifies the key labour force indicators for 2005 for the Aboriginal (self-identified) component of the labour force in Saskatchewan compared to the non-Aboriginal component.

Table 3: Labour Force Activity for Aboriginal and non-Aboriginal Identity, Saskatchewan, 2005 Average

	Aboriginal Identity	Non-Aboriginal Identity	Difference
Total Population Over 15 years (thousands)	57.1	690.7	n.a.
Labour Force (thousands)	35.2	474.5	n.a.
Labour Force Participation Rate (% of Population over 15)	61.6%	68.7%	(7.1) ppt
Employment Rate (% of Population over 15)	51.6%	65.7%	(14.1) ppt
Unemployment Rate (% of Labour Force)	16.3%	5.1%	11.2 ppt

Source: Statistics Canada, Labour Force Survey and author's calculations.

In the case of the Labour Force Survey, those identified as "Aboriginal Identity" represent 7.6 percent of the total population over 15, but a slightly smaller proportion (6.9 percent) of the labour force, reflecting their lower Labour Force Participation Rate (61.6 percent as compared to 68.7 percent for the non-Aboriginal component of the labour force).

Nevertheless, this Aboriginal participation rate is significantly higher than the rate of 44.4 percent identified for "North American Indians – single response" in the 2001 Census. It is also much closer to the non-Aboriginal participation rate than was the case in the 2001 Census. Although these are not strictly comparable data bases, there may be evidence of some convergence of participation rates; further study of 2006 Census data, when it becomes available, is warranted.

Further evidence of possible convergence is seen in Employment and Unemployment Rates. In the former case, the "Aboriginal" Employment Rate of 51.6 percent in 2005 is much higher than the 30.3 percent found for First Nations people in the 2001 Census. It is 14.1 percentage points behind the rate for non-Aboriginal people compared to a gap of 35.6 percentage points in the 2001 Census.

In the case of Unemployment Rates, the "Aboriginal" unemployment rate averaged 16.3 percent of the Labour Force in 2005, fully 11.2 percentage points above the rate for non-Aboriginal people in Saskatchewan. Nevertheless, this gap is much smaller than 26.8 percentage point gap seen in the 2001 Census data.

The caution against firm conclusions based on this data bears repeating, since the data groups are not strictly comparable as a time series. Nevertheless, there is reason for hopeful anticipation of 2006 Census data.

Income Levels

The 2001 Census collected data on family incomes for persons identified as "North American Indian – single response" on a comparable basis with income data for the "non-Aboriginal" population. Table 4 presents data on income from employment in the 2000 calendar year.

Table 4: Employment Income for First Nations[187] Respondents and the Total Non-Aboriginal Population over 15 Years in 2000, Saskatchewan

	First Nations	Non-Aboriginal Population	Difference
Total Population over 15 Years (number)	41,200	673,930	n.a.
Did Not Work in 2000 (% of population)	55.8%	27.6%	28.2 ppt
Worked Full Time (% of population)	14.3%	39.8%	(25.5) ppt
Average Income for Full Time Employees ($)	$28,399	$35,794	($7,395)
Worked Part Time or Part-Year (% of population)	29.8%	32.7%	(2.8) ppt
Average Income for Part-Time and/ or Part-Year Employees ($)	$12,300	$16,131	($3,831)

Source: Statistics Canada, Selected Income Characteristics, Aboriginal Origin, for population 15 and over, 2001 Census.

In 2000, First Nations people were more than twice as likely as non-Aboriginal people to have not worked at all; almost 56% of the First Nations population (of all ages) did not work at all in 2000 compared to almost 28% of non-Aboriginal people. Only 14.3 percent of First Nations respondents worked full time for all of 2000 compared to 39.8 percent of non-Aboriginal people, and they earned an average of $28,399 from employment – 79.3 percent of the income earned by their non-Aboriginal counterparts. While the part-time and part-year employment levels were similar between First Nations and non-Aboriginal respondents (at 29.8 percent and 32.7 percent of the total

---

[187] For census data, "First Nations" will be used to refer to those survey respondents who responded by "North American Indian" only for cultural identity on census survey forms, excluding any groups who may have identified themselves by more than one cultural orientation.

populations, respectively), the employment earnings of First Nations part-time or part-year employees was 76.2 percent of the earnings of non-Aboriginal employees with the same employment status. In 2000, First Nations people were 60 percent as likely to work as non-Aboriginal people, and when they did find work, they earned income at a rate of 75% to 80% of the non-Aboriginal population.

Sources of income for individuals in 2001 Census data (Table 5) compare the composition of income for those identifying themselves as North American Indian – single response with those identifying themselves as non-Aboriginal.

Table 5: Sources of Total Income for First Nations[188] Respondents and the Total Non-Aboriginal Population over 15 Years in 2000, Saskatchewan

	First Nations	**Non-Aboriginal Population**	**Difference**
Total Population over 15 Years (number)	41,200	673,930	n.a.
Average Income in 2000 ($)	$12,752	$ 26,899	($ 14,147)
Employment Income (% of total income)	58.8%	73.8%	(15.0) ppt
Government Transfer Payments (% of total income)	38.6%	13.9%	24.7 ppt
Other Income (% of total income)	2.6%	12.3%	(9.7) ppt

Source: Statistics Canada, Selected Income Characteristics, Aboriginal Origin, for population 15 and over, 2001 Census.

Data shows that First Nations people receive a much higher proportion of their income from transfer payments than non-Aboriginal people (38.6 percent compared to 13.9 percent). Accordingly, a smaller proportion of First Nations' income is derived from employment and other sources (such as interest, dividend and investment income) than is the case for non-Aboriginal people. In absolute terms, the average income from government transfer payments

---

[188] For census data, "First Nations" will be used to refer to those survey respondents who responded by "North American Indian" only for cultural identity on census survey forms, excluding any groups who may have identified themselves by more than one cultural orientation.

was $4,922 for First Nations people, 31.6 percent higher than the average transfer payment income of $3,739 received by non-Aboriginal people.

2001 Census data also provides a breakdown of population counts by income class, presented in Table 6.

Table 6:   Percentage of Total Population by Income Class for First Nations[189] Respondents and the Total Non-Aboriginal Population, Saskatchewan, 2001 Census

Income class	First Nations (percent)	Non-Aboriginal Population (percent)	Difference (percentage points)
Without Income	7.5%	4.0%	3.5 ppt
Under $5,000	32.4%	11.2%	21.2 ppt
$5,000 - $9,999	16.8%	10.8%	6.0 ppt
$10,000 - $19,999	23.6%	24.4%	(0.8) ppt
$20,000 - $29,999	10.0%	16.5%	(6.5) ppt
$30,000 - $39,999	5.2%	12.4%	(7.2) ppt
$40,000 - $49,999	2.2%	7.7%	(5.5) ppt
$50,000 - $59,999	1.2%	5.5%	(4.3) ppt
$60,000 and over	1.0%	7.5%	(6.5) ppt

Source: Statistics Canada, Selected Income Characteristics, Aboriginal Origin, 20% sample data, 2001 Census.

There is clear over-representation of First Nations people in the lowest income classes, with a cumulative total of 80.3 percent of the First Nations population reporting income of less than $20,000 in 2000. This compares to 50.4 percent of the non-Aboriginal population reporting incomes less than $20,000.   On the other hand, 13.0 percent of the non-Aboriginal population had incomes in excess of $50,000 compared to 2.2 percent of the First Nations population.   The median income (the level of income at which half the population is above and half below) was $8,913 for First Nations respondents; this is 43.2 percent of the median income of $20,648 for non-Aboriginal respondents.

---

[189] For census data, "First Nations" will be used to refer to those survey respondents who responded by "North American Indian" only for cultural identity on census survey forms, excluding any groups who may have identified themselves by more than one cultural orientation.

Table 7 examines income data in terms of the incidence of "low income" among economic family units within each population base.

Table 7: Incidence of Low Income for First Nations[190] Respondents and the Total Non-Aboriginal Population over 15 Years in 2000, Saskatchewan

	First Nations	Non-Aboriginal Population	Difference
Number of Economic Family Persons and Unattached Individuals	31,040	820,815	n.a.
Number of Low Income	19,220	106,495	n.a.
Other	11,820	714,320	n.a.
Incidence of Low Income (%)	61.9%	13.0%	48.9 ppt

Source: Statistics Canada, Selected Income Characteristics, Aboriginal Origin, for population 15 and over, 2001 Census.

In 2000, 61.9 percent of First Nations respondents were part of a household categorized as low income, as opposed to 13.0 percent of the non-Aboriginal population. The incidence of low income among First Nations people was more than 4.75 times the rate among non-Aboriginal people. As a result, low income First Nations people comprise 13.3 percent of people living in low income households in Saskatchewan, compared to 3.4 percent of all economic households and individuals living alone.

Household Characteristics

Table 8 compares the marital status of 2001 Census respondents identified as "North American Indian – single response" with that of the non-Aboriginal population in Saskatchewan.

Of the adult population of First Nations, the overwhelming majority (61.1 percent) have never married – more than twice the rate of non-Aboriginal people. The corollary is that

---

[190] For census data, "First Nations" will be used to refer to those survey respondents who responded by "North American Indian" only for cultural identity on census survey forms, excluding any groups who may have identified themselves by more than one cultural orientation.

less than half as many First Nations people (25.3 percent of the adult population) were married at the time of the 2001 Census than non-Aboriginal people (55.9 percent of the adult population). With a lower rate of marriage, First Nations people have a lower incidence of divorce and widowhood, but interestingly, they have twice the rate of separation while legally married than non-Aboriginal people. Of First Nations adults who had ever been married, 65.0 percent were still legally married and not separated; this was true for 78.3 percent of non-Aboriginal adults who had ever been married. The data revealed that the incidence of marital breakdown (separated and divorced as a percentage of those ever married) for First Nations people, at 25.4 percent, was more then twice the rate of 11.6 percent for non-Aboriginal people.

Table 8: Marital Status of First Nations[191] Respondents and the Total Non-Aboriginal Population over 15 Years in 2001, Saskatchewan

	First Nations	**Non-Aboriginal Population**	**Difference**
Total Population over 15 Years (number)	41,200	673,930	n.a.
Never Married (% of population)	61.1%	28.6%	32.5 ppt
Legally Married (and not separated) (% of population)	25.3%	55.9%	(30.6) ppt
Separated (but still legally married) (% of population)	4.6%	2.2%	2.4 ppt
Divorced (% of population)	5.3%	6.1%	(0.8) ppt
Widowed (% of population)	3.7%	7.2%	(3.5) ppt

Source: Statistics Canada, Selected Demographic and Cultural Characteristics, Aboriginal Origin, 2001 Census.

---

[191] For census data, "First Nations" will be used to refer to those survey respondents who responded by "North American Indian" only for cultural identity on census survey forms, excluding any groups who may have identified themselves by more than one cultural orientation.

Additional data on family composition gathered in the 2001 Census is shown in Table 9. Private households were examined for the status of residents (family members versus non-members), the number of adults versus children and the relationships of adults in the household. Most noticeable is the fact that First Nations household members are 51.1 percent children, compared to only 30.2 percent for non-Aboriginal households. Further, the incidence of single parents is three times higher in First Nations households than in non-Aboriginal households, at 11 percent compared to 3.6 percent. On a combined basis, husbands, wives and common-law partners make up 25.7 percent of First Nations households while the same groups make up 50.8 percent of non-Aboriginal households.

Table 9: Composition of Households of First Nations[192] Respondents and the Total Non-Aboriginal Population in 2001, Saskatchewan

	First Nations	Non-Aboriginal Population	Difference
Total Population of Private Households (number)	61,720	686,790	n.a.
Husbands or Wives (% of population)	14.4%	45.3%	(30.9) ppt
Common-Law Partners (% of population)	11.3%	4.5%	6.8 ppt
Lone Parents (% of population)	11.0%	3.6%	7.4 ppt
Children (% of population)	51.1%	30.2%	20.9 ppt
Non-Family Members (% of population)	12.2%	16.4%	(4.2) ppt

Source: Statistics Canada, Selected Demographic and Cultural Characteristics, Aboriginal Origin, 2001 Census.

[192] For census data, "First Nations" will be used to refer to those survey respondents who responded by "North American Indian" only for cultural identity on census survey forms, excluding any groups who may have identified themselves by more than one cultural orientation.

Also of interest, 16.4 percent of non-Aboriginal households consist of non-family members (either relatives, non-relatives or those living alone) compared to 12.2 percent of First Nations households. Details provided by the Census reveal that, in the case of First Nations households, 4.6 percent are likely to be relatives living within the household, compared to 1.4 percent in non-Aboriginal households. Non-Aboriginal households are much more likely to consist of people living alone (12.0 percent of total household populations) than First Nations households (4.0 percent of total household populations).

Indication of household stability is demonstrated by data on population movement in Table 10. First Nations people were more likely to have moved in the past year; only 74.6 percent were at the same address in 2001 as they were in 2000 compared to the more stable population of non-Aboriginal people, 87.3 percent of whom were at the same address in 2001 as they were in 2000. In other words, 25.4 percent of First Nations people had changed residences in the previous year, while 12.7 percent of non-Aboriginal people had moved in the same period. In 2001, First Nations people were twice as likely to change residences as non-Aboriginal people. Of those who had changed residences within the year before the 2001 Census, First Nations respondents were about equally as likely as non-Aboriginal respondents to have moved within the census division and within the province, but only half as likely to have moved to Saskatchewan from another province or territory. Only a small portion of either population had moved from outside the province.

Table 10: Relocation of Households of First Nations[193] Respondents and the Total Non-Aboriginal Population in 2001, Saskatchewan

	First Nations	Non-Aboriginal Population	Difference
Total Population 1 Year and Over (number)	68,495	715,875	n.a.
Lived at the Same Address One Year Ago (% of population)	74.6%	87.3%	(12.7) ppt
Moved within Census District in Past Year (% of population)	16.1%	7.5%	8.6 ppt
Moved within Province in Past Year (% of population)	7.9%	3.4%	4.5 ppt
Moved between Provinces Last Year (% of population)	1.4%	1.8%	(0.4) ppt

Source: Statistics Canada, Selected Demographic and Cultural Characteristics, Aboriginal Origin, 2001 Census.

Education

The 2001 Census collected data on school attendance and school achievement in First Nations and non-Aboriginal populations in Saskatchewan, shown in Table 11. The data reveals that First Nations adults are almost twice as likely to be attending school on a full-time basis than non-Aboriginal adults and slightly less likely to be attending school on a part-time basis. Almost one-quarter (23.6 percent) of the First Nations population over 15 was attending school in 2001, compared to 14.1% of the non-Aboriginal population.

---

[193] For census data, "First Nations" will be used to refer to those survey respondents who responded by "North American Indian" only for cultural identity on census survey forms, excluding any groups who may have identified themselves by more than one cultural orientation.

Table 11: School Attendance for First Nations[194] Respondents and the Total Non-Aboriginal Population over 15 Years in 2001, Saskatchewan

	First Nations (% of over 15 pop.)	Non-Aboriginal Population (% of over 15 pop.)	Difference (percentage points)
Not Attending School	76.4%	85.9%	(9.5) ppt
Attending School Full Time	20.9%	10.9%	10.0 ppt
Attending School Part Time	2.7%	3.2%	(0.5) ppt

Source: Statistics Canada, Selected Educational Characteristics, Aboriginal Origin, for population 15 and over, 2001 Census.

A comparison of school achievement is provided in Table 12.

Table 12: Highest level of Schooling for First Nations[195] Respondents and the Total Non-Aboriginal Population over 15 Years in 2001, Saskatchewan

	First Nations (% of over 15 pop.)	Non-Aboriginal Population (% of over 15 pop.)	Difference (percentage points)
Less than High School Graduation	59.2%	38.0%	21.2 ppt
High School Graduation Only	6.8%	11.1%	(4.3) ppt
Some Post-Secondary	12.5%	10.9%	1.6 ppt
Trades Certificate	9.8%	12.7%	(2.9) ppt
College Diploma	6.7%	12.6%	(5.9) ppt
University Diploma	1.6%	2.9%	(1.3) ppt
Bachelor's Degree	3.0%	9.1%	(6.1) ppt
University Certificate Above Bachelor's	0.2%	0.8%	(0.6) ppt
Master's Degree	0.2%	1.5%	(1.3) ppt
Earned Doctorate	0.02%	0.42%	(0.40) ppt

Source: Statistics Canada, Selected Educational Characteristics, Aboriginal Origin, for population 15 and over, 2001 Census.

[194 & 195] For census data, "First Nations" will be used to refer to those survey respondents who responded by "North American Indian" only for cultural identity on census survey forms, excluding any groups who may have identified themselves by more than one cultural orientation.

North American Indian – single response respondents were over 55 percent more likely to have less than high school graduation than non-Aboriginal respondents, as nearly 60 percent of First Nations respondents were in this category. While 62 percent of non-Aboriginal people had achieved at least high school graduation or equivalent, this was true for 40.8 percent of First Nations respondents. First Nations people were 77 percent as likely to have achieved a trade certificate as non-Aboriginal people and less than 43 percent were as likely to have a college or university certificate, diploma or degree of any sort.

Table 13 examines the fields of study or specialization of training of the First Nations and non-Aboriginal populations.

Table 13: Major Field of Study for First Nations[196] Respondents and the Total Non-Aboriginal Population over 15 Years in 2001, Saskatchewan

	First Nations (% of over 15 pop.)	Non-Aboriginal Population (% of over 15 pop.)	Difference (percentage points)
No Post-Secondary	78.5%	60.0%	18.5 ppt
Education, Recreation, Counselling	3.8%	5.8%	(2.0) ppt
Fine and Applied Arts	0.7%	2.1%	(1.4) ppt
Humanities	0.6%	1.9%	(1.3) ppt
Social Sciences	4.5%	2.8%	1.7 ppt
Commerce and Business Admin.	3.6%	8.2%	(4.6) ppt
Agriculture, Nutrition and Food	0.9%	2.6%	(1.7) ppt
Engineering and Applied Sciences	0.1%	0.8%	(0.7) ppt
Applied Science and Trades	5.4%	8.9%	(4.4) ppt
Health Professions and Technology	1.8%	6.0%	(4.2) ppt
Mathematics and Computer Science	0.1%	0.9%	(0.8) ppt
No Specialization	0.1%	0.0%	0.1 ppt

Source: Statistics Canada, Selected Educational Characteristics, Aboriginal Origin, for population 15 and over, 2001 Census.

---

[196] For census data, "First Nations" will be used to refer to those survey respondents who responded by "North American Indian" only for cultural identity on census survey forms, excluding any groups who may have identified themselves by more than one cultural orientation.

First Nations people tend to be under-represented in all fields of study except the social sciences, reflecting their overall lower level of post-secondary qualification. Differences in the distribution of training specialties is further revealed in Table 14, which compares the two population bases in terms of post-secondary training by major field of study.

Table 14: Distribution of People with Post-Secondary Training by Major Field of Study for First Nations[197] Respondents and the Total Non-Aboriginal Population over 15 Years in 2001, Saskatchewan

	First Nations (% of those with post-secondary)	Non-Aboriginal Population (% of those with post-secondary)	Difference (percentage points)
Education, Recreation, Counselling	17.7%	14.5%	3.2 ppt
Fine and Applied Arts	3.2%	5.2%	(2.0) ppt
Humanities	2.8%	4.8%	(2.0) ppt
Social Sciences	20.9%	7.0%	13.9 ppt
Commerce and Business Admin.	16.7%	20.5%	(3.8) ppt
Agriculture, Nutrition and Food	4.2%	6.5%	(2.3) ppt
Engineering and Applied Sciences	0.5%	2.0%	(1.5) ppt
Applied Science and Trades	25.1%	22.2%	2.9 ppt
Health Professions and Technology	8.4%	15.0%	(6.6) ppt
Mathematics and Computer Science	0.5%	2.2%	(1.7) ppt
No Specialization	0.5%	0.0%	0.5 ppt

Source: Statistics Canada, Selected Educational Characteristics, Aboriginal Origin, for population 15 and over, 2001 Census and author's calculations.

---

[197] For census data, "First Nations" will be used to refer to those survey respondents who responded by "North American Indian" only for cultural identity on census survey forms, excluding any groups who may have identified themselves by more than one cultural orientation.

The distribution of specialties among those who have achieved post-secondary designations is similar for First Nations individuals and non-Aboriginal post-secondary graduates. The dramatic exceptions are the social sciences, where the proportion of First Nations graduates is almost three times that of non-Aboriginal people, and the health professional and health technology fields, in which First Nations respondents qualify at 56 percent the rate of non-Aboriginal people.

Housing

The 2001 Census collected information on housing conditions in Canada, and some data is available through Indian and Northern Affairs Canada, but without provincial breakdowns. This data is provided in Table 15.

Table 15: Comparative Housing Statistics, Registered Indians, Registered Indians on Reserve and Total Canadian Population, 2001

	Registered Indians	Registered Indians on Reserve	All Canadians
Dwellings Built within Last 15 Years (% of total)	31.6%	53.8%	24.1%
Dwellings Needing Major Repairs (% of total)	23.5%	36.3%	8.2%
Dwellings with More Than 1 Person per Room (% of total)	7.4%	13.8%	1.4%
Average Number of Persons Per Room	0.6	0.7	0.4
New Housing Starts (% of existing dwellings)	-	2.4%	1.4%
Dwellings with Water Supply (% of total)	-	97.7%	100%
Dwellings with Sewage Disposal (% of total)	-	94.9%	100%

Source: Indian and Northern Affairs Canada, Comparison of Socio-economic Conditions, 1996 and 2001, 2005.

The data suggests that Registered Indians tend to have newer housing than the general population. Almost a third of the total housing occupied by Registered Indians are less than 15 years old. More than one-half of dwellings on reserves are less than 15 years old compared to the general population, in which less than a quarter of dwellings are less than 15 years old.

The condition of dwellings appears to be much worse for Registered Indians, as nearly a quarter of all their dwellings and more than a third of dwellings on reserves are in need of major repairs to plumbing, electrical wiring, structural walls, floors, ceilings, et cetera. By comparison, only 8.2 percent of the dwellings of the general Canadian population are rated as in need of major repairs.

Two measures of density are provided by the data; the percentage of houses occupied by an average of more than one person per room and the average number of persons per room. In both cases, the Registered Indian population inhabits much more crowded facilities, with five times the Canadian share of dwellings having more than one person per room (almost ten times on reserves) and an average number of persons per room 50 percent higher than the Canadian average (75 percent higher on reserves).

The rate of replacement of dwellings for Registered Indians seems to be higher than for the general populace. New housing starts on reserves equalled 2.4 percent of the total housing stock compared to 1.4 percent for the general public.

In 2001, 2.3 percent of reserve housing was without water supply services and 5.1 percent was without sewage disposal facilities, while virtually all other Canadian housing had these services available. It should be noted, however, that this situation was an improvement over 1996, when 3.9 percent of reserve housing was without water services and 8.5 percent was without sewage disposal. By 2001, the discrepancy in water and sewage services between reserve housing and the rest of Canada had been reduced by about 40 percent.

Statistics Canada Census data[198] for 2001 identified only 1 percent of housing occupied by "Aboriginals" in Saskatchewan as without running water and 1 percent as without a flush toilet, suggesting that housing conditions in Saskatchewan might be better on average than for the national sample of "Registered Indians." The data is not strictly comparable, however, and should not be considered conclusive.

Health

Indian and Northern Affairs Canada has published general health indicators comparing the health status of Registered Indians, Registered Indians on reserves and the total Canadian public for the year 2001. The data is shown in Table 16.

Overall life expectancy is 9.5 percent below the Canadian average for male Registered Indians and 8.0 percent below the national average for females. Registered Indians on reserves have life expectancies 10.1 percent below the national average for males and 9.5 percent below the national average for females.

The mortality rate for Registered Indians is below the national average (25 percent below the national rate for all Registered Indians), likely reflecting the lower age profile of the Registered Indian population. The infant mortality rate on reserves is 38 percent above the national average. A 2006 report prepared by the Canadian Institute for Health Information[199] identifies the 2001 infant mortality rate for Canada at 5.3 per 1,000 and for Saskatchewan at 5.9 per 1,000. The same report identifies life expectancy at birth in the year 2001 for Saskatchewan as 76.2 years for males and 81.8 years for females, slightly below the national averages cited above by Indian and Northern Affairs Canada. Indian and Northern Affairs Canada notes in another report that the life expectancy of male Registered Indians has risen from 84.7 percent of the national average in 1980 to 92.0 percent of the national average in 2001.[200] The convergence of female life expectancies over the same period has been similar, as female Registered Indian life expectancy has gone from 86 percent to 92 percent of the national rate.

---

[198] Statistics Canada, 2001 *Aboriginal Peoples Survey, Community Profile - Regina and Saskatchewan – Housing.*
[199] Canadian Institute for Health Information, *Health, 2006*, 2006.
[200] Indian and Northern Affairs Canada, *Basic Departmental Data, 2003*, March, 2004.

Table 16: Comparative Health Statistics, Registered Indians, Registered Indians on Reserve and Total Canadian Population, 2001

	Registered Indians	Registered Indians on Reserve	All Canadians
Life Expectancy – Males (years)	70.4	69.2	77.0
Life Expectancy – Females (years)	75.5	74.3	82.1
Crude Mortality Rate (per 1,000)	5.3	5.5	7.1
Infant Mortality Rate (per 1,000)	-	7.2	5.2
Crude Tuberculosis Incidence Rate (per 100,000)	34.4	-	5.5

Source: Indian and Northern Affairs Canada, Comparison of Socio-economic Conditions, 1996 and 2001, 2005.

Infant mortality rates are 38.5 percent higher among Registered Indians on reserves than among the Canadian public at large. Another publication from Indian and Northern Affairs Canada identified the infant mortality rate for 2000 as slightly lower, at 6.4 per 1,000 live births for "First Nations On-Reserve," compared to a national average of 5.5 per 1,000 live births.[201] This shows First Nations infant mortality as closer to the national average, at 16.4 percent above the national average. The publication also noted that First Nations infant mortality rates had fallen from 23.7 to 6.4 per 1,000 live births from 1980 to 2000, a drop in infant mortality of 73 percent over 20 years (the national rate dropped by 47 percent).

The data in Table 16 also indicates that Registered Indians have an incidence of tuberculosis more than 6 times the national average. According to Indian and Northern Affairs Canada[202] this incidence of TB among First Nations fell from 82.1 to 34.0 cases per 100,000 population (or by 38.6 percent) between 1980 and 2000.

Indian and Northern Affairs Canada has published data on the causes of death among First Nations people compared to the general population. The data is national basis and expressed in

---

[201] *Ibid.*
[202] *Ibid.*

the terms of "Potential Years of Life Lost," a measure which takes into consideration the age of death by identifying the number of years below a life expectancy of 75 that death occurs. Potential Years of Life Lost are expressed per 100,000. Table 17 shows years of life lost for the year 2000 among First Nations people and 1999 among the general population.

First Nations people experience the greatest loss of years of life from injury of various kinds, as is the case for the general population. This may reflect that deaths from injuries often happen at younger ages than death from disease, resulting in more potential years of life lost. First Nations loss of potential years of life from injuries is 3.4 times the rate of loss in the general population, however.

First Nations people lost more potential years of life from every classification of disease except cancer (the number one cause of death among the Canadian general population), congenital diseases, genitourinary diseases and blood diseases. In those causes of death which affect First Nations more than the general public, the ratio of First Nations losses to losses among the general public ranged from just over 100 percent to as high as 366 percent.

Table 17: Potential Years of Life Lost per 100,000 Population for First Nations (2000) and Canada (1999)

Disease Classification	First Nations	Canada	Difference (years)	Ratio of First Nations to Canada (%)
Injury	4,304	1,260	3,044	341.6%
Circulatory	978	907	71	107.8%
Cancer	828	1,555	(727)	53.2%
Ill Defined	469	128	341	366.4%
Digestive	404	171	233	236.2%
Endocrine	324	143	181	226.6%
Respiratory	293	189	104	155.0%
Perinatal	284	210	74	135.2%
Infectious	274	112	162	244.6%
Nervous System	219	140	79	156.4%
Mental	185	58	127	319.0%
Congenital	40	177	(137)	22.5%
Genitourinary	31	37	(6)	83.8%
Musculoskeletal	31	15	16	206.7%
Blood Diseases	11	16	(5)	68.8%

Source: Indian and Northern Affairs Canada, Comparison of Socio-economic Conditions, 1996 and 2001, 2005 and author's calculations.

While this data does not clarify whether First Nations people suffer these ill fates more often than the general public, or at an earlier age than the general public, it is clear that First Nations people are far more likely to experience loss of potential years of life from ill health than the general public, as reflected in the lower life expectancies in Table 16 .

Entrepreneurship

The census collected data on the extent of self employment among persons identifying themselves as North American Indian – single response in comparison to the non-Aboriginal population. The data is shown in Table 18.

Table 18: Experienced Labour Force by Class of Worker for First Nations[203] Respondents and the Total Non-Aboriginal Population, Saskatchewan, 2001 Census

	First Nations	Non-Aboriginal Population	Difference
Total Experienced Labour Force over 15 Years (number)	15,825	462,060	n.a.
Paid Employees (% of Experienced Labour Force)	95.9%	79.1%	16.8 ppt
Paid Self-Employed (Incorporated) (% of Experienced Labour Force)	0.7%	4.6%	(3.9) ppt
Self-Employed (Incorporated) (% of Experienced Labour Force)	3.3%	14.9%	(11.6) ppt
Unpaid Family Workers (% of Experienced Labour Force)	0.1%	1.4%	(1.2) ppt

Source: Statistics Canada, Selected Labour Force Characteristics, Aboriginal Origin, 20% sample data, 2001 Census.

---

[203] For census data, "First Nations" will be used to refer to those survey respondents who responded by "North American Indian" only for cultural identity on census survey forms, excluding any groups who may have identified themselves by more than one cultural orientation.

First Nations people who have experience in the labour force are far more likely to be paid employees than non-Aboriginal workers, and about 20 percent as likely to be self-employed either as paid workers (incorporated) or unincorporated businesses than non-Aboriginal counterparts.

Industry Canada has published data on Aboriginal entrepreneurs in Saskatchewan on their website.[204] The 2001 Census found 2,530 self-employed Aboriginal people in Saskatchewan, 60 percent of whom were Métis. That would imply that the North American Indian – single response individuals identified in Table 18 comprise another 25 percent of total Aboriginal people self-employed in 2001.

Industry Canada also identifies the composition of Aboriginal small and medium-sized enterprises (SMEs) in Saskatchewan according to industrial classification, as shown in Table 19. The study does not distinguish those businesses owned by First Nations people from those owned by other Aboriginal people.

Table 19:   Industrial Composition of Aboriginal SMEs, Saskatchewan and Canada, 2002

Industry	Canada (% of all Aboriginal SMEs)	Saskatchewan
Primary	15.0%	16.3%
Construction	16.6%	12.9%
Manufacturing, Transportation and Warehousing	9.6%	21.7%
Wholesale and Retail Trade	12.2%	11.0%
Arts, Entertainment, Accommodation, Food and Cultural	14.6%	6.3%
Services	17.9%	22.5%
Other	14.1%	9.2%
	100.0%	100.0%

Source: Industry Canada, Aboriginal Business Canada – Saskatchewan, website.

---

[204] See: http://strategis.ic.gc.ca/epic/internet/inabc-eac.nsf/en/ab00433e.html, accessed on June 16, 2006.

Aboriginal businesses in Saskatchewan are engaged in industries across the spectrum, as is the case for all of Canada. The Industry Canada report notes that the distribution of businesses in Saskatchewan only differs significantly statistically from the national distribution of Aboriginal businesses in that more than twice as many Saskatchewan businesses are in the Manufacturing, Transportation and Warehousing industry and about half as many are in the Arts, Entertainment, Accommodation, Food and Cultural industries. It is worth noting that Saskatchewan Business magazine's 2005 list of 100 largest companies in Saskatchewan included two First Nations owned businesses, NorSask Forest Products and the Saskatchewan Indian Gaming Authority (SIGA). The same magazine identified SIGA as the 11th largest employer in the province.[205]

Table 20 shows key characteristics of Aboriginal SMEs as identified by Industry Canada.

Table 20: Profile of Aboriginal SMEs, Saskatchewan and Canada, 2002

	Canada	Saskatchewan
	(% of all Aboriginal SMEs)	
Sole Proprietorships	66.7%	68.4%
Partnerships	18.5%	14.9%
Incorporation	14.8%	16.7%
Less than 5 years old	32.7%	33.6%
6 to 9 years old	23.5%	19.5%
More than 10 years old	43.8%	46.9%

Source: Industry Canada, Aboriginal Business Canada – Saskatchewan, website.

Saskatchewan data was statistically equivalent to national data. Notably, it revealed a relatively high proportion of sole proprietorships among Aboriginal businesses and the fact that about half the businesses were more than ten years old.

---

[205] "Top 100: Saskatchewan's Top 100 Companies of 2005," *Saskatchewan Business Magazine* Vol. 26, issue 5 (August 2005), pp. 19-27.

The sources of start-up funding used by Aboriginal businesses in Saskatchewan and Canada are outlined in Table 21.

Table 21: Levels and Sources of Start-up Financing for Aboriginal SMEs, Saskatchewan and Canada, 2002

	Canada (% of all Aboriginal SMEs)	Saskatchewan
Start-up: Less than $25,000	69.3%	48.4%
Start-up: $25,000 to $49,999	11.1%	14.1%
Start-up: $50,000 to $99,999	8.9%	19.6%
Start-up: Over $100,000	10.8%	17.8%
Borrowed Start-up – none	49.8%	36.2%
Borrowed Start-up – less than 25%	9.5%	5.2%
Borrowed Start-up – 25% to 49%	8.1%	13.3%
Borrowed Start-up – 50% to 74%	14.5%	23.5%
Borrowed Start-up – 75% to 99%	9.8%	12.7%
Borrowed Start-up – 100%	8.2%	9.1%
Sources of Start-up Funds:		
- Personal Savings	82.9%	88.8%
- Loans and Lines of Credit	37.0%	48.9%

Source: Industry Canada, Aboriginal Business Canada – Saskatchewan, website.

Generally, Aboriginal businesses in Saskatchewan used a higher level of start-up funding than national Aboriginal businesses and relied more heavily on borrowed funds to get their businesses started.

An important question in fostering First Nations participation in the economy is, what allows First Nations businesses to be successful entrants in the modern market economy? The leading work on this question comes from the Harvard Project on American Indian Economic Development, led by Stephen Cornell and Joseph P. Kalt. In their paper

"Reloading the Dice: Improving the Chances for Economic Development on American Indian Reservations," they identify three categories of "key development ingredients."[206] The first category is "external opportunity," which includes political sovereignty or First Nation control over decision making, a market opportunity, access to financial capital and a manageable distance from markets. The second category is "internal assets," which consists of natural resources, human capital, institutions of governance and culture, or norms and behaviours that exist and are respected within the community. The third category is the "development strategy," which consists of the overall economic system or organization of the reserve's economy, and the choice of development activities or projects to pursue. Their recommendations for maximizing the utility of these key development ingredients consist of three tasks – mobilizing and sustaining support for the institutions and strategies the First Nation creates; implementing strategic choices through formalized decisions, rules and procedures and professional financial, personnel and record systems; and establishing a political environment safe for political development.

In the Canada-Aboriginal Peoples Roundtable Sectoral Follow-Up Session on Economic Opportunities, participants clearly identified the need for Aboriginal-controlled governance, capacity building (human capital) strategies, partnerships and funding to improve access to capital and investment, clear separation between political governance and economic management, access to technology, training and support for business development and management, clarification of rights and access to resources, sustainable resource management policies, and improvements in legislative and regulatory frameworks governing Aboriginal economic development.[207] These policy priorities of Aboriginal participants in this Canadian roundtable reflect the key ingredients and tasks for development identified by Cornell and Kalt.

---

[206] Stephen Cornell and Joseph P. Kalt, "Reloading the Dice: Improving the Chances for Economic Development on American Indian Reservations" *What Can Tribes Do?: Strategies and Institutions in American Indian Economic Development,* http://www.ksg.harvard.edu/hpaied/docs/reloading%20the%20dice.pdf, accessed June 21, 2006.

[207] *Economic Opportunities Sectoral Follow-Up Session: Facilitators' Report,* http://www.Aboriginalroundtable.ca/sect/econ/rprt/ssn_e.html, accessed June 21, 2006.

Conclusion

Overall, the information garnered from the 2001 Census and other sources provides a clear picture of the socio-economic conditions faced by First Nations peoples in Saskatchewan. The indicators of employment and labour force activity, income levels, household characteristics, education, housing, health and entrepreneurship generally show that First Nations people endure socio-economic conditions far below those of the rest of Canadian society, with low incomes, low employment rates, poorer housing conditions and more health problems.

On the other hand, there is hope for improvement as evidenced by rapidly improving labour market conditions, high rate of participation in the education system, life expectancy converging on the national standard and increasing entrepreneurial success among First Nations people and businesses.

APPENDIX 4. MAJOR FEDERAL AND SASKATCHEWAN REPORTS AND DOCUMENTS

The following is a brief chronology of major federal and Saskatchewan reports and documents on First Nations and Aboriginal issues:

1947 – Joint Committee of the Senate and House of Commons on the *Indian Act* holds hearings. In spite of demands for treaty implementation and treaty fulfillment, 1951 changes to the *Indian Act* did not materially change 1876 legislative template.

1967 – Hawthorn Report on Indian Conditions in Canada rejects assimilation and proposes continuation of "special status" for Aboriginal peoples, but proposes that reserves be converted into municipalities.

1969 – Federal government White Paper, *Statement of the Government of Canada* on *Indian Policy*, released, proposing elimination of "special status" for Aboriginal peoples.

1971 – White Paper officially withdrawn.

1982 – Section 35 of *Constitution Act, 1982* provides clear constitutional protection for "existing Aboriginal and treaty rights of the Aboriginal peoples of Canada" and section 37 provides for a First Ministers' Conference with National Aboriginal leaders on Aboriginal rights.

1983 – *Report of the Special Committee of the House of Commons on Indian Self-Government* (Penner Report) proposed recognition of First Nations as a distinct, constitutionally protected order of government within Canada and with a full range of government powers.

1983 – Amendments made to the *Constitution Act, 1982* to add precision to the Aboriginal rights provisions and provide for three more First Ministers' Conferences.

1987 – First Ministers sign Meech Lake Accord, which is opposed by Aboriginal peoples for ignoring Aboriginal issues.

1990 – In an effort to save the Meech Lake Accord, First Ministers agree to a "companion resolution" that includes a commitment to resume First Ministers' Conferences on Aboriginal issues.

1990 – Office of the Treaty Commissioner for Saskatchewan releases report on treaty land entitlement, which forms basis for negotiations toward Treaty Land Entitlement Framework Agreement.

1991 – Federal government establishes the Royal Commission on Aboriginal Peoples.

1992 – Aboriginal leaders given status as full participants in negotiations that lead to Charlottetown Accord; resulting Accord proposes to recognize inherent right of self-government for Aboriginal peoples in Constitution and put in place a process to negotiate self-government and implementation of Aboriginal and treaty rights; Accord defeated in national referendum, October 26.

1992 – Canada, Saskatchewan and 25 Saskatchewan First Nations sign Treaty Land Entitlement Framework Agreement.

1995 – Federal government releases federal policy guide to Aboriginal self-government, *The Government of Canada's Approach to Implementation of the Inherent Right and the Negotiation of Aboriginal Self-Government.*

1996 – Royal Commission on Aboriginal Peoples releases 5-volume report.

1996 – Canada, Saskatchewan and the Federation of Saskatchewan Indian Nations sign a Protocol Agreement to Establish a Common Table.

1997 – Federal government releases *Gathering Strength: Canada's Aboriginal Action Plan* in response to the Royal Commission report.

1997 – Office of the Treaty Commissioner for Saskatchewan renewed with a mandate to study the nature of the treaty relationship and several specific treaty issues and to explore the requirements and implications of treaty implementation.

1998 – Office of the Treaty Commissioner releases the *Statement of Treaty Issues: Treaties as a Bridge to the Future.*

2000 – Canada, Saskatchewan and the Federation of Saskatchewan Indian Nations sign a Framework for Governance of Treaty First Nations.

2001 – Canada and the Meadow Lake First Nations sign self-government Agreement-in-Principle and Canada, Saskatchewan and Meadow Lake First Nations sign Tripartite-Agreement-in-Principle.

2004 – Saskatchewan Commission on First Nations and Métis Peoples and Justice Reform releases its final report, *Legacy of Hope: An Agenda for Change*; Saskatchewan Commission of Inquiry into Matters Relating to the Death of Neil Stonechild releases its report.

2005 – First Ministers meet with national Aboriginal leaders at Kelowna, British Columbia and sign "Kelowna Accord."

2006 – Office of the Treaty Commissioner releases an interim report, *Treaties: The Road to Reconciliation.*

APPENDIX 5. A SYNOPSIS OF SIGNIFICANT SELECTED JUDICIAL DECISIONS ON FIRST NATIONS AND ABORIGINAL ISSUES

Major Judicial Decisions on Aboriginal Issues, by Topic and Year (with annotations for cases cited in the body of the document)

Hunting and Fishing Rights:

1. *R.* v. *Prince* [1964] S.C.R. 81.
2. *R.* v. *Sikyea* [1964] S.C.R. 642.
3. *R.* v. *White and Bob* (1964) 52 W.W.R. 193 (B.C.C.A.).
4. *R.* v. *George* [1966] S.C.R. 267.
5. *R.* v. *Sigereak* [1966] S.C.R. 645.
6. *R.* v. *Daniels and White* [1968] S.C.R. 517.
7. *Cardinal* v. *Attorney General of Alberta* [1974] S.C.R. 695.
8. *R.* v. *Myran* [1976] 2 S.C.R. 137.
9. *R.* v. *Frank* [1978] 1 S.C.R. 95.
10. *R.* v. *Kruger* [1978] 1 S.C.R. 104.
11. *R.* v. *Jack* [1980] 1 S.C.R. 294.
12. *R.* v. *McKinney* [1980] 1 S.C.R. 401.
13. *R.* v. *Elk* [1980] 2 S.C.R. 166.
14. *R.* v. *Mousseau* [1980] 2 S.C.R. 89.
15. *R.* v. *Sutherland* [1980] 2 S.C.R. 451.
16. *R.* v. *Moosehunter* [1981] 1 S.C.R. 282.
17. *R.* v. *Taylor and Williams* [1981] 2 C.N.L.R. 114 (Ont. C.A.).
18. *R.* v. *Dick* [1985] 2 S.C.R. 309.
19. *R.* v. *Jack and Charlie* [1985] 2 S.C.R. 332.
20. *Simon* v. *The Queen* [1985] 2 S.C.R. 387.

   The appellant's treaty right to hunt is protected by section 88 of the Indian Act and, therefore, cannot be contravened by provincial legislation.

21. *R.* v. *Horse* [1988] 1 S.C.R. 187.
22. *R.* v. *Agawa* [1988] 3 C.N.L.R. 73 (Ont. C.A.).
23. *Claxton* v. *Saanichton Marina Ltd.* [1989] 3 C.N.L.R. 46 (B.C.C.A.).
24. *R.* v. *Horseman* [1990] 1 S.C.R. 901.

   Under Treaty 8, hunting rights have been limited to hunting for food, so hunting for commercial purposes must be done in accordance with provincial regulations.

25. *R.* v. *Sioui* [1990] 1 S.C.R. 1025.

   By the terms of their 1760 treaty, the Huron were ensured freedom to carry on their customs and religion over the entire territory, as long as the activities were not incompatible with the particular use made by the Crown of the territory.

26. *R. v. Sparrow* [1990] 1 S.C.R. 1075.

> *Section 35 of the Constitution Act, 1982 protects Aboriginal rights not extinguished prior to 1982, and regulation does not constitute extinguishment. Legislation affecting these rights can be valid if the interference with the rights can be justified as having a valid legislative objective and being consistent with the honour of the Crown in its dealings with Aboriginal peoples.*

27. *Ontario (Attorney General)* v. *Bear Island Foundation* [1991] 2 S.C.R. 570.

> *The appellants exercised sufficient occupation of the land in question to establish an Aboriginal right to land, but this right had been extinguished by the Robinson-Huron Treaty of 1850.*

28. *R. v. Howard* [1994] 2 S.C.R. 299.
29. *R. v. Badger* [1996] 1 S.C.R. 771.

> *Treaty No. 8 guaranteed the Indians the "right to pursue their usual vocations of hunting, trapping and fishing" subject to a geographic limitation and the right of government to make regulations for conservation purposes." These rights were not extinguished by the NRTA. However, the geographic limitation would include lands visibly being put to an alternative use, such as privately-owned lands, but there was no evidence provided to suggest that the provincial conservation regulations were a justifiable interference with treaty rights to hunt on unoccupied lands, as required by R. v. Sparrow.*

30. *R. v. Lewis* [1996] 1 S.C.R. 921.
31. *R. v. Nikal* [1996] 1 S.C.R. 1013.
32. *R. v. Van der Peet* [1996] 2 S.C.R. 507.

> *To be an Aboriginal right, an activity must be an element of a practice, custom or tradition integral to the distinctive culture of the Aboriginal group claiming the right, which means that they must have central significance to the Aboriginal people and have continuity with the practices, customs and traditions of the Aboriginal people prior to European contact. Trading fish was not integral to the Sto:lo, so commercial fishing is not an Aboriginal right.*

33. *R. v. N.T.C. Smokehouse Ltd.* [1996] 1 S.C.R. 672.
34. *R. v. Gladstone* [1996] 1 S.C.R. 723.
35. *R. v. Cote* [1996] 3 S.C.R. 139.
36. *R. v. Adams* [1996] 3 S.C.R. 101.
37. *R. v. Sundown* [1999] 1 S.C.R. 393.
38. *R. v. Marshall* (No. 1) [1999] 3 S.C.R. 456.

> *The treaties of 1760-61 between the Crown and the Mi'kmaq should be interpreted as providing a right to fish for the purpose of generating a "moderate livelihood," rather than merely to trade in fish acquired under the regulations applicable to all citizens, as this is required to uphold the honour of the Crown. In the absence of a justification for the infringement of this treaty right, fisheries regulations are inapplicable to the Mi'kmaq.*

39. *R. v. Marshall* (Rehearing) [1999] 3 S.C.R. 533.
40. *Halfway River First Nation* v. *British Columbia* [1999] B.C.J. 1880 (B.C.C.A.).
41. *R. v. Catarat* [2001] S.J. 283 (C.A.).
42. *Mitchell* v. *M.N.R.* [2001] 1 S.C.R. 911.

> *The laws of evidence must ensure that the Aboriginal perspective is given due weight but this does not negate general principles governing evidence. Even if deference were granted to finding of pre-contact trade relations between the Mohawks and First Nations north of the St. Lawrence River, the evidence does not establish this northerly trade as a defining feature of the Mohawk culture. Thus, no Aboriginal right to bring goods across the border for the purposes of trade has been established.*

43. *Wewaykum Indian Band* v. *Canada* [2002] 4 S.C.R. 245.
44. *Benoit* v. *Canada* [2003] F.C.J. No. 923 (C.A.).
45. *R. v. Morris and Olsen* 2004 B.C.J. No. 121 (C.A.).
46. *R. v. Marshall; R. v. Bernard* [2005] 2 S.C.R. 220.

> *Mi'kmaq only have the treaty right to trade in, and harvest for trade, items traditionally traded at the time the treaties were made, so the respondents had no treaty right to log. Neither did they possess Aboriginal title to the lands they logged, as Aboriginal title to land is established by aboriginal practices that indicate "exclusive" pre-sovereignty "occupation" of the land.*

47. *R. v. Kapp* 2006 BCCA 277.
48. *R. v. Sappier; R. v. Gray* 2006 SCC 54.
49. *R. v. Powley* 2003 SCC 43.
50. *R. v. Blais* 2003 SCC 44.

Treaty Interpretation, Fiduciary Duty and Duty to Consult:

1. *Dreaver* v. *The King* (1935), 5 C.N.L.C. 92 (Exch.).

> *The medicine chest clause in Treaty 6 requires that all medicines, drugs, or medical supplies be supplied free of charge to treaty Indians.*

2. *Calder* v. *British Columbia* [1973] S.C.R. 313.

> *Prior to the arrival of Europeans, Aboriginal peoples had title to the land they had occupied and this title was recognized at common law, though it could be extinguished by a statute or treaty (the Court split on whether Nisga'a title had been extinguished or not in this particular case).*

3. *R. v. Nowegijick* [1983] 1 S.C.R. 29.
4. *Smith* v. *The Queen* [1983] 1 S.C.R. 554.
5. *Guerin* v. *The Queen* [1984] 2 S.C.R. 335.
6. *Mitchell* v. *Peguis Indian Band* [1990] 2 S.C.R. 85.
7. *Blueberry River Indian Band* v. *Canada* [1995] 4 S.C.R. 344.

8. *Delgamuukw* v. *British Columbia* [1997] 3 S.C.R. 1010.

> *Aboriginal title encompasses the right to exclusive use and occupation of the land held pursuant to that title, and is protected by section 35 of the Constitution Act, 1982. In order to establish a claim to Aboriginal title, the Aboriginal group asserting the claim must establish that it occupied the lands in question at the time at which the Crown asserted sovereignty over the land subject to the title, and oral history can be used as evidence of occupancy. The protected uses must not be irreconcilable with the nature of the group's attachment to that land. Constitutionally recognized Aboriginal rights, including Aboriginal title, are not absolute and may be infringed by the federal and provincial governments if the infringement (1) furthers a compelling and substantial legislative objective and (2) is consistent with the special fiduciary relationship between the Crown and the Aboriginal peoples. Under the second part, legislative objectives are subject to accommodation of the Aboriginal peoples' interests, in accordance with the honour and good faith of the Crown. One aspect of accommodation of "Aboriginal title" entails notifying and consulting Aboriginal peoples with respect to the development of the affected territory, and in most cases the duty will be significantly deeper than mere consultation. Another aspect is fair compensation.*

9. *Haida Nation* v. *British Columbia* [2004] 3 S.C.R. 511.

> *The Crown has a duty to consult with Aboriginal peoples who have asserted an Aboriginal right with which Crown decisions could interfere, which is an essential corollary to the honourable process of reconciliation that s. 35 of the Constitution Act, 1982, demands. The foundation of the duty in the Crown's honour and the goal of reconciliation suggest that the duty arises when the Crown has knowledge, real or constructive, of the potential existence of the Aboriginal right or title and contemplates conduct that might adversely affect it. The scope of the duty is proportionate to a preliminary assessment of the strength of the case supporting the existence of the right or title, and to the seriousness of the potentially adverse effect upon the right or title claimed.*

10. *Taku River Tlingit First Nation* v. *British Columbia* [2004] SCC 74.

11. *Mikisew Cree First Nation* v. *Canada* [2005] 3 S.C.R. 388.

> *The Crown, while it has a treaty right to "take up" surrendered lands, is nevertheless under the obligation to inform itself on the impact its project will have on the exercise by the appellants of their treaty hunting, fishing and trapping rights and to attempt to deal with the appellants in good faith and with the intention of substantially addressing their concerns, as part of the duty to consult.*

Division of Powers:

1. *Attorney General of Canada* v. *Canard* [1976] 1 S.C.R. 170.
2. *Natural Parents* v. *Superintendant of Child Welfare* [1976] 2 S.C.R. 751.

3. *Four B Manufacturing Ltd.* v. *United Garment Workers* [1980] 1 S.C.R. 1031.
4. *Derrickson* v. *Derrickson* [1986] 1 S.C.R. 285.
5. *Paul* v. *Paul* [1986] 1 S.C.R. 306.
6. *R.* v. *Francis* [1988] 1 S.C.R. 1025.
7. *Kitkatla Band* v. *British Columbia* [2002] S.C.R. 146.
8. *Paul* v. *British Columbia (Forest Appeals Commission)* [2003] 2 S.C.R. 585.

> *The Province has legislative competence to endow an administrative tribunal, such as the Forest Appeals Commission, with capacity to consider a question of Aboriginal rights in the course of carrying out its adjudicative function, though its decision on this matter can be reviewed by the courts to determine whether the decision was correct in law.*

9. *R.* v. *Fiddler* [1994] 1 C.N.L.R. 121 (Sask. Q.B.).

Other Issues:

1. *Hamlet of Baker Lake* v. *Canada* [1979] 3 C.N.L.R. 17 (F.C.T.D.).
2. *Canadian Pacific Ltd.* v. *Matsqui Indian Band* [1995] 1 S.C.R. 3.
3. *R.* v. *Pamajewon* [1996] 2 S.C.R. 821.
4. *Opetchesaht Indian Band* v. *Canada* [1997] 2 S.C.R. 119.
5. *St. Mary's Indian Band* v. *Cranbrook* [1997] 2 S.C.R. 657.
6. *R.* v. *Gladue* [1999] 1 S.C.R. 688.
7. *Corbiere* v. *Canada* [1999] 2 S.C.R. 203.
8. *Westbank First Nation* v. *British Columbia Hydro and Power Authority* [1999] 3 S.C.R. 134.
9. *Lovelace* v. *Ontario* [2000] 1 S.C.R. 590.
10. *Osoyoos Indian Band* v. *Oliver* [2001] SCC 85.
11. *Lac La Ronge Indian Band* v. *Canada and Saskatchewan* [2001] SKCA 109.
12. *British Columbia* v. *Okanagan Indian Band* [2003] SCC 71.
13. *McDiarmid Lumber Ltd.* v. *God's Lake First Nation* [2006] SCC 58.

Treaty Implementation: Fulfilling the Covenant

Appendix 6. Mandate Letter from Chief of Federation of Saskatchewan Indian Nations and Minister of Indian Affairs and Northern Development
and Federal Interlocutor for Métis and Non-Status Indians, July 18, 2005

APPENDIX 6. MANDATE LETTER FROM CHIEF OF FEDERATION OF SASKATCHEWAN INDIAN NATIONS AND MINISTER OF INDIAN AFFAIRS AND NORTHERN DEVELOPMENT AND FEDERAL INTERLOCUTOR FOR MÉTIS AND NON-STATUS INDIANS, JULY 18, 2005

Government   Gouvernement
of Canada   du Canada

Federation of Saskatchewan Indian Nations

JUL 1 9 2005

JUL 1 8 2005

Judge David M. Arnot
Treaty Commissioner
Office of the Treaty Commissioner
606 Spadina Crescent East, Suite 1150
SASKATOON SK S7K 3H1

Dear Judge Arnot:

The current Office of the Treaty Commissioner has been operating since 1996, with a mandate set out in two critical documents:

A "Joint Workplan and Budget" for a Table on Exploratory Treaty Discussions, dated June 20, 1996, addresses the work of the Exploratory Treaty Table, as facilitated by the Commission, in creating a Statement of Treaty Issues.

A "Memorandum of Agreement between Canada and the Federation of Saskatchewan Indian Nations", dated October 31, 1996, sets out the broader roles and function of the Office of the Treaty Commissioner, which include but are not limited to the facilitation of the Treaty Table.

In October 1998, the Commission issued the *Statement of Treaty Issues*, based in large part on the discussions at the Treaty Table. The common understandings contained in the *Statement of Treaty Issues* contribute to the foundation of the treaty relationship. Since that time, the Table has worked to issue specific context papers in each of the areas identified in the Memorandum of Agreement, and has completed five of the original seven targeted areas.

.../2

Treaty Implementation: Fulfilling the Covenant

Appendix 6. Mandate Letter from Chief of Federation of Saskatchewan Indian Nations and Minister of Indian Affairs and Northern Development and Federal Interlocutor for Métis and Non-Status Indians, July 18, 2005

- 2 -

In 2005, with two years remaining in an extension of this mandate, your Office and the Treaty Table plan to complete the remaining two context papers, in justice and in hunting/trapping/fishing/gathering, as well as one for an additional issue, lands and resources, referred to the Table by the parties in 1999.

With recent deliberations about the nature and scope of an agreement-in-principle on self-government, the parties have agreed that they need to explore the requirements and implications of treaty implementation based upon the views of the two parties. The parties also agree that they have not fully utilized the mandate of the Office of the Treaty Commissioner.

The 1996 Memorandum of Agreement states, in section 3.4, that the Commissioner can, if and as directed by the parties to the Agreement,

"assist in the task of defining the rights and obligations accruing from the Treaties, and exploring the implementation of those rights and obligations. The Minister's ability to deal with issues related to the definition and implementation of treaty rights and obligations is dependent on the authorities in place from time to time."

The 1996 Memorandum of Agreement, under subsection 3.8.5, contemplates "developing a capacity to conduct independent and focused research and prepare reports which will contribute to the resolution of an issue and promote solutions," subject to the specific requests of the parties and the determination by the Treaty Commissioner that such is necessary. Under section 3.8.4, the Commissioner can, similarly, develop "an independent capacity to analyze and report on the positions of the Parties on specific treaty issues" at the direction of the parties.

Based upon these specifications, it is the will of the parties to direct the Office of the Treaty Commissioner to explore options for treaty implementation and to produce a report. The report could provide an in-depth analysis of concepts and principles of Treaty implementation, in both the historic and modern context. It could also, to the extent possible, provide recommendations and options to the parties for future direction in the evolution of treaty policy. Subject to the will of the parties, this report could inform the further negotiation and development of the governance arrangements at the Governance and Fiscal Relations Table. Canada's ability to deal with these issues is dependent upon the authorities in place from time to time.

.../3

Treaty Implementation: Fulfilling the Covenant

Appendix 6. Mandate Letter from Chief of Federation of Saskatchewan Indian Nations and Minister of Indian Affairs and Northern Development and Federal Interlocutor for Métis and Non-Status Indians, July 18, 2005

- 3 -

The Office of the Treaty Commissioner, in consultation with the parties at the Treaty Table, can decide on appropriate formats for completing this work. Our representatives will work with the Commission to continue to hold discussions about Treaty implementation, and will seek common understandings about how the concept could help us reach an agreement in a number of areas.

The parties will commence the work by meeting with the Treaty Commissioner to frame the general questions that will guide the preparation of the report. A work plan will be created by the Treaty Commissioner by July 15, 2005, and be submitted to the parties prior to the commencement of the work.

The parties request that an interim progress report be available by October 31, 2005, with a view toward the completion of a final report by March 31, 2006.

Yours sincerely,

The Honourable Andy Scott, PC, MP
Minister of Indian Affairs and Northern
Development and Federal Interlocutor for
Métis and Non-Status Indians

Chief Alphonse Bird
Federation of Saskatchewan Indian
Nation